Work to Welfare
How Men Become Detached from the Labour Market

This book provides a new perspective on joblessness among men. During the last twenty years vast numbers of men of working age have moved completely out of the labour market into 'early retirement' or 'long-term sickness' and to take on new roles in the household. These trends stand in stark contrast to rising labour market participation among women. Based on an unprecedented range of new research on the detached male workforce in the UK, and located within an international context, the book offers a detailed exploration of the varied financial, family and health circumstances 'detached men' are living in. It also challenges conventional assumptions about the boundaries between unemployment, sickness and retirement, and the true health of the labour market. *Work to Welfare* represents an important contribution to debates about the labour market and benefit systems, and will be of interest to readers and practitioners in social policy, economics and geography.

Pete Alcock is Professor of Social Policy and Administration at the University of Birmingham. He has published extensively on poverty, social exclusion and the benefits system.

Christina Beatty is a research fellow at the Centre for Regional Economic and Social Research, Sheffield Hallam University, and a statistician by background.

Stephen Fothergill is a Professor at CRESR and an economist by background. He has published extensively on urban and regional problems in the UK.

Rob Macmillan is a researcher in the Department of Geography, Durham University. He was previously a researcher at CRESR.

Sue Yeandle is Professor of Sociology at CRESR and the School of Social Science and Law, Sheffield Hallam University. She has published extensively on work, employment and the family.

D0162521

Work to Welfare

How Men Become Detached from the Labour Market

Pete Alcock, Christina Beatty, Stephen Fothergill, Rob Macmillan and Sue Yeandle

CAMBRIDGE
UNIVERSITY PRESS

PUBLISHED BY THE PRESS SYNDICATE OF THE UNIVERSITY OF CAMBRIDGE
The Pitt Building, Trumpington Street, Cambridge CB2 1RP, United Kingdom

CAMBRIDGE UNIVERSITY PRESS
The Edinburgh Building, Cambridge, CB2 2RU, UK
40 West 20th Street, New York, NY 10011-4211, USA
477 Williamstown Road, Port Melbourne, VIC 3207, Australia
Ruiz de Alarcón 13, 28014 Madrid, Spain
Dock House, The Waterfront, Cape Town 8001, South Africa

http:/www.cambridge.org

First published 2003

Printed in the United Kingdom at the University Press, Cambridge

Typeface Plantin 10/12 pt   *System* LaTeX 2_ε [TB]

A catalogue record for this book is available from the British Library

Library of Congress Cataloguing in Publication data
Work to welfare: how men become detached from the labour
market / Pete Alcock . . . [et al.].
　　p.　　cm.
Include bibliographical references and index.
ISBN 0 521 80249 0 – 0 521 00286 9 (pb.)
1. Men – Employment – Great Britain.　2. Unemployment – Great Britain.
3. Work – Great Britain – Psychological aspects.　4. Labor policy – Great Britain.
5. Public welfare – Great Britain.　I. Alcock, Peter, 1951–
HD5765.A6 W673S　2002
331.12′0941–dc21　2002071641

ISBN　0 521 80249 0 hardback
ISBN　0 521 00286 9 paperback

Contents

Figures

Tables

Notes on the authors

Pete Alcock is a professor in the Department of Social Policy and Social Work at the University of Birmingham. Before joining that university he worked at Sheffield Hallam University. He has written extensively on issues of poverty, social exclusion, local regeneration and the benefits system.

Christina Beatty is a research fellow within the Centre for Regional Economic and Social Research (CRESR) at Sheffield Hallam University. A statistician by background, she has worked on issues concerning the labour market, unemployment and housing.

Stephen Fothergill is a professor within CRESR at Sheffield Hallam University. An economist by background, he has previously published on a wide range of issues around urban and regional problems in the UK, particularly trends in employment and unemployment.

Rob Macmillan is a researcher in the Department of Geography at the University of Durham, and was previously a researcher at CRESR. A politics graduate, he also has first-hand experience of the UK social security system through his time as a benefits adviser.

Sue Yeandle is a professor within CRESR at Sheffield Hallam University. A sociologist by background, she has specialised in issues of unemployment, women and family life in both the UK and EU context, and has published widely on these topics.

Preface

The detachment of large numbers of men from paid employment is one of the most significant social changes of the last twenty years or so. The once near universal expectation that men's working lives would extend from the time of their leaving school through to their state pension age has been shattered, probably for good. In Britain – the focus of the new research reported here – more than one in five of all 16–64-year-old men, or nearly 4 million men in total, are no longer in employment.

There has always been unemployment, of course, and during the 1980s and 1990s redundancies hit men very hard. But only a minority of the men who are now detached from employment are conventionally unemployed. Early retirement, ill-health and domestic responsibilities – and sometimes a combination of these with an important element of unemployment thrown in – are all key factors, too.

There is scant evidence that this increase in labour market detachment among men was ever anticipated by policy-makers or academic analysts. It has grown quietly, year on year, and even now the true scale of this phenomenon is not widely recognised. What is more, the trend among men stands in marked contrast to what is happening among women, who are becoming engaged in paid employment in ever larger numbers. Women's rising 'labour force participation' is well known and has been the subject of much research and vast discussion in the media. That at the same time men are dropping out of employment, or are being pushed out, has prompted comparatively little comment or investigation. We should not jump to the simplistic conclusion that this is a case of women taking over in the workplace. Most of the jobs that used to be filled by men were in very different sectors and occupations from those now held by women.

Nor should we assume that men's growing detachment from work is mainly a voluntary phenomenon, prompted by rising affluence and greater choice. Early retirement on a comfortable pension is only a small part of the story. More often, men's labour market detachment is supported by the public purse, through the benefits system. Quite apart from the loss of potential output which labour market detachment represents, as the source of a major financial claim on the Exchequer it is an issue of legitimate concern.

This book attempts to fill some of the gaps in current knowledge about men's changing relationship to the world of work. As befits an issue that spans several disciplines, the book's authors comprise an economist, a statistician, a political scientist, a sociologist and a social policy expert. This diversity of perspectives is reflected in the contrasting approaches of the chapters. However, despite the varied and at times contradictory academic baggage the members of the team brought to this study, we have found a good deal of common ground about what is actually happening.

The immediate backgound to the book is a research project carried out at the Centre for Regional Economic and Social Research at Sheffield Hallam University, between 1997 and 1999. This was mainly financed by a grant from the UK government's Economic and Social Research Council (ref. no. 000236958). It was supplemented by a grant from the Rural Development Commission that allowed the survey to be enlarged to include men in a number of rural areas as well as in towns.

Like nearly all academic research, the project built on the foundations of work we had previously undertaken. This included in particular a study by Christina Beatty and Stephen Fothergill of labour market adjustment in the wake of pit closures, which was one of the first to observe that job loss was much less likely to result in higher recorded unemployment than in men dropping out of the labour market altogether. The project was able to deploy Sue Yeandle's substantial experience of interview-based research exploring the relationship between labour market change and family life, and to build on Pete Alcock's and Rob Macmillan's work on the benefits system and its influence on individual decision-making.

Special thanks go to Alison Herrington, who worked as researcher on the project for several months and carried out some of the in-depth interviews. Dave Drew and the staff and fieldworkers of the Survey and Statistical Research Centre at Sheffield Hallam University played an important role in gathering the extensive survey data. We would also like to thank the local authority staff who provided practical assistance in each of our survey areas. Sheila Walker provided invaluable administrative and secretarial support throughout, and Carol Goodale and Nicola Smith helped from time to time with the overload. Many colleagues from academia and the policy world provided valuable advice and comment. Among these we wish especially to mention Paul Convery, Jane Davidson, Arthur Fleiss, John Philpott, Lorna Reith and Simon Wood, who all sat on the project's advisory group. The final product is, however, solely our own, and we take responsibility for any errors of judgement or emphasis.

HOW THE BOOK IS ORGANISED

The book is organised in three sections. The first deals with the context for labour market detachment. Chapter 1 describes the main relevant trends in the UK labour market. Chapter 2 considers the international context and ch. 3 explores how welfare policy relating to the labour market has developed in Britain.

The second section of the book sets out our new evidence, based on the surveys described in the appendix. Chapters 4 to 6 present the findings from the large-scale survey of the main groups of men of working age who are outside full-time employment. Chapter 4 provides an overview of this 'detached male workforce'. Chapter 5 gives special attention to men who are recipients of sickness and disability benefits, while ch. 6 concentrates on the situation of older men. These chapters show that there is extensive concealed unemployment among men who are officially recorded as 'economically inactive'. The geography of labour market detachment, and in particular the high incidence of joblessness in older industrial Britain, forms an important component of these chapters.

Chapters 7 to 10 introduce evidence from our in-depth follow-up interviews. Chapter 7 explores the relationship between family circumstances and labour force detachment, and considers the impact of age and of relationships. Chapter 8 examines the health circumstances of men in further detail. Chapter 9 focuses attention on how men without jobs cope with their financial situation, while ch. 10 explores the barriers they face in trying to re-enter employment. These chapters provide rich and contextualised evidence about what it is really like to be outside the labour market. Finally ch. 11, which comprises the third section of the book, looks at the policy implications of our findings.

Overall, we believe this has been an important, timely and innovative study. It provides answers to several key questions about current trends in the labour market, although new questions also arise from our research. We have called the book *Work to Welfare* because this has been the experience of so many of the men in our study. If policy is to succeed in moving men like these back from welfare to work, we believe it needs to build on the knowledge and understanding that this book attempts to provide.

Abbreviations

BHPS	British Household Panel Survey
CRESR	Centre for Regional Economic and Social Research
DfEE	Department for Education and Employment
DSS	Department of Social Security
DTI	Department of Trade and Industry
DWP	Department for Work and Pensions
ED	Enumeration District
EHPS	European Household Panel Survey
ELFS	European Labour Force Survey
ESF	European Social Fund
EU	European Union
FRS	Family Resources Survey
IB	Incapacity Benefit
ILO	International Labour Organisation
IVB	Invalidity Benefit
JSA	Jobseeker's Allowance
NI	National Insurance
OECD	Organisation for Economic Co-operation and Development
SCELI	Social Change and Economic Life Initiative
WAP	Working-age population

Part I

The context for labour market detachment

1   The UK labour market

Sue Yeandle

Introduction

This book is about processes of labour market detachment among adult men. As later chapters show, in recent years detachment from the labour market has become an increasingly important phenomenon, with significant economic and social consequences. Yet it cannot be explained in terms of any single factor – men's attitudes or personal characteristics, for example, or employers' decisions to close or restructure workplaces. As a research team, our interest in the processes of labour market detachment arose partly from the observation that, in the early and mid-1990s, inadequate opportunities in the British labour market were being reflected not only in continuing high levels of unemployment, but also in rising levels of economic inactivity. This was particularly the case in certain local labour markets where major industrial restructuring had occurred. We were also stimulated by a developing literature on how employment behaviour and labour market participation were influenced by welfare systems and social security regimes (Esping-Andersen 1990). Finally, we were interested in how far changes in men's social and family roles, affected both by women's rising rates of labour force participation and by the proliferation of different types of household structure, were shaping changes to traditional expectations about men's working lives.

What do we mean by detachment from the labour force? Labour market analysis uses a range of measures to assess levels of participation in the labour force: employment, unemployment and a variety of types of 'economic inactivity'. Our study started from an assumption that the boundaries between these categories were not clear cut. How to count the unemployed (those who want a job but cannot obtain one) had already become an increasingly vexed question for academics and policy-makers alike. As discussed below, the available measures all have limitations. This had been widely recognised in relation to female unemployment for years (Sinfield 1981, Walker 1981, Martin and Wallace 1984), but until the 1990s the prevalence of standardised patterns of male employment had disguised the problem for the male labour force. At the start of the twenty-first century, a range of alternatives to full-time 'lifelong' male employment have emerged, with part-time working, early retirement, re-training and adult learning, all unknown for men early in the twentieth century, becoming familiar concepts. Further, during the later twentieth century, it became possible in certain circumstances for men to withdraw from employment and to access a range of social security, insurance and employment benefits associated with chronic ill-health, a limiting disabil-ity or family responsibilities of various kinds. Important changes in the rules governing such withdrawals from the labour force, whether perma-nent or temporary, occurred during the last quarter of the twentieth cen-tury. For example, new rights to time off to carry out parental and family duties were included in the Employment Relations Act 1999. These de-velopments are discussed in more detail in ch. 3.

Our study is the more timely because the relationship between work and welfare was given very high profile by the Labour government imme-diately it came to power in 1997. It has continued to be an important and controversial theme since that time. This book explores new evidence from men who have become more or less detached from the labour force. It is based on a study of men who, when interviewed, were of an age at which full-time employment would once have been taken for granted. All the men were aged between 25 and 64, and almost all had been without regular full-time work for six months or more (see the appendix). The study was thus designed to explore the blurred and eroding boundaries between unemployment, economic inactivity and part-time employment for men. As later chapters show, the decisions the men had made were often complex, frequently a mixture of both enforced and voluntary pro-cesses, and sometimes 'drawn out'; one step had led to another for some, resulting in their labour force detachment, even though this may not have been an intended or expected outcome of the actions they took or the choices they made.

High levels of unemployment, as experienced during the later 1970s, 1980s and 1990s, were not, of course, new; indeed, in the 1940s, many aspects of the modern British welfare state had emerged from experiences of widespread poverty and hardship associated with mass unemployment in the 1920s and 1930s. But in the mid-1990s, interesting new evidence was rapidly accumulating: among older men, rates of 'economic inac-tivity' had accelerated fast, with inactivity associated with sickness and disability growing at a rate hard to comprehend in the context of rising general living standards (e.g. in housing and nutrition) and after fifty years of the National Health Service. Our study took shape as a way of answer-ing the following questions about adult men and the labour market:

- How much unemployment is concealed by economic inactivity among men?
- What do the recent work histories of men who have become 'detached' from the labour market tell us?
- How far are 'detached' men cushioned from the effects of losing their wage by their family and personal circumstances, and more generally, how do they 'get by'?
- Among detached men, how large are the groups still seeking work, prevented from working by health or disability, choosing early exit (perhaps linked with part-time work) or occupied by family responsibilities?

Later chapters show how the study has been used to provide some of the answers to these questions. In this opening chapter, we discuss approaches to measuring employment and unemployment, and the problems and issues associated with them; the dynamic nature of labour market analysis, both in relating to the changing composition of the labour force and to changes in demand for labour of different types; and men's changing experience of work as a component of their lives.

Employment and unemployment in the UK

As other commentators have pointed out, 'there is no perfect way to measure unemployment' (MacKay 1999: 1919). What is more, economies which permit free movement of labour will inevitably and always have some unemployment; this is known as 'adjustment' unemployment, which may be both frictional (people moving between jobs for which they have appropriate skills, within the same local labour market) and structural (movement between jobs which involve, for the worker, a change of occupation or industry or local labour market) (MacKay 1999: 1920). This much has long been recognised; indeed, Beveridge himself argued that 'full employment does not mean the end of change, competition, initiative and risks. It means only fresh opportunity always' (Beveridge 1944: 131).

In Britain, statistics on unemployment have been collected, in a variety of ways, since the 1880s. Statistics were derived initially from trade union records, and later from data based on unemployment insurance records after 1911 (Denman and McDonald 1996). During the first half of the twentieth century, changes to the law on unemployment insurance brought increasing numbers of unemployed workers within the scope of these records; but it was only with the 1948 implementation of the National Insurance Act that coverage extended to all male and female employees. The resultant data, on those 'registered as unemployed', most

of whom were also eligible for social security benefits because of their unemployment, can be distinguished from the 'claimant count' figures on
which administrative data since 1982 have been based.[1] While the earlier
assessments had been based on a clerical count, the new data collection
system was computerised in 1982. From October of that year, registra-
tion for employment became voluntary for all adults, and from November
1982 the official unemployment figures were based instead on a claimant
count of those receiving unemployment-related benefits. Denman and
McDonald report that this led to changes in coverage which 'had the
effect of reducing the level of unemployment, on average, by 112,000
(or 3.7 per cent)' (1996: 13). The 1982 changes followed an inquiry into
unemployment statistics instigated in 1980 by the then new Conservative
government. At that time the government identified 'those aged 60 to 65
who had taken "early retirement", the unfit and the "unemployable" as
groups that should be excluded' (Walker 1981: 9). As Walker notes, the
Job Release Scheme, introduced in 1977, had already denied those within
a year of statutory retirement who chose to join it (leaving work in return
for a tax-free allowance) the entitlement to register as unemployed.

The 'claimant count' is based on official records of the number of individuals who are (successfully) claiming 'unemployment benefits'. Of
course, the titles given to such benefits change over time, as governments
decide (see ch. 3). The basis upon which a claim for unemployment
benefits is approved is subject to change, usually caused by governments
deciding to adjust the eligibility criteria entitling individuals to such benefits. These criteria include evidence about whether or not the individual
has, as a member of the workforce, been making National Insurance (NI)
payments over relevant periods. Some people who are not in work but
who would like to have a job may be deterred from applying for such
benefits, thinking they are ineligible, or fearing stigma or that they may
be judged to be ineligible. Here confusion about benefit entitlement, discussed more fully in ch. 3, plays an important role. Some of the sources
of stigma or embarrassment about claiming benefits are also outlined in
that chapter. Other people may be excluded from the claimant count (and
indeed from receiving benefit) because they are judged not to be behaving
appropriately. In recent years this has been connected with various assessments of whether an individual is 'actively seeking work' or 'available
for work' (again, see ch. 3 for details). Some who wish to work may have

[1] For a full analysis of changes affecting the collection of unemployment statistics from 1881
onwards, see Denman and McDonald (1996) (including annex A which details 'legislative
and administrative changes likely to have affected the monthly series of unemployment
statistics between 1912 and 1982') and Fenwick and Denman (1995) for a list of all such
changes affecting the unemployment figures between 1979 and 1995.

characteristics that enable assessors to allocate them to another category of benefit because they meet its eligibility criteria (the prime examples being sickness and disability benefits). Examples of men who were advised to apply for, or were redirected to, other benefits are discussed in chs. 7 and 8.

The political sensitivity of unemployment, particularly as 'magic' figures such as the 1 or 2 million mark are reached, has meant that governments have sometimes stood accused of 'massaging' the unemployment figures. Some argue that, for the purpose of analysis of conditions in the labour market, the 'claimant count' figures are best discarded and replaced by survey data, especially data based on figures collected using the International Labour Organisation (ILO) definition of unemployment. This covers people who are out of work, want a job, have actively sought work in the previous four weeks and are available to start work within the next fortnight; or are out of work and have accepted a job that they are waiting to start in the next fortnight. The ILO definition has the advantage of enabling cross-national comparison of data, as well as eliminating the impact of administrative and legislative changes, but it remains an imperfect measure. Labour Force Survey data, in the UK as elsewhere in Europe, rely on asking a randomly selected, statistically generalisable, sample of individuals to assess their own situation. Such data produce statistically reliable estimates, and tend to be favoured over counts of claimants since the latter fail to pick up many persons who wish to have paid work. Examples include eligible persons who are not claiming relevant benefits, and others who may want work but are officially deemed not to be fully active in seeking it. Given that unemployed people in areas of high unemployment and low demand for labour are more likely than others to become discouraged in their search for work, this can be an important source of regional variation in the reliability of claimant unemployment data. Being counted within the ILO definition of unemployment for respondents to these surveys nevertheless implies that, in their own judgement, they are 'actively seeking work'.

As MacKay (1999) and others note, it has traditionally been the relationship between the number of unfilled jobs in the economy (job vacancies) and the number of people judged to be unemployed which has determined whether or not unemployment is seen as a political problem requiring government action, or an inevitable labour market characteristic (as in 'adjustment unemployment', discussed above). If estimates of vacancies (there is no sure way, in a free market economy, of counting all vacancies, so labour market analysts rely always on estimates, guided by research evidence on how best to make these) are smaller than counts of 'the unemployed', by other than a very small margin, then there is judged to be an 'unemployment problem'. Such a problem has existed for British governments now for over thirty years. During that time commentators have repeatedly drawn attention to a variety of facets of this problem. It varies in severity by region; it affects men and women differently; it is experienced more frequently by young workers and by older workers; and it arises both because people wishing to enter the labour market cannot find a job, and because people who hold jobs lose their position when employers decide to shed labour or to close a worksite. Throughout the past fifty years, as shown below, workers in certain occupations and industries have been especially vulnerable to redundancy. The regional location of these industries gave rise to the expectation that job losses of this type and scale would lead to (at least initial) rises in unemployment in the regions affected. That this did not occur, to the extent expected, following mass pit closures in the British coalfields in the 1980s and 1990s, was part of the labour market puzzle which Beatty and Fothergill first investigated in their study of labour market adjustment in the coalfields (Beatty and Fothergill 1996).

The period between the early 1970s and 1997 (when our study was begun) saw important fluctuations in male and female economic activity rates, employment rates and unemployment rates. While economic activity for women increased, men's economic activity fell. More detail about the situation of men is given in ch. 4.

The scale of the changes is evident. Male employment in Great Britain fell by an extraordinary 1.7 million between spring 1979 and spring 1983 (Office for National Statistics 1997). In the following decades the number of jobs held by men continued to fall – by almost 1 million between 1981 and 1998, with very large falls in manufacturing jobs and the extractive industries only partly offset by increases in male employment in parts of the service sector, notably in financial and business services and in distribution, hotels, catering and repairs. By contrast, the overall number of jobs held by women increased by 2.2 million between 1981 and 1998, although many of these jobs were part time, and the increase disguised major job losses affecting women employed in manufacturing (Office for National Statistics 1999: table 4.15).

For the whole of the last quarter of the twentieth century, unemployment was a significant economic and political issue, with profound social consequences. Officially recorded male unemployment peaked in the mid-1980s and again in 1993. More detailed figures for the 1990s show that while for both men and women claimants unemployment was a particularly acute problem for the young (those under 25), among workers aged 25 and above, rates were consistently higher for men than for women, with rates for men aged 45–54 fluctuating between 4.8 and

Table 1.1. *Reasons for economic inactivity:[a] by gender, 1993 and 1998*

	Males		Females		All of working age	
	1993	1998	1993	1998	1993	1998
Does not want a job	70	67	72	71	72	69
Wants a job but not seeking in last four weeks						
Long-term sick or disabled	10	16	3	6	5	9
Looking after a family or home	2	2	14	14	10	9
Student	4	5	2	3	3	3
Discouraged worker[b]	3	1	1	1	2	1
Other	5	5	4	4	4	4
All	24	29	24	26	24	27
Wants a job and seeking work but not available to start[c]	6	4	4	3	4	3
All reasons (= 100%) (millions)	2.7	3.0	4.9	4.9	7.6	7.9

Notes:

[a] At spring each year; males aged 16 to 64, females aged 16 to 59.

[b] People who believed no jobs were available.

[c] Not available for work in the next two weeks. Includes those who did not state whether or not they were available.

Source: Labour Force Survey, Office for National Statistics (*Social Trends* 29, 1999).

9.3 per cent, compared with 3.1 and 5.0 per cent for women of the same age.

The economically inactive, as discussed in more detail below, comprise a number of sub-categories which are conceptually and empirically distinct. 'Inactive' persons may be full-time students, persons caring full time for another person or for a home and family, persons who are not required to register for work because they are sick or disabled and in receipt of sickness or disability benefits, as well as those who have chosen, or been required to take, an early exit or temporary withdrawal from the labour force. Some of these, the 'early retired', may have taken severance or reached the retirement age specific to their occupation, and will often (although not always) be in receipt of an occupational pension. Between 1993 (the most recent peak in male unemployment) and 1998 the Labour Force Survey estimated that the number of men of working age who were economically inactive rose from 2.7 million to 3 million. Of these, the proportion saying they wanted a job, but who had not sought work in the previous four weeks, rose from 24 to 29 per cent (table 1.1). While this table shows that the figures for most sub-categories of male economic inactivity remained relatively stable, those indicating that they were not seeking work because of long-term sickness or disability rose particularly sharply. A similar, but less marked, picture emerges when the figures for women of working age are examined.

Previous research had in the 1980s already focused on a particular subcategory of the unemployed, those who had been unemployed for longer periods (the long-term unemployed, usually defined as those out of work for a year or longer) (Burghes and Lister 1981, White 1983, Dawes 1993). Much earlier, Beveridge had discussed the 'long-period unemployed', citing Wales and Northern England as areas where 'nearly two out of every five persons unemployed had been out of work for more than a year' (Beveridge 1944: 66–7). In these mid- and late-twentieth-century studies it had already been noted that there were important regional, age and sex differences among the long-term unemployed.

In the early 1980s, Walker reported that, in 1979,

two-thirds of those unemployed for more than one year were aged 35 or over, and one-third were aged 55 or over. Nearly three-quarters had formerly held manual jobs... The long-term unemployed came disproportionately from construction, manufacturing or basic industries. The main reasons given for leaving their last job were redundancy and ill-health. In fact, more than one in three had some handicap or illness which affected their activities. (1981: 19)

Walker also drew attention to 'a significant group of older people who are part of the "hidden" unemployed because, under different labour market conditions, they would be employed', stressing the role of 'age discrimination' in this process, which meant that 'long-term unemployment [was] borne disproportionately by older workers' (23). Regional disparities in the unemployment rate contributed further complexity, although regional analyses still underestimated the impact on some vulnerable small areas. Sinfield, writing about the geography of unemployment in 1981, commented that

the picture that emerges is a depressing one of downward spiral. It illustrates well what may happen in a community with above-average unemployment for many years, and how further increases in unemployment will generally hit these groups yet again. (Sinfield 1981: 28)

Another study found that 'personal disadvantages', including low levels of education, poor health and disability, played only a minor role in explaining long-term unemployment. Rather more important in individual work histories were displacement from the 'shrinking manufacturing sector' (and from other industries of declining employment, such as mining, iron and steel) and mobility between industries (White 1983: 151). Large-scale redundancies, and to a lesser extent employers' programmes of early retirement, had also been important in bringing older men into long-term unemployment. Only a minority of the long-term unemployed in White's study had a personal history of 'recurrent unemployment', and this was concentrated among the younger long-term unemployed. Notably, most of the formerly stable workers who were now long-term unemployed were older men, a disproportionate number of whom had experienced redundancy or early retirement. White observed that 'there were however many who had left stable employment of their own choice, most commonly for reasons of ill-health' (154). Furthermore, 'the great majority of the long-term unemployed came (in their last employment) from large or medium-sized firms or from the public sector' (155). White emphasised that while older men at this time were 'not particularly prominent in the flow into long-term unemployment', their chances of getting a job were 'extremely slender'. Summarising his conclusions about workers who had fallen into long-term unemployment directly from long-lasting stable jobs, he explained:

The main routes into unemployment for these formerly stable workers are early retirement, redundancy, and leaving for reasons of ill-health. The occupational pensioners naturally come from the over-55 age group, and from the skilled manual and higher non-manual occupations. Those leaving work for reasons of ill-health are more often in the age group between 45 and 55 and from a wide mix of manual occupations. Redundancies and closures, especially large-scale ones, bring stable employment to an end for many in both age groups. (White 1983: 164)

In 1986 a large research programme involving ten universities, the Social Change and Economic Life Initiative (SCELI), was sponsored by the Economic and Social Research Council. This studied developments in six labour markets (Aberdeen, Kirkcaldy, Northampton, Coventry, Rochdale and Swindon) and examined changes in labour supply and demand, the impact of economic restructuring and continuing high unemployment. The SCELI studies adopted a broader than conventional definition of unemployment, recognising that 'the unemployed are not just people without work but people who would participate in the formal economy if there were jobs available for them' (Gallie, Marsh and Vogler 1994: 7).

The SCELI studies also noted that it was difficult to make 'clean distinctions' between the unemployed and the economically inactive. In practice, SCELI treated as unemployed all those who were receiving benefits on the grounds of unemployment and any others who had looked for work in the previous four weeks.

By comparison with the present study, SCELI paid rather little attention to the group within the economically inactive category that

has increased most rapidly and has become the focus of growing policy attention: recipients of long-term sickness and disability benefits.
SCELI nevertheless took research into employment and unemployment
into important new territory and reached some significant conclusions.
The study emphasised that there were 'no grounds for considering the
non-registered (unemployed) as in any sense a less real category of the
unemployed'. Furthermore, unemployed people did not display 'distinctive' attitudes to work, and '[t]he unemployed were clearly not . . . in-
herently unstable members of the workforce' (Gallie and Vogler 1994:
152).

Factors important for 'job chances' were

The availability of particular types of work . . . the resources that can be provided
by the household to facilitate job search, and . . . the structural misfit between the
low qualifications possessed by the unemployed and the sharp rise in qualifications
required by the changing nature of work in industry. (Gallie and Vogler 1994: 153)

The SCELI data also provided an opportunity to study work history
data collected from respondents for the period 1945–85. Analysis
revealed a substantial strengthening of the relationship between 'men's
occupational status and their susceptibility to unemployment' over the period, as well as a 'cohort difference in the impact of the adverse economic
circumstances of the 1970s and 1980s', which had affected younger cohorts most seriously (Gershuny and Marsh 1994: 113). As we reveal in
ch. 7, our new study found further evidence of this effect. Gershuny and
Marsh also stressed their finding that 'unemployment is concentrated
among a small group of people (in distinctive geographical and occupational locations)' (1994: 113).

The relationship between labour market behaviour and aspects of family life had been studied before SCELI (Yeandle 1991, 1993, Allatt and
Yeandle 1992), but came into wider view through the new six-labour-
market study. Specific scrutiny of unemployment and relationship breakdown revealed that

Postmarital unemployment caused a significant number of marital dissolutions
which would otherwise not have occurred at all, or would have occurred at a later
date . . . [and that] a number of individuals experienced unemployment episodes
as a direct consequence of the dissolution of their marriages. (Lampard 1994:
296)

This issue has also been explored in the present study, and is discussed
in relation to specific cases in ch. 7.

Dawes's investigation of *Long-term Unemployment and Labour Market
Flexibility* (1993) drew on samples of men and women who had been
out of work for six months or more in four of the localities included in

the SCELI studies (Rochdale, Northampton, Swindon and Kirkcaldy), the interviews taking place in 1990 and 1991. Dawes found that where they could, the long-term unemployed acted flexibly, but that they were constrained by 'social factors which [were] not within their control' (8). The 'extent of household responsibilities' was a major influence on the labour market behaviour of the unemployed, a point explored in the present study, while social (and household) networks were of great importance in gaining a job and in alleviating poverty and social exclusion during unemployment. Dawes concluded that 'the level of unemployment benefits has no explanatory value in considering the labour market behaviour of the long-term unemployed'; indeed, decreasing levels of benefit would be likely only to 'exacerbate the process of social exclusion'. The research found that over time the 'reservation wage' increased rather than decreased, since for this group 'their household commitments remain[ed] the dominant influence on their assessment of the earnings they require[d]' (9).

These and other studies, then, had shown well before our study began that unemployment was unevenly distributed across the country, and affected some groups of men much more severely than others. It also indicated that the term 'unemployed' could, at times, be a label attached to men whose ability, inclination or need to work had become reduced, as well as one used to describe those whose sole reason for being out of work was that they had no opportunity of employment. Poor health, early retirement, other sources of income, including redundancy payments, wage replacement schemes, opportunities to access pensions before statutory retirement age and changes in social security benefits were all adding to an already complex picture. The way the boundaries between unemployment and other economic statuses were shifting was a key interest for our study, as it was clear that processes of labour market attachment and detachment were neither simple nor static.

Men's changing experience of work

Throughout the 1990s evidence accumulated that, for men, the 'standard employment relationship' was becoming eroded (Beck 1992, Beatson 1995, Cousins 1999, Goodin 2000). Under multiple pressures – from labour market restructuring and an increasingly important service sector, from increased opportunities for extended education, from new patterns of family life and from the quest within organisations for downsized, flexible workforces responsive to technological change – men's employment patterns became more diverse. It became the received view that never again would men's working lives involve lifelong full-time employment in a single industry, for the half century of their lifespan between the ages of 15 and 65. Work for men would start later, finish earlier and be more varied in between. Skills would become obsolete, or require updating, ever more rapidly, whole industries in which men had predominated for 150 years would disappear and in the future more work would involve interpersonal, clerical and technical skills, with much reduced call for manual labour, fewer unskilled jobs and a greater need to reskill and re-train, not just once, but perhaps numerous times during the working life. These developments, viewed as tragic and alarming by some (Seabrook 1978, 1982, Showler and Sinfield 1981, Merritt 1982), were seen by others as potentially heralding a world in which men would have more leisure, more choice and more variety in their lives (Gershuny, 1978). Data from the British Household Panel Study (BHPS) confirm many of these observations. For example, whereas less then 5 per cent of men exited full-time education to unemployment before 1970, by the 1990s 'this had grown to almost one in three' (Taylor 2000: 76).

These changes reflected increased workplace and skill flexibility and greater use by employers of options for early retirement and voluntary redundancy. These trends were expected to continue (although as ch. 2 shows, most European governments no longer believe this to be the case). These developments, it was concluded, would not only exert their im-pact through changing practices in the workplace, but would also affect men's later lives: changes in the proportion of male workers covered by occupational pension provision were of particular concern. In the UK the proportion of male workers who were members of occupational pension schemes peaked as long ago as 1967, steadily reducing from the 1970s onwards (Department of Social Security (DSS) 2000a: para. 2.1).

The financial circumstances of detached men are an important ele-ment of the present study, and are discussed in chs. 6 and 9. A recent review of studies in this field has shown that the average real incomes of people in the 50–74 age group increased substantially in the last quarter of the twentieth century, with earnings playing a declining role, and pri-vate pensions and investment income an increasing role, while 'unearned private income was more important than transfers from the state' (Barker and Hancock 2000: 49). This review also used evidence from the Family Resources Survey (FRS) to show that 'nearly a quarter of men aged 50–54 who are seeking work or would like a job, and a fifth of those who are long-term sick in this age group, are drawing an occupational pension' (Barker and Hancock 2000: 50).

The FRS data also demonstrate that among the 50-plus group, men who were early retired were substantially more likely than those who were long-term sick to be owner-occupiers, and that about a quarter had no financial wealth. Those in employment had the highest incomes in this group, followed, in declining order of income level, by the retired, the long-term sick and those looking for work (Barker and Hancock 2000: 51). Furthermore, the authors, using data from the BHPS, confirmed that

controlling for other factors, retirement before state pension age increases the probability of movement into the low-income group, possession of an occupational pension reduces the probability and home-owners are less likely than renters to move into low income. (Barker and Hancock 2000: 59)

Barker and Hancock's review (which also considered evidence from the Survey of Retirement and Retirement Plans conducted in 1988 and 1994) emphasised the importance of recognising the variety of financial circumstances in which early retired people, and indeed others in this age group, are found. Our study, as chs. 6 and 9 confirm, firmly underlines this point.

Since 1997, the pensions and employment situation of older workers have been a particular focus of the Labour government's attention, and a range of measures designed to halt or reverse the trend towards lower employment rates among this group has been introduced (Ashdown 2000), including the New Deal 50 Plus, which aims specifically to encourage those in the 50–64 age group to return to employment. Pensions policy has also been under review, and the Performance and Innovation Unit (2000) has reported on the trends and issues which lie behind the government's emphasis on 'active ageing'.

The study reported in this book is concerned with men who have become detached from the labour force on both voluntary (as in early retirement) and involuntary bases. Involuntary labour market exit may arise because of redundancy, poor health, workplace accidents and injuries, family obligations or dismissal. During the twentieth century men (and women) have acquired a range of legal rights and protections in employment which now govern their conditions of employment and the ways and circumstances in which their employment can be terminated. Full discussion of these is beyond the scope of this chapter, but it is worthwhile briefly to note the main developments. (In some industries, collective bargaining agreements negotiated between employers and trade unions may offer a higher degree of protection to workers than is offered by the law.) The key provisions in British law have included those relating to redundancy, unfair dismissal, sickness, disability, entitlements to periods of leave (paid and unpaid) and regulations concerning working hours. These policy developments are all relevant to the present study since they affect the circumstances in which men leave employment, or may have their employment legally terminated. For anyone who has ever secured employment, it is departure from paid work which, ultimately, leads to labour market detachment. Some of the legal measures concern how employers must behave if they intend to shed labour; others give legal protection to workers whose behaviour, for example absences from work, might otherwise cause their employers to dismiss them.

The Redundancy Payments Act 1965 was a policy originally introduced in a period of low unemployment, designed to facilitate the redeployment and mobility of workers, especially those over 41 years of age. In the 1970s, however, this had in effect 'become (hidden) *unemployment* redundancy for those within less than ten years of retirement' (Harris 1991: 110, emphasis in original).

A government-sponsored study of the effects of this legislation also showed that

One of the most important demonstrated consequences of the Act has been to increase the significance of age as a criterion for redundancy because the larger payments to older workers with long service acts as a mechanism to induce them to leave employment. (Department of Employment, 1978, cited Hepple and Fredman 1986: 141)

The 1965 Act and the subsequent Employment Protection (Consolidation) Act 1978 (which incorporated the 1965 Act) laid down how redundancy payments should be calculated. This included a scaling down of the amounts payable to workers in their final year before statutory retirement age (Hepple and Fredman 1986), and the exclusion of workers over this age from the provisions of the Act, providing a further incentive to male workers to avoid delaying departure from employment until after reaching age 64. We will see in ch. 2 how governments, which once encouraged such early retirement, have more recently tried to reverse the trend towards 'early exit' in an attempt to raise the employment rate among the working-age population (WAP).

The main ways in which the state has sought to support workers prevented from working through sickness or disability are described in ch. 3. Policy on industrial and occupational diseases and injuries developed gradually (and somewhat piecemeal) from the late nineteenth century onwards. The Workmen's Compensation Act of 1887 first introduced the concept of 'occupational risk' and provided for workers to be compensated for injuries suffered at work. This was extended to cover certain industrial diseases in 1906 (Marshall 1975). As late as 1972, however, some 5 million workers still 'worked in premises not covered by any occupational health or safety legislation' (Hepple and Fredman 1986: 44), a fact which the comprehensive Health and Safety at Work Act of 1974 was designed to rectify. These and other subsequent developments have cushioned the worst effects of sickness and injury, although there remains a strong link between poverty and other forms of deprivation and poor health.

Legislation introduced by the last Conservative administration sought for the first time to protect workers and potential employees from discrimination on the grounds of disability (the Disability Discrimination Act 1995). Social and ideological perceptions of disability have changed significantly over recent decades (Walker and Howard 2000). This has contributed to shifts in policy concerning the state's responsibility to enable people with disabilities to secure adequate income to meet their living costs, as well as to enable them to participate in employment. The social security aspects of these shifts are considered in ch. 3. In line with such policy developments, the incoming 1997 Labour administration placed further emphasis on its desire to see 'an increase in the number of disabled people able to work', although how far the measures introduced have actually helped disabled people remains controversial (Drake 2000).

Through the Employment Relations Act 1999, introduced in part to comply with the UK's commitments to the European *Social Policy Agenda* (Commission of the European Communities 2000), male employees for the first time gained the right to some types of leave from work with legal protection against being penalised by their employer (Department of Trade and Industry (DTI) 1998). This was an important development, as it treated men who were fathers as having responsibilities other than for breadwinning, and meant that a role for men which involved the care of their families was now recognised in law. The Act gave all workers, including men, the right to thirteen weeks' unpaid leave during the first five years after having a child, and the right to take 'reasonable time off' to deal with family crises involving their children or other dependants. The government went on to review all aspects of parental leave in 2001, following publication of the *Work and Parents* Green Paper. It is planned that statutory rights to paid paternity leave for men at the time of their child's birth will be introduced in 2004 (DTI 2000).

While this brief discussion indicates the range of legal measures which should help to prevent men's detachment from the labour force, or compensate them if they are unable to work, our research showed that many men were unsure about their entitlements. Some men had quit their jobs in circumstances where the more recent developments described above

Table 1.2. *Employee jobs in selected industries in the UK: 1948–98*

Index (1948 = 100)	1948	1958	1968	1978	1988[a]	1998
Coalmining	100	98	61	37	15	2
Ports and docks	100	100	87	42	23	16
Railways	100	87	51	44	27	16
Steel production	100	114	123	101	37	18
Shipbuilding	100	88	64	60	24	8
Agriculture	100	74	49	47	40	40
Motor vehicle manufacture	100	113	169	169	39	36
Textile manufacture	100	94	74	49	23	18
Column totals	100	92	73	58	27	19
Column totals (000 jobs)	4,092	3,778	2,993	2,363	1,118	791

Note: [a]The 1998 figures are interpolations based on the 1987 and 1989 Censuses of Employment. There was no Census of Employment in 1988.
Source: Parliamentary question in the House of Lords, 19 April 2000, published in Office for National Statistics 2000, 108.7: 311.

might have enabled them to remain in employment. We return to these issues in later chapters of the book.

Changes in the structure, organisation and composition of the labour market

The key features of change in the UK labour force since the 1960s are well known. Back in 1966, well over half of the workforce (58 per cent) were manual workers, while fewer than one-tenth were in managerial or professional jobs (Weir 1973: 21). Thirty years later (using revised and therefore not directly comparable occupational definitions), it was estimated that fewer than half of employed men (about 48 per cent) were in manual occupations, while almost one-third (31 per cent) were in managerial or professional jobs. The occupational distribution of the workforce had also changed, with jobs in traditional male industries – coal, steel, shipbuilding, heavy engineering, vehicle manufacturing and agriculture – sharply reduced. Table 1.2 shows the dramatic reduction in the number of jobs in such industries between 1948 and 1998.

As the service sector has grown in importance in the UK economy, so the nature of the jobs within it has altered. The proportions of workers in full-time employment vary by both sex and age, and for men, the proportions in full-time employment fall quite sharply in older age groups (table 1.3). Service sector employment contains many part-time jobs, a high proportion of jobs based in offices, shops and leisure outlets, and

Table 1.3. *Older workers in employment by age group and whether working full time: UK, winter 1999–2000, not seasonally adjusted (thousands (%))*

Age	50–59	60–64	65+
Men	2,731	644	283
of which			
Total in full-time employment	2,512	526	88
Percentage in full-time employment	(92)	(82)	(31)
Women	2,297	370	179
of which			
Total in full-time employment	1,201	116	22
Percentage in full-time employment	(52)	(31)	(12)
All persons	5,028	1,014	461
of which			
Total in full-time employment	3,712	642	110
Percentage in full-time employment	(74)	(63)	(24)

Source: Labour Force Survey (published in Office for National Statistics 2000, 108.7: 311).

many in which the tasks involved have traditionally been unpaid work performed by women.

Part-time and temporary employment and (for some people) having a second job have become important features of the UK labour market, which has shown continuing growth in the proportion of part-time jobs, especially those held by workers in certain age groups and women. Part-time employment increased rather steeply for men in the UK between 1985 and 1995, with part-time employment among men aged 25–49 rising by 145 per cent to approximately 250,000 jobs. This was also an important type of employment for younger and older men, with almost 450,000 part-time jobs held by men under 25, and around 250,000 by men aged 50–64, in 1995 (Yeandle 1999). Men are slightly less numerous than women among those in the UK labour force who hold a second job. Labour Force Survey estimates suggest that in 1998 around 550,000 men and some 680,000 women were in this situation (Office for National Statistics 1999: 77). Temporary employment, although not a particularly strong feature of the UK labour market when it is compared to that of other European countries, affected around 6.5 per cent of male employees in the UK in 1997 (and was higher, at 8.4 per cent, for women).

Changes in the occupational and industrial structure of the labour market have, of course, brought some benefits for those in the workforce. The declining industrial sectors included many characterised by dangerous, unhealthy or unpleasant working conditions. Despite health and safety legislation, including the 1974 Health and Safety at Work Act, workplace injury rates remain much higher in many traditionally male occupations – construction, extraction and utility supply, transport, storage and communication, agriculture and manufacturing (all with workplace injury rates at or near 20 per 1000 in the late 1990s) (Office for National Statistics 1999: 84) – than in education, finance and business. Predominantly male industries such as agriculture and fishing, transport and communication, energy and water supply and construction also have longer average weekly hours of work than is the case in banking and finance, public administration, education and health or other services (Office for National Statistics 1999: 78), although male weekly hours of employment continue to exceed female weekly hours in all of these sectors.

Regional and local labour markets

As indicated above, a regional and local focus has long been recognised as important in explaining labour market behaviour and change. The main structural developments in the UK labour market referred to above have had a differential impact in different regions of the country. This has meant that employment growth of certain types has been concentrated in some localities, with a converse concentration of job loss in others. Investigation of the relationship between local unemployment rates and individual ill-health during the 1980s has shown, by correlating rates of unemployment in local labour markets with data on the health of individuals, that '*high levels* of unemployment exert an adverse effect on the relative chances of poor health, whether subjective or objective, across a national population of working age' (Bellaby and Bellaby 1999: 479, emphasis in original). This research, which controlled for a range of confounding factors including the 'healthy worker effect', suggested that 'it is . . . likely that high levels of unemployment generate ill health that leads to more irregular employment and more frequent early exit from the labour market' (*ibid.*). This is important in relation to the present study, which was designed to explore processes of labour market detachment in areas with different levels of joblessness (see the appendix). As we show later in the book, our study found greater reliance on sickness and disability benefits in the areas of higher, longer-standing unemployment. A variety of ways in which this finding might be explained are explored in chs. 5 and 8.

Another important feature of the dynamic labour market which this book explores concerns changes in the skills and skill levels of the male labour force over time. Much of the labour market restructuring outlined above has occurred in sectors in which skilled male manual workers were employed. For middle-aged and older men leaving these industries, closures and redundancies meant that the occupation for which they had trained (often through formal apprenticeships) and in which they had expected to have lifelong employment was now closed to them. For younger men these same shifts have brought important changes in youthful expectations about when in the life course vocational training occurs, and have introduced the idea that there may be a number of points in the male working life when skills need to be acquired. Men in their 40s and older, shaken out of traditional male industries, now require both new job opportunities and the chance to retrain and reskill for these, if they are to regain access to employment.

The adequacy of the state's efforts to support these developments has been widely debated. From 1974 onwards, following the establishment of the Manpower Services Commission, vocational training structures in the UK were recast (Ainley 1988). The old apprenticeship model, which had given many working-class males their access to skilled, unionised and relatively secure and well-paid employment, was replaced by a variety of youth training schemes, mainly designed to alleviate the problems associated with rising youth unemployment (Allatt and Yeandle 1992). Later, in the 1990s, modern apprenticeships, and sustained efforts to increase the age participation rate in further and higher education, were also introduced, as governments gave increasing attention to the need for higher levels of skill and qualification in the workforce. Inevitably, some of the detached men interviewed for the present study had experience of these measures. Since 1997, a range of New Deal programmes have been introduced, as part of Welfare to Work policy. The initial emphasis was on the New Deals for young people and for lone parents, although subsequent initiatives have also been developed: New Deal 50 Plus, mentioned above, and New Deal 25 Plus. The Labour government has claimed success for these interventions (Department for Education and Employment (DfEE) 2001a), although critics argue that falls in official unemployment have been mainly attributable to the buoyant labour market context which coincided with Labour's 1997–2001 term of office.

Earnings and family responsibilities

The changes in men's relationship to the labour market described above have gradually eroded the male breadwinner role, while women's much increased participation in employment has underscored this change. Indeed, the trend towards dual earning in family households has been particularly important in raising the standard of living of those households able to retain an active connection with the labour market. A variety of demographic changes is also linked to the changes in men's family responsibilities and in the role of male earnings in household economies. These changes include a lower marriage rate, smaller family size coupled with increased longevity (so that raising a family occupies a relatively shorter part of the average life), higher levels of divorce and relationship breakdown and an increasing likelihood that men will have second families. The situation of some men, including lone fathers, single men and divorced or widowed men living alone, raises particular issues relating to labour market attachment. Although it continues to be the case that most men are the main earners for their households, for a significant group supplementary income is available, especially at certain life stages, and men who are lifelong sole breadwinners have become something of a rarity. The significance of these developments for male attachment to the labour force has been little discussed and studied. The design of the present study has enabled some light to be shed on the circumstances of men in different family and household situations, which are examined in ch. 7.

In the past decade analysts have drawn attention to the emergence of a social divide between 'work-rich' and 'work-poor' households (Gregg and Wadsworth 1996). Official analysis of 'workless households' – homes in which no one has a paid job – showed that in 1998 they could be categorised as follows: 31 per cent single person households; 25 per cent lone parent households containing dependent children; 21 per cent married/cohabiting couples without children; 12 per cent married/cohabiting couples with dependent children; 5 per cent lone parents with non-dependent children; 4 per cent households of two or more unrelated adults; and 3 per cent married/cohabiting couples with non-dependent children. Further analysis showed that economic inactivity was more important among these households than unemployment. Of the 3.1 million workless households containing at least one person of working age, 75 per cent were households where all adult members were economically inactive and 14 per cent were households where all were unemployed, while 11 per cent contained both unemployed and inactive adults (Office for National Statistics 1999: 74). The implications of this are that policy directed at reducing unemployment will not, unless it is accompanied by significant policy measures to tackle economic inactivity, make much of an inroad into poverty.

Furthermore, generic policy based on a notional household containing a couple and their children is now more inappropriate than ever. Recent comparison of data from the General Household Panel Survey for 1973 and 1996 (Berthoud 2000) shows that households containing 'single adults' were less likely to have a job at the later date (68 per cent compared with 80 per cent in 1973). Among 'couples with children', there was an increase in both joblessness (up from 5 to 9 per cent having no job) and dual earning (up from 43 per cent to 60 per cent). The increasing prevalence of living alone, which features among the population of working age as well as among the post-retirement population, like the continuing rise in the number of lone parent families, which has already reached official policy agendas, must be recognised in the development of employment and social policy.

Labour market dynamics

As is made clear in ch. 3, which discusses social security benefits, there is continuous and substantial movement between different labour market (and thus benefit) circumstances. This dynamic aspect of the labour market is very important. It is movement into unemployment (or another specific labour market status, such as economic inactivity) at a higher on-flow rate than the off-flow from that status which raises the size of the unemployed (or inactive) population. What matters, in terms of whether unemployment or economic inactivity is increasing or decreasing, are the answers to three questions? How many people are entering unemployment (etc.)? How many people are leaving unemployment (etc.)? And once on, how long are people remaining in unemployment (etc.)?

Movement between economic activity statuses over time can be estimated from the UK Labour Force Survey. Table 1.4 shows the estimates based on data for men whose status was known for spring in both 1999 and 2000. From this table it can be seen that some statuses are much more static than others: for example, most men (95 per cent) who were in employment in spring 1999 were also in employment in spring 2000. Those who were economically inactive in 1999, however, were also very likely to remain so a year later; of those looking after a family or home, 88 per cent were still inactive, and of those who were long-term sick or disabled, 96 per cent were still inactive. By contrast, of those who were unemployed and actively seeking work in spring 1999, 40 per cent were in work a year later, 46 per cent remained unemployed and 14 per cent had become economically inactive. Of those who had been temporarily sick or injured in 1999 39 per cent had regained employment, while 14 per cent had become unemployed and 48 per cent were economically inactive.

The BHPS also provides important evidence of dynamic labour market processes, showing that whereas only 3 per cent of employed men had become unemployed at the next wave of the interviews (one year later), 54 per cent of men who were unemployed at first contact were still in this situation at the following wave of interviews (Taylor 2000: 90). On the

Table 1.4. *Movement between employment statuses over twelve months: men in UK, spring 2000*

Status one year previously (main activity self-assessed)	Total (000)	Current labour market status		
		Employed (%)	Unemployed (%)	Economically inactive (%)
In employment[a]	15,000	95	2	2
Unemployed, actively seeking work				
Full-time student	1,361	38	9	52
Looking after family or home	251	7	6	88
Temporarily sick or disabled	98	39	14	48
Long-term sick or disabled	1,287	2	2	96
Retired	3,706	1	_[b]	99
None of these	178	45	14	41
All	22,754	68	4	28

Notes:
[a] Includes those who responded that they were working in a paid job or business, laid off, on short time in a firm, on a government-supported training scheme or doing unpaid work for themselves or a relative.
[b] Sample size too small for a reliable estimate.
Source: Labour Force Survey (in Office for National Statistics 2000, 108.9: 394).

basis of extensive analysis of the BHPS, Taylor conjectures that 'Unstable early years in the labour market, and an exposure to unemployment at a young age (which is becoming more common) could have repercussions for an individual's career' (Taylor 2000: 92).

These analyses form an important backdrop to our study. As ours is a study of men who have had no full-time regular job for almost all the six months prior to the survey, it has, by definition, excluded those men who, during the previous six months, have returned to employment following redundancy, unemployment, ill-health or a short spell, for whatever reason, between jobs. The study was designed to explore processes of male labour force detachment. As such it is men without work whose personal, family or economic situations have led them to make no attempt, or only unsuccessful attempts, to re-enter the labour market with whom this book is concerned.

2 The international context

Sue Yeandle

Introduction

In ch. 1 the concept of detachment from the labour market was explored in relation to the UK. There we saw some of the limitations of conventional measures of unemployment and located the non-employed population in the context of the changing structure of the UK labour market.

Chapter 2 turns to comparative assessment of labour market detachment. The chapter opens with evidence about economic inactivity and unemployment in a number of other economies, and looks at some evidence about 'non-standard' employment. It goes on to give an indication of how some other states have addressed these issues, exploring the role played by both national and European policy on employment, and identifying some differences in policy response and in welfare systems. Having considered this broader international context, the third part of the chapter outlines recent developments in the employment policy of the European Union (EU), which seeks explicitly to address labour market detachment and 'early exit'. Finally, the chapter concludes by considering a number of explanations of labour market change and welfare policy, and the political ideologies which support them.

Statistical comparisons

Unemployment

In 1999, more than one in eight of the 8 million European men who were unemployed according to the ILO definition (see ch. 1) lived in the UK – and the UK was one of five EU states in which over a million men were defined as unemployed. Male unemployment was thus a very significant and costly social issue for the EU and for several other member states. In that year, the male ILO unemployment rate in the UK lay slightly below the EU average, at 6.9 per cent (see table 2.1). About a third of unemployed men in the UK had been unemployed for a year or

Table 2.1. *Male unemployment in the EU: European Labour Force Survey 1999*

	Number of males aged 15–64 who are ILO unemployed	% of males 15–64 who are ILO unemployed	% of unemployed men seeking part-time work	% of unemployed men without work for 12 months or more
Finland	151	11.0	12	24
Spain	1,078	10.9	2	40
France	1,471	10.5	4	38
Italy	1,272	8.8	4	62
Germany	1,907	8.6	4	50
Sweden	192	8.3	7	33
Belgium	186	7.5	4	60
Greece	188	7.0	4	45
UK	1,113	6.9	10	35
Ireland	59	5.9	4	60
Austria	101	4.7	5	28
Denmark	69	4.5	14	21
Portugal	115	4.1	1	40
Netherlands	121	2.7	34	48
Luxembourg	2	1.8	5	45
EU-15	8,024	8.2	5.3	44.7

Source: Eurostat (Franco 2000).

more (compared with the EU average of almost 45 per cent), and the UK was one of four EU member states in which more than 10 per cent of unemployed men were seeking part-time employment. Comparatively, this evidence suggests that although the UK was not among the EU states facing the most critical problems of male unemployment, the size of its problem was large and some other states appeared to be faring better.

It has already been indicated in ch. 1 that the widely used ILO definition of unemployment may not reveal the true extent of joblessness in an economy. Other measures of labour market participation and of attachment to the labour market are therefore used in making international comparisons in this chapter. Below, the 'non-employment' rate, the inactivity rate and the proportions of men who are working either on limited duration contracts of employment, or on a part-time basis, are also considered within their European and wider international context.

Employment rates and non-employment rates

The UK employment rate (which shows the proportion of people of working age who are in employment) is not especially low by EU or international standards. Indeed, with Iceland, Switzerland, Norway and Denmark, the UK is one of five Organisation for Economic Co-operation and Development (OECD) countries with an overall employment rate higher than that of the USA (Jozefowicz and Pearce 2000).

Overall employment rates are calculated for both men and women and include those in part-time employment. Differences between countries in female labour force participation, and in the proportion of workers employed only part time, may therefore distort the picture of what is happening specifically to men. Table 2.2 isolates full-time employment rates, for men of working age only, and breaks them down by age. This shows that the UK also has relatively high rates of full-time male employment. For example, the UK level is higher than the average for the EU in all age ranges, and is exceeded among the older age group (55–64) only by rates in Denmark, Sweden, Portugal and Spain. In fact, full-time employment rates for men in this older age group are markedly lower, by 14 or more percentage points, in Belgium, France, Italy and the Netherlands (Kyi and Charlier 2001).

Some commentators argue that the 'non-employment' rate (which adds together the inactive and unemployed WAP) should be used to measure the 'labour reserve' in an economy. Table 2.3 shows these figures for selected countries in 1997, again broken down by age, and showing the sexes separately. Looked at in this way, it is clear that there are very large differences in the gap between the highest and lowest

Table 2.2. *Male full-time employment rates for selected countries, by age, spring 2000 (% of age group)*

Country	15–64	15–24	25–54	55–64
Luxembourg	74	34	92	37
Portugal	74	46	89	56
Austria	73	54	87	38
Denmark	73	44	84	43
UK	72	43	84	52
Germany	70	44	84	43
Greece	70	30	87	54
Ireland	70	44	85	57
Spain	68	34	84	54
Netherlands	67	32	82	37
Finland	66	37	81	35
France	65	27	84	29
Italy	65	28	82	38
Sweden	65	26	79	56
Belgium	54	27	70	21
EU-15	68	36	83	43

Note: Self-assessed definitions of full-time employment (except Netherlands).
Source: Kyi and Charlier 2001 (*Eurostat*, Community Labour Force Survey).

non-employment rates across the countries shown. This is true for both sexes and all age groups, except for men aged 25–54, where the gap is much narrower, with an upper rate of 20 per cent and a lower rate of 10 per cent.

In all the economies referred to in table 2.3 it is still the norm for men of 'prime working age' to be in employment. The UK, with 15 per cent of 25–54-year-old men outside employment, occupies a midpoint between the extremes observed in Norway, the Netherlands and Greece (each with only 10 per cent of such men without employment) and Finland and Spain (with 20 per cent in this situation). For older men, aged 55–64, the variation between the different countries is very much greater. At one extreme, in Belgium, more than two-thirds of this age group are non-employed. By contrast, in Norway only a little over a quarter of these older men are non-employed. Again, the UK occupies a midpoint between the two poles, with 41 per cent of older men without employment.

The separate figures for young people and for women in table 2.3 show that the UK has comparatively high proportions of these groups in employment. In many other countries, non-employment among the young population is higher because of more widespread take up of extended educational opportunities. Indeed, in the UK, among the non-employed

Table 2.3. *Working-age population non-employment rates for selected countries, by age and sex, 1997*

	Men			Women		
Country	15–24	25–54	55–64	15–24	25–54	55–64
Finland	59	20	62	67	25	66
Spain	68	20	50	78	57	82
Ireland	59	18	42	64	47	78
Italy	70	17	59	80	52	86
Sweden	60	17	35	61	21	39
UK	37	15	41	41	29	61
Germany	50	15	53	57	34	73
Belgium	72	14	68	78	37	88
France (1996)	75	14	61	82	32	71
Denmark	28	11	39	37	23	59
Portugal	57	12	42	67	30	63
USA	40	12	35	44	27	51
Austria	43	11	60	49	29	83
Greece	70	10	41	81	49	76
Netherlands	42	10	57	45	35	80
Norway	41	10	27	48	20	40
EU-15	59	15	52	67	38	74
Highest rate	75	20	68	82	57	88
Lowest rate	28	10	27	37	21	39

Source: Fina-Sanglas 2000 (derived from OECD data) (figures have been rounded).

population aged 15–24, only 84 per cent are in education, compared with 89 per cent for the EU as a whole (Franco 2000).

Women's relatively high levels of employment in the UK contribute, by definition, to their low non-employment rate. However, only 56 per cent of UK women in employment have full-time jobs, compared with 67 per cent for the EU-15. Non-employment among women shows very considerable variation between countries, reflecting the different, but rising, proportions of women who are active in the labour market. This development is one indication of the declining relevance of the male breadwinner model (Crompton 1999).

Some labour market analysts stress the evidence of dynamic processes in the labour market. Evidence from the European Household Panel Survey (EHPS) reveals how economic activity and unemployment are distributed throughout the whole European population. Using data for 1994–5, Marlier (1999) showed that despite an average EU economic activity rate of 68 per cent (UK 72 per cent) during this time, almost 75 per cent (UK nearly 80 per cent) were economically active at some point

Table 2.4. *Male inactive population aged 15 plus by reasons for not looking for work, 1999*

Country	Inactive (000)	Do not wish to work[a] (%)	Sickness or disability (%)	Studying or training (%)	Retired (%)	Family responsibilities (%)
UK	6,720	79	22	11	53	3
Finland	641	82	19	14	52	1
Netherlands	1,733	84	15	14	60	5
Portugal	1,156	97	14	31	47	–
Spain	5,957	90	10	27	56	<1
Belgium	1,594	91	9	26	57	1
Luxembourg	61	97	8	28	59	–
Italy	8,893	87	7	23	61	1
Denmark	801	71	6	10	54	1
Germany	10,784	93	6	20	66	1
Greece	1,515	97	5	25	66	<1
Austria	955	88	3	20	71	–
Sweden[b]	1,218	–	3	26	50	–
France[c]	8,135	96	–	–	–	–
Ireland[c]	426	88	–	–	–	–
EU-15 men	50,390	89	8	21	50	1
EU-15 women	83,013	91	5	14	33	22
UK women	11,088	84	11	6	54	21
UK both sexes	17,808	82	15	8	53	14

Notes:

[a] Do not wish to work: this column includes all those who said they were not looking for work and did not wish to work. It therefore includes those counted in subsequent columns. The rows in this table do not, therefore, add to 100 per cent.

[b] In Sweden, 52 per cent of men who were inactive and not seeking work said this was because they did not wish to work. As 'non-response' was extremely high for these men (43.6 per cent), this figure has not been included in the table. Non-response in other countries ranged between 0 per cent and 0.6 per cent, except in Spain (4.5 per cent) and the UK (5.9 per cent).

[c] In France and Ireland high percentages are recorded as giving 'no reason' for not looking for work (69 per cent in France and 88 per cent in Ireland). This means that percentages calculated for columns 3–6 do not offer meaningful comparisons. The percentage giving 'no reason' for not seeking work is below 1 per cent in all other countries except in the UK (5.8 per cent) and in Sweden (14.7 per cent).

Source: Table 65, European Labour Force Survey 1999 (*Eurostat*).

within the period. Four-fifths of these working-age people were active throughout the whole period, while the rest were economically active for some but not all of that time. During these years, unemployment in the EU (as measured by the EHPS) averaged 11 per cent (8 per cent in the UK) – yet almost 20 per cent of economically active persons experienced some unemployment. Marlier also produced a measure of 'disadvantage' in relation to the labour market. This showed that, across the EU, 30 per cent of men and 32 per cent of women spent half or more of their time in unemployment and/or lived in a household where less than 50 per cent of the time available to its members was spent in employment. This was true of 23 per cent of men and 25 per cent of women in the UK.

Inactivity rates

The non-employment rates discussed above refer both to those who are 'inactive' and to those who are 'unemployed'. Our study disentangles these groups, and – as later chapters show – stresses the blurring of the boundaries between these categories (Green 1999). In ch. 4, Beatty and Fothergill show the unemployment and economic inactivity rates for men in Great Britain over the period 1977–2000 (fig. 4.1), and break down economic inactivity into separate categories (fig. 4.2). They show that the share of economic inactivity attributable to permanent sickness rises significantly with age. To explore how far this is true of other comparable economies we need to review comparative international data on sub-categories of the economically inactive.

Webster (2001), using data from the European Labour Force Survey (ELFS) 1999, notes that in the UK 7 per cent of the WAP (both sexes) report being 'inactive' because of their own sickness or disability. He points out that this rate is the highest in Europe and twice the average for the EU-15 (3.5 per cent); only Portugal and Finland have similarly high rates (6.5 per cent and 6.3 per cent respectively).

Table 2.4 refers specifically to men (and includes all men aged 15 plus in the EU population). This shows that the UK has a noticeably lower proportion of inactive men who say they do not wish to work than most other European countries. In fact, more than 13 per cent of inactive males in the UK say they would like to have a job (compared with less than 6 per cent for the EU as a whole (ELFS 1999)).

The ELFS asks those who are inactive and not seeking work to give their reasons. This is useful because it enables the proportions of this group who are inactive because of sickness/disability, study or training, retirement and family responsibilities to be distinguished. Table 2.4 presents this information. The picture in the UK is rather different from that in most other countries. In the UK, more than one in five of this group gave sickness/disability as their reason (22 per cent). This compares with fewer than one in ten men in most other countries, with only Finland, the Netherlands and Portugal coming anywhere near the levels reported in the UK (19 per cent, 15 per cent and 14 per cent respectively).

Inactive men in the UK are far less likely than such men in other countries not to be seeking work because of study or training. This applies to only one in ten men in the UK, but to more than twice as many in countries such as Germany, Spain, Greece, Italy, Portugal and Sweden. The proportion of inactive men saying they are not seeking work because they have retired is more variable. Just over half UK men give this response, compared with around 45 per cent in countries such as Portugal and Sweden, and with over 60 per cent in Denmark, Germany, Italy, the Netherlands and Austria.

All this suggests that there are particularly complex issues surrounding male inactivity in the UK. Inactive men in the UK are more likely to say they would like to work than most other European men. Positive reasons for inactivity, such as studying and training, are given less often in the UK than in most other countries. Men in the UK are slightly more likely than their other European counterparts to be inactive because of family responsibilities (2.5 per cent compared to an EU average of 1.0 per cent). They are not especially highly concentrated in the 'retirement' category by comparative standards, yet they show very strongly indeed among those men who are inactive because of illness or disability. It is hardly credible that UK men's health should be worse by such a large margin than the health of other European men. It is far more likely that UK men, particularly where they are recipients of benefits related to health/disability, are more willing or able to define themselves in this way.

The discussion above is consistent with observations made by Green (1999), whose innovative analysis of the ELFS showed that, across the EU, 'there are marked national variations in the shares of the jobless lying outside the scope of the conventional ILO definition of unemployment' (1999: 460). Green has argued that it is important to explore alternative measures which can offer indicators of 'severe unemployment, unemployment, broader unemployment, and non-employment' in order to make a more comprehensive assessment of 'the extent of joblessness' (1999: 461). Analysing ELFS data for 1995, she created an index of broad unemployment which included both the ILO unemployed and the inactive who would like to work, were seeking work or were available for work. This showed the UK ranking fourth worst among the EU-15, with only the Netherlands, Italy and Denmark showing greater unwanted joblessness among men of prime working age (25–59). To gauge the significance of this, it should be noted that for the same year, overall ILO unemployment rates for this age group ranked three of these countries well below the EU average (9.2 per cent). In that year this measure was, for these three countries, 7.5 per cent (UK) and 6.3 per cent (Denmark and the Netherlands) (Green 1999: 456–7).

As later chapters of this book reveal, the subjective nature of definitions of ill-health and disability, and the influence which social policies and benefit regimes exert over these definitions, is particularly problematic when labour market debates are couched principally in terms of recorded levels of unemployment. This becomes all the more difficult when governments also operate with an ill-defined and political concept of 'full employment' as a prime goal of policy. Some of the implications of this are taken up more fully later in this book.

Employment patterns among men

Table 2.1 has already shown that 10 per cent of unemployed men in the UK are looking for part-time work, and that about one-third of them have been out of work for over a year. Table 2.5 gives details of men's employment contracts and of the hours they work for all EU member states. Here again very marked differences emerge between countries.

In the Netherlands, almost one in five employed men works part time, compared with just 3 per cent in Spain, Greece and Italy and an EU average of 6 per cent. The UK has almost one in ten male workers in part-time employment. Apart from the tiny state of Luxembourg, the UK has the lowest proportion of male workers on limited duration contracts in the EU (at 6 per cent) – compared with an EU average of 12 per cent and a rate of 31 per cent in Spain. When they are working full time, however, male workers in the UK work long hours – an average of 45 per week, compared with 41 across the EU and just 39 hours in the Netherlands.

These figures suggest that some countries – the Netherlands being a rather striking example – have a distribution of paid work across their male population rather different from that found in the UK. The Netherlands has very low rates of employment among older men, a high proportion of men working part time and low average hours worked by full-time male workers. It has also, as discussed in more detail below, grappled with a variety of policy responses to its 'unemployment problem'.

Over the past twenty years, sickness and disability benefits/pensions and 'early exit' policies have played an important role in some countries in encouraging men to leave the labour force. The next section of this chapter considers developments in five other EU states. These examples show that lower rates of ILO unemployment may be achieved by adopting particular employment and welfare responses.

Table 2.5. *Male employment, showing part-time employment, contracts of limited duration and usual hours worked*

	Employment rate (15–64 years)	Employees working part time (%)	Employees on limited duration contracts (%)	Usual weekly hours of full-timers (hours)	Usual weekly hours of part-timers (hours)
Denmark	81	10	9	40	13
Netherlands	80	18	9	39	19
UK	77	9	6	45	17
Austria	77	4	7	40	23
Portugal	76	6	17	42	21
Ireland	74	7	7	41	19
Luxembourg	74	2	3	41	29
Denmark	72	5	13	41	15
Greece (98)	72	3	12	42	23
Sweden	72	9	11	40	19
Belgium	70	5	14	40	20
Finland	70	8	15	40	20
France	68	6	13	40	23
Spain	68	3	31	41	19
Italy	67	3	9	40	27
EU-15	72	6	12	41	19

Source: Franco 2000 (ELFS 1999).

Tackling unemployment and underemployment

Faced with rising unemployment rates after 1973, European states re-acted in a variety of ways to changes in their labour market circumstances. Responses have included attempts to reduce the labour supply, to redistribute employment, to increase productivity and to create jobs, as well as measures designed to minimise the social, economic and political impact of unemployment. The focus of this section, which cannot explore all of these, is on the strategies used to tackle unemployment by reducing labour supply. As others have noted, this has involved recourse to two main instruments of policy, 'early retirement and easily accessible disability insurance regulations':

Although male labour participation in the age group 55–64 was not very different between Europe and the US in 1973 (about 80 per cent), the differences in the early 1990s are remarkable. While in France and the Netherlands male labour force participation is well below 50 per cent, it is about 70 per cent in the US and the UK. (de Neubourg 1997: 238)

De Neubourg stresses that, as well as stimulating early retirement through a variety of policy measures, some countries, including the Netherlands and Sweden, also slackened disability insurance regulations, 'providing both high benefits and social legitimation to those with an unfavourable position in the labour market' (239). Thus by the early 1990s nearly 8 per cent of the Netherlands' population of working age were disability transfer recipients, compared with 2.7 per cent in the US.

Examination of labour force trends in national economies demonstrates the extent to which various developments – early retirement, withdrawal from the labour force on grounds of disability, active labour market policies promoting vocational education and training and stimulating job creation, short-time working – have contributed to reducing labour supply and concealing unemployment. In many cases these policies have had positive consequences for people who would otherwise have been 'stranded' without work and reliant on minimum levels of social protection. Some policies have produced labour market opportunities, others have provided alternative, higher rate, benefits or pensions for those without work, and some have made easier the transition from active labour force participation to retirement. There has also been increasing attention to the influence of American-style 'workfare' models which have been adopted in European states as a way of tackling the relationship between work and welfare (Evans 2001, Lødermel and Trickey 2001). This chapter now turns to brief consideration of developments in five other EU states: Germany, Spain, France, Finland and the Netherlands.

Germany

Employment policy in Germany has been profoundly affected by the unification of the Federal German Republic and the former Democratic German Republic in 1990. As one commentator put it, 'West German social and economic policy incorporated its prodigal other half. The high hidden unemployment, inadequate social benefit rates and other characteristics of the old soviet-style welfare state became subject to the German social state' (Evans 2001: 15).

Against this background, Germany adopted a range of measures to combat unemployment during the 1990s, including restrictions on eligibility for unemployment benefit and enforced job search for claimants. The German welfare state is firmly based on social insurance, and a useful summary of the arrangements for unemployment benefits, sickness/disability pensions and social assistance in Germany is given in Evans (2001). In his assessment of the 'welfare-to-work' target group in Germany, Evans emphasises that 'longer-term and permanent invalidity is covered by schemes that either pay a full pension for those who are completely unable to work, or a part pension for those with reduced earning capacity' (Evans 2001: 16). He nevertheless cites Bolderson *et al.*'s conclusion that in reality it is extremely difficult to divide people neatly into those who are 'incapacitated' and those who are 'unemployed'. As in the UK, this means that the number of people wanting to work significantly exceeds the number recorded as unemployed.

Estimates suggest that the *stille Reserve* or 'silent reserve', consisting of underemployment and hidden unemployment as well as open unemployment, numbered almost 8 million persons in 1997, although registered unemployment in that year was around 4 million. In the years following German reunification, labour market policy made extensive use of early retirement and of the transitional allowance for older unemployed workers. This reduced the number of unemployed by some 20 per cent each year in the early 1990s. German labour market analysts have calculated that, in 1996, there were at least half a million 'inactive' Germans who wished to work and who would be willing to start work immediately (Düll and Vogler-Ludwig 1998).

By 2001, the German government was stressing that the central goal of its employment policy was 'creating jobs', acknowledging that it still faced an 'immense challenge' in responding to unemployment in the new *Länder*. In a revised approach to tackling existing unemployment and seeking to prevent future unemployment, the German government emphasised the importance of its active labour policy: 'Instead of administering unemployment, money will be spent to improve qualifications and the rate of employment. During 2000, training and continuing education were at the core of the active labour policy' (Germany, *National Action Plan for Employment* 2001: 7).

The German government has underlined the extent to which policy for the twenty-first century differs from previous policy:

In the interest of older employed individuals, in anticipation of demographic changes, and increasing labour shortages in specific regional and professional parts of the labour market, the Federal Government and the social partners decided . . . to initiate a paradigm change in its policy pertaining to older employed individuals. The goal was to reverse the trend of premature retirement and to increase the number of employed older individuals. (Germany, *National Action Plan for Employment* 2001: 10)

In 1996, Germany decided to raise the age threshold for eligibility for retirement benefits arising from unemployment from 60 to 65, to take effect from 2001. It is expected that this will raise the employment rate of older workers after 2001, since 'early retirement will be linked to a significant decrease in retirement benefits' (Germany, *National Action Plan for Employment* 2001: 71).

Another German measure taken to raise the employment rate of older workers has been the Act on Part-Time Work in Old Age, which supports older workers in transferring to part-time work and offers them protection in relation to unemployment insurance. Through the Second Law for the Part-Time Employment of Seniors, this policy has been extended to 2009. In Germany, 106,000 fewer older people (aged over 55) were unemployed in 2000 than in 1999. The government attributes this to increased numbers of placements by employment offices, and to the Federal Employment Service's success in reducing 'prejudices against older workers' willingness and ability to perform' (Germany, *National Action Plan for Employment* 2001: 22). Separate legislation on part-time work and fixed term contracts has also been enacted. This aims to 'facilitate fixed term recruitment of older workers for the age group from 58 upwards, who are particularly likely to be unemployed' (Germany, *National Action Plan for Employment* 2001: 23), while under another statutory provision, until 2006 only, 'the age threshold for integration subsidies for older workers has been reduced from 55 to 50' (Germany, *National Action Plan for Employment* 2001: 24).

Just over a million severely disabled people are 'available to the general labour market' in Germany (1999 estimates). This represents about one in six of the population assessed as severely disabled. Only 175,000 of this group, however, are officially recorded as 'severely disabled people who are unemployed' (Germany, *National Action Plan for Employment*

2001: 35). Germany's Act to Combat Unemployment of Severely Disabled People came into force in October 2000. This has the stated general aim of addressing disproportionate unemployment among disabled people, and the specific objective of reducing the number of unemployed people from this group by 25 per cent (50,000 people) by October 2002.

Spain

Spain still has one of the highest ILO unemployment rates in Europe, yet its highly visible unemployment problem also conceals additional underemployment and hidden unemployment. Data from the ELFS for 1987–97 suggest that in 1997 the standard ILO unemployment rate (21 per cent) was 3 percentage points below the true 'enlarged unemployment rate' of 24 per cent. Between 1987 and 1997, 'some 200,000 to 250,000' people aged 30–54 years (70 per cent of them men) declared themselves permanently disabled, while 150,000 people took early retirement (Toharia 1998).

During the 1980s and 1990s, Spain's socialist governments 'sought to liberalize, privatize and deregulate the economy and integrate into Europe' (Cousins 1999: 31), joining the EU in 1986. In a labour market which still retains a highly regulated core workforce, in effect a primary labour force coexists with two additional labour forces – one containing large numbers of workers on fixed term contracts, and the other those who work in the informal or underground economy (Cousins 1999: 155). Workers in the core labour market enjoy relatively generous social protection (organised along Bismarckian lines), while others are much less well provided for. For example, workers without employment experience are not entitled to receive unemployment benefits (Cousins 1999: 156), and a means-tested scheme of non-contributory benefits provides access to pensions and invalidity benefits.

Since the Luxembourg Jobs Summit in 1997, the Spanish government has sought to respond to EU guidance on employment policy, recognising, for example, that the 'problems in the Spanish labour market vary widely according to region' (Spain, *National Action Plan for Employment* 2001: 5). Accordingly, its 'active policies' to promote employment 'are not targeted evenly across Spain'. For example, although the overall unemployment rate for Spain had fallen to 13.6 per cent in late 2000, it was above 22 per cent in regions such as Andalusia, Extremadura, Ceuta and Melilla. By adopting an active labour market policy, Spain placed 9,000 adult men with disabilities (aged over 25) in jobs, and recruited over 100,000 adult men into 'social employment' during 2000. In 2001, Spain aims to offer help in finding employment to over 280,000 long-term unemployed people, and to almost 50,000 people with disabilities. It also plans to address early retirement in 2001, shifting policy so that '[t]hose people who entered the social security system after 1966 will only be able to retire early if they have paid in for at least 30 years and are unemployed' (Spain, *National Action Plan for Employment* 2001: 16).

In a measure to encourage retention of older workers in employment, companies will (from 2002) pay reduced social security contributions for 'workers between 55 and 64 who have been with the company for at least five years' (Spain, *National Action Plan for Employment* 2001: 16). 'The possibility of fixing a maximum age limit for workers' has also been eliminated, through Royal Decree/Law 5/2001, a measure adopted to prevent employers from using 'forced retirement' as a way of 'regulating their workforce' (Spain, *National Action Plan for Employment* 2001: 17).

France

An analysis of the French labour market stresses that:

The unemployment boundary is closely tied to public policies, which results in people being removed from the labour market when they do not, in fact, have a job. Some policies aim to reduce the working population, others directly affect the unemployment statistics, and still others promote job creation and indirectly affect the way in which unemployment is measured by the statistics. (Gineste and Ait Kaci 1998)

In France, policy interventions to reduce unemployment have included extended education (to lower youth unemployment), early and 'gradual' retirement schemes, exemptions from job seeking and job creation/job subsidy schemes (e.g. the *contrat emploi solidarité* – employment solidarity contracts). Large numbers of workers aged 60–65 took early retirement in the 1980s and early 1990s (378,000 in 1985 alone). Early retirement options were made more readily available to workers aged 55–59 in the mid-1980s, and in the region of 200,000 people in this age group took the early retirement option each year between 1985 and 1996. After 1984, older unemployed people were also allowed 'job seeking exemptions' and removed from the unemployment statistics. By the 1990s, around 250,000 people were included in this category each year (Gineste and Ait Kaci 1998).

Table 2.6 shows that the total number of French people 'experiencing employment difficulties' was more than double the number defined as ILO unemployed. In the later 1990s, concern grew in France that previous measures, especially early retirement, were not effective ways of responding to labour market change. As a result, since 1998, 'France has pursued a comprehensive strategy with three closely co-ordinated

Table 2.6. *Number of people affected by employment difficulties in France,*[a] *1996 (thousands)*

Category	Number
Unemployed (ILO definition)	3,080
Hidden unemployed	820
of which:	
jobseekers in training schemes	350
early retirees	470
No job search	560
of which:	
the 'discouraged' unemployed	240
those unable to seek a job	320
Involuntary shorter hours	1,570
of which:	
involuntary part-time	1,360
involuntary shorter-full-time	210
Other forms of lack of security (temporary work, fixed term contracts, etc.)	660
Total	6,690

Note: [a]Statistically, 'hidden' unemployment and the lack of job search, or 1.4 million people, are normally classified as inactive, while involuntary shorter working hours and other forms of work that lack security, or 2.2 million people, are classified as employed.
Source: Gineste and Ait Kaci 1998 – original sources DARES, INSEE, CGP.

objectives: stronger and more sustainable growth; growth with a higher job content; and growth for all' (France, *National Action Plan for Employment* 2001: 2).

Policy shifted towards job creation and measures designed to redistribute paid employment. The French government claims that 1.6 million new jobs were created between June 1997 and early 2001. Actions taken within the framework of the French *National Action Plan for Employment* 2000, according to official assessment, produced 'exceptional' employment statistics, with 580,000 new jobs and 420,000 fewer people unemployed. France also claims employment successes for its shorter working week policy. First introduced on a voluntary basis in the early 1990s, this scheme was introduced on a statutory basis in 1997, and aimed to reduce average working hours to 35 hours per week via negotiated agreements between employers and workers (Evans 2001: 13). By the end of 2000, more than half of employees (in businesses with ten or more employees) worked fewer than thirty-six hours per week, and 'more than 54,300 collective bargaining agreements had been reached, creating or preserving more than 347,000 jobs' (France, *National Action Plan for Employment* 2001: 3).

The official French position is that, in response to the European Council's recommendations on employment policy,

incentive measures for early retirement managed by the State and the social partners were further reduced (in 2000) and new measures to keep people employed
have been added. France has also enriched the panoply of actions to find work
for older job seekers. (France, *National Action Plan for Employment* 2001: 3)

Between 1997 and 2000 the long-term trend towards labour market detachment among older workers had been put into reverse, and the employment rate for 50–64 year olds had risen nearly 3 points to 52.4 per cent. Among the measures being adopted in France, the progressive programme for early retirement (*préretraites progressives*) is of particular interest. This enables employees over 55 to be kept in their work part time. The scheme had 12,000 beneficiaries in 2000, and the number is expected to rise to 16,000 in 2001 (France, *National Action Plan for Employment* 2001: 21).

Finland

In Finland, a sustained period of low unemployment came to an end in 1990. Between 1990 and 1994 the national registered unemployment rate rose very sharply, from 4 to 20 per cent. Observers recognise that within the Finnish labour market, 'in addition to conventionally measured un-employment, there are various groups whose attachment to the labour market is affected by the lack of job opportunities' (Santamäki-Vuori 1998: 82). As elsewhere, these groups include people affected by active labour market policies, those in early retirement schemes 'for labour-market related reasons', those in voluntary short-time work, and those available for work but not actively seeking a job. During the early 1990s, Finland responded to rapidly rising unemployment by 'a doubling of ac-tive labour market policy measures', mostly through subsidised employ-ment and labour market training schemes. Involuntary part-time work also increased during this time (to 112,000 people or 5 per cent of total employment in 1996).

Finland introduced a special unemployment pension scheme in 1972, which aimed to enable long-term unemployed people who were ap-proaching normal retirement age to retire early. This policy also involved targeting the agricultural sector, where significant restructuring was tak-ing place. In the late 1980s an 'early disability pension' scheme was also introduced, first in the private and later in the public sector. By 1996, 123,000 people under 65 were on one of these schemes, about half of them on early disability pension. At the end of that decade, Finland

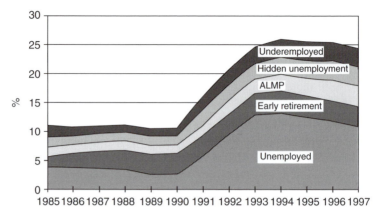

Figure 2.1   Finland: broad unemployment as a percentage of the population aged 15–64, 1985–97

raised the qualifying age for these pensions from 55 to 60, and in the 1990s other qualifying conditions were also made more stringent. These developments halted the rise in the number of recipients, which started to fall after 1994. In 1996, 7 per cent of 55–59 year olds, and 40 per cent of 60–64 year olds were recipients of these pensions. Figure 2.1 shows 'broad unemployment' in Finland, 1985–97, by its component parts.

In 1997, the Finnish government introduced its National Programme for Ageing Workers 1998–2002. This aimed to offer employment to older workers and to shift social attitudes. The perspective adopted in this programme was that 'maintaining working ability and professional competence among ageing workers is of vital importance' (Lilja 1999: 83).

In the same spirit, the Finnish government's *National Action Plan for Employment* 2001 stresses that its key employment policy aims are, '[f]or close to 70% of the working-age population to be able to find employment, and – in the long term – to bring the average age for retirement from the labour market about 2–3 years closer to the official retirement age' (Finland, *National Action Plan for Employment* 2001: i).

To this end, Finland has drawn up both national and regional action plans for employment, in accordance with EU guidelines (see the third section of this chapter). In 2000, Finland's official employment rate stood at 69 per cent for men, with 8 per cent of men working part time. The retirement age for men had begun to rise, accompanied by a fall in the use of early retirement pensions, and 42 per cent of people aged 55–64 were in employment. The Finnish labour market in 2000 included both high unemployment and labour shortages. As the *National Action Plan for Employment* points out, there are structural unemployment problems:

During the recession, Finland recorded a high percentage of unemployed whose return to the labour market is complicated by obstacles related to age and a lack of educational and vocational qualifications. (Finland, *National Action Plan for Employment* 2001: 2)

Marked regional disparities in unemployment rates (19 per cent in parts of northern Finland, compared with 6 per cent in southern Finland) have been addressed using active labour policy measures. As a result, in areas of high unemployment, almost 8 per cent of the workforce were in such schemes in 2000.

Finland's plans for tackling unemployment and raising the employment rate in 2001 include improvements in the services provided to unemployed people, increasing social assistance for those in labour market training or practical training, and tax incentives to encourage acceptance of low paid work. Special efforts are to be made to promote lifelong learning for older people to enable them to stay in work, vocational training for adults is to be targeted at the over 40s, and a new scheme aims to equip middle-aged people with basic computer skills.

The Netherlands

The situation in the Netherlands has been widely discussed in the comparative social policy literature. Peters (1998: 67) has pointed out that 'the number of disabled persons is even higher than the number of people receiving unemployment benefits'. As media and public attention became focused on the high levels of sickness and disability benefits recipients, the Netherlands embarked (in the 1990s) on a process of 'redefining disability and a re-examination of beneficiaries'. Measures adopted included 'bonuses for employers hiring partially disabled workers and . . . a financial penalty upon employers whose workers entered the rolls of the disabled' (Goodin, Headey and Driven 1999: 70). This changed approach reduced the numbers of benefit recipients from 921,000 in 1993 to 860,000 in 1995, although 'since then, the effects of this large-scale operation have largely been exhausted' (Peters 1998: 68). By late 1996, the Netherlands judged that about three-quarters of its disability claimants were '100 per cent disabled' – and calculated that almost 70 per cent of these were people over 45. Despite these developments, many people have continued to rely on the Dutch disability scheme:

Currently their number is 920,000 or nearly 14 per cent of the economically active population. With the exception of clientelist Italy . . . This number is more than twice as high as in any comparable country . . . In fact the Dutch disability scheme has turned out to be a specific safety net for nearly half a million long-term unemployed. A 'high dike, bringing the army of unemployed out of sight, so that we can live together in harmony', the situation was described by the columnist

Huygen in NRC *Handelsblad* (27 April 1999). Redistribution of work went not only towards part-time employment, it also went to younger and healthier people. (Becker 2000: 234–5)

Indeed, as Becker goes on to suggest, 'registered unemployment has shifted heavily towards other categories of non-employment... in fact, Dutch unemployment has not declined at all since the mid-1980s, despite cuts in welfare benefits'.

Becker identifies a range of possible factors contributing to the low registered unemployment rate in the Netherlands. These include the decline in the relative value of the minimum wage; increased employment, largely attributable to new part-time jobs; the comparatively low average hours worked (about 1,400 hours per annum in 1995); wage restraint; high levels of early retirement; and high numbers of working-age people on disability benefits.

In the late 1990s, the Dutch government enacted a number of measures designed to 'prevent premature departure from the labour market by stimulating the changeover from early retirement to pre-pension schemes' (Netherlands, *National Action Plan for Employment* 2001: 9). These included the Invalidity Insurance (Differentiation in Contributions and Market Forces) Act, the Sickness Benefits Act and the Disability (Reintegration) Act. The latter came into force in July 1998 and aims to reintegrate all disabled jobseekers into the labour market. Between July 1998 and the end of 1999, under measures introduced via this legislation, nearly 17,000 disabled people 'were placed in employment or re-employed with the help of instruments such as a placement/re-employment budget, a tailor-made package, or a subsidy to allow the individual concerned to retain his or her own job' (Netherlands, *National Action Plan for Employment* 2001: 36). Official assessment considers these results 'not very impressive', and stresses that 'over the next few years policy will focus on improving implementation' (Netherlands, *National Action Plan for Employment* 2001: 19).

The Netherlands is also 'seeking a higher labour force participation rate among older people' (Netherlands, *National Action Plan for Employment* 2001: 14). From July 2002 new voluntary retirement schemes will cease to receive favourable tax treatment, and by 2009, all voluntary early retirement schemes are being required to convert into pre-pension schemes. Future plans under consideration in 2001 include 'reintroducing the obligation for people over the age of $57\frac{1}{2}$ to apply for jobs' and requiring employers to contribute to unemployment costs when a worker aged $57\frac{1}{2}$ or above has to start claiming unemployment benefits. An Older Workers Task Force, funded by the state, is also to be set up. This will have the tasks of changing employer and employee attitudes, publicising good practice and offering information and advice, especially to small and medium-sized enterprises.

This short review of how five other states have responded to unemployment and economic inactivity in their labour forces demonstrates that the UK is not alone in having significant numbers of people outside employment who would like to have a job, but who are not counted in unemployment statistics. It is clear that during the 1980s and 1990s other states also encouraged some people who became unemployed to move into economic inactivity through defining them as retired, disabled or as trainees. Recent policy statements by national governments make it very clear, however, that active steps are now being taken or are planned to reverse this situation. Faced with the certain prospect of an ageing population, European states are now seeking with some urgency to raise the employment rate of the WAP. In many other European states this can be tackled, in quite large part, through policy on female employment, since female non-employment rates remain relatively high in Spain, Italy, Ireland, Greece and Belgium, and are also higher than in the UK in the Netherlands, France and Germany. The UK cannot tackle raising the employment rate in the same way because female labour force participation has been rising in the UK since at least the 1960s, albeit mainly through part-time work. The UK will need to focus on regional disparities in unemployment and economic inactivity, on the high numbers of working-age men who are recipients of sickness and disability benefits and on the trend for its workers to take early retirement, if working age employment rates in the UK are not to fall behind in the first decades of the twenty-first century.

Much has been made in discussing recent labour market and welfare policy of the influence of American style 'workfare' policy on European governments. Lødermel and Trickey (2001: xi) have underlined the trend towards expecting unemployed people receiving social assistance 'to participate in work or other activities as part of their assistance contract'. Reviewing evidence for seven European countries, these authors observe that governments have introduced both incentives (such as voluntary training programmes and in-work benefits) and disincentives (such as stricter eligibility criteria and conditionality rules). They also draw attention to the support which social democratic parties have given to workfare policies in recent decades. They stress that the importance of these developments lies in the way workfare affects the balance of rights and obligations within the social assistance contract (xii). This issue is discussed in more detail in the final section of this chapter. Before turning to some brief comments on theories and ideologies of welfare and their role in the development of policy on labour force participation, it is necessary to outline the role being played by EU policy on employment in shaping national governments' responses. The next section is devoted to this aspect.

The development and influence of EU employment policy

It is important to focus attention on those at the margins of the labour market, by investing in people to increase their employability and by reducing barriers for labour market entry. Confronting these challenges requires multi-faceted policies, which go beyond labour market issues, and which aim to increase social inclusion and participation. (Commission of the European Communities, 2000)

The EU Social Policy Agenda

In a major policy statement issued in June 2000, the European Commission set out its 'strategic response to modernise the European social model', building on 'the progress achieved in the employment and social fields'. The statement emphasised that although considerable progress had been made in 'fostering job creation', the average employment rate in the EU was too low, at only 62 per cent (1999), especially among the population aged 55–65 (Commission of the European Communities 2000: 9). Furthermore, long-term structural unemployment remained an important problem, with 'marked regional imbalances' and high unemployment in 'declining industrial areas' (Commission of the European Communities 2000: 11). Although the European Employment Strategy had, since 1998, been an 'effective' tool for structural reform in the national labour markets, it required further strengthening. Furthermore, the long-term context was one in which

Demographic changes will strongly affect the structure of the labour market and labour supply and will put heavy pressure on pension and health systems. Failure to adapt and modernise social protection systems would increase the risk of more unemployment, poverty, and social exclusion. (Commission of the European Communities 2000: 11)

In response to this somewhat sobering assessment, the *Social Policy Agenda* stressed the critical importance of 'striving to achieve competitiveness, full employment and quality of work, quality in industrial relations, and quality of social policy'. This approach depended on 'promoting more jobs' based on 'high skills, fair labour standards and decent levels of occupational health and safety' (Commission of the European Communities 2000: 13).

If successful, implementation of the *Social Policy Agenda*, the Commission claimed, would combine 'economic, employment and social policies in a way which maximise[d] economic dynamism, employment growth and social cohesion'. This strategy would rely upon 'synergy and consistency' with other policy areas, including regional policy and policy on education and training.

The specific aim of the strategy outlined in the *Social Policy Agenda* is to raise the EU employment rate to 70 per cent by 2010 (to 60 per cent for women). This was to be achieved by adherence to the EU *Employment Guidelines* 2001, by continuing pressure on the full employment theme in all policy areas, and by assessment of the 'impact of the Structural Funds support, in particular of the European Social Fund (ESF), on employment and social policies'. Emphasis was also given to the importance of removing obstacles 'encountered by workers exercising their right to free movement' (Commission of the European Communities 2000: 19) and to 'modernising social protection'. This last aim involved 'adapting social protection systems to make work pay and provide secure income, make pensions safe and pension systems sustainable, promote social inclusion and ensure high quality and sustainability of health care' (Commission of the European Communities 2000: 20).

The previous section has already shown that EU employment policy has begun to influence the actions of national governments in combating unemployment and other labour market difficulties. Future UK responses to problems of unemployment and economic inactivity, for as long as the UK remains a member of the EU and committed to concerted action in this sphere, will also be influenced by the agreements reached at recent European Councils of Ministers (Lisbon, Nice, Stockholm). Two key developments referred to in the *Social Policy Agenda* need some further elaboration here. These are the demographic changes likely to occur in European countries in the next twenty-five years, and the direction given to labour market policy at national level by adherence to the European *Employment Guidelines*.

Demographic changes

At the end of the twentieth century, the share of the European population who were of working age (both sexes, aged 15–64 years) had been growing for over fifty years. Demographers predict, however, that this trend will continue only until about 2010, after which time it is expected to decline, mainly because of increased longevity, but also taking into account expected trends in fertility. Thus the relative size of the WAP is likely to be back at 1950s' levels by 2050. In the 1990s the ratio of the total inactive population (including those of working age) to the active WAP was 112 to 100 people. This is expected to rise to 140 to 100 by the middle of the twenty-first century (Jozefowicz and Pearce 2000).

It is worth noting that, by comparison with the USA and Japan, European countries have high levels of economic inactivity among their WAPs:

In 1997, only 59.5 per cent of the WAP of the European member states of the OECD was in employment. The comparable figures for the US and for Japan were 73.5 per cent and 70.0 per cent respectively . . . Of the remaining 40.5 per cent of non-employed Europeans of working age, only about 6.6 per cent were counted as unemployed. The other 33.9 per cent of the WAP forms a heterogeneous group, with very different degrees of attachment to the labour market. A large proportion is in education; another is not actively seeking work because of 'personal responsibilities'. Some are out of the labour force because of illness or incapacity, and some because they considered that no jobs were available (the so-called discouraged workers). In addition to the explicitly discouraged, a proportion of all other groups would probably be available for work if labour market prospects were better. Europe today suffers from very high levels of under-utilisation of its potential labour force. (Jozefowicz and Pearce 2000: 34)

The EU employment strategy and national action plans for employment

Following the Luxembourg Summit on employment in late 1997, an important new approach to employment policy was agreed by the member states of the EU. Under the employment title of the Treaty, member states are now committed each year to contributing to the *Joint Employment Report*, on the basis of which the European Commission prepares *Employment Guidelines* containing specific recommendations for each country. Following their adoption by the European Council, member states are obliged to take these *Guidelines* into account when shaping their national employment policies. Some of the ways in which this has begun to take effect have already been indicated earlier in this chapter.

Each member state has prepared a national action plan for employment annually since 1998. Member states 'are required to implement their employment policies in a way which is consistent with the Broad Economic Policy Guidelines'. The national action plans for employment must be built around the four 'pillars' of the European employment policy: employability, entrepreneurship, adaptability and equal opportunities. At the Lisbon Summit in 2000, the European Council strongly reasserted its commitment to 'full employment', and placed greater emphasis on 'tackling discriminatory aspects of the labour market' (Commission of the Economic Communities 2000: 4). Following analysis of the *Joint Employment Report*, it judged that:

Participation rates amongst older people remain low in many Member States and new challenges are emerging more clearly than in the past, notably labour shortages, skill gaps and regional disparities . . . The guideline on older workers has been widened from the tax-benefit aspect to a more comprehensive set of policies in support of active ageing. (Commission of the European Communities 2000: 4)

Within the *Employment Guidelines for 2001*, Guideline 2 – 'A more employment friendly approach: benefits, taxes and training systems' – requires each member state to 'review and, where appropriate, reform its benefit and tax system to remove poverty traps, and provide incentives for unemployed or inactive people to seek and take up work' (Commission of the European Communities 2000: 10).

Guideline 3 promotes the development of 'active ageing', in an attempt both to create incentives to encourage older workers to remain in the labour force and to enhance their capacity for paid work. This includes adopting measures to 'maintain working capacity and skills of older workers', the introduction of flexible working arrangements, and the raising of employers' awareness of what older workers can offer. Member states are also to ensure that older workers have 'sufficient access' to vocational education and training, and must review their tax and social protection systems 'with the aim of removing disincentives and creating new incentives for older workers to remain active in the labour market' (Commission of the European Communities 2000: 11).

Active policies are also required to tackle the 'unemployment and exclusion' which exist 'in certain sectors, occupations and regions' alongside labour shortages. The approach advocated includes 'job-matching' by employment services, as well as the promotion of occupational and geographical mobility. Measures to combat discrimination and to meet the needs of disabled people and other groups disadvantaged in accessing labour market opportunities are also to be adopted. Alongside these aspects, all of which are presented under the 'employability' pillar, each country is also asked to focus on developing entrepreneurship and job creation (pillar II). Here there is an explicit call for 'local action for employment' – promoting a partnership approach to local and regional job creation, and identifying opportunities to improve the functioning of local labour markets (Commission of the European Communities 2000: 15).

The emphasis in recent EU statements has thus been on the contribution that employment policies can make to achieving wider social goals. There is also a growing recognition that employment and welfare policies are inextricably linked. The final section of this chapter now turns briefly to the background to these developments.

Linking labour market change and welfare policy

Paid employment, most of it outside the home, first became the norm for men in most Western societies during the nineteenth century. Paid work came to dominate adult male life, and to be the principal means of household survival and of material wellbeing. The twentieth century saw the development of systems of welfare to support those unable to secure a living through income from employment. William Beveridge famously defined welfare as necessary to defeat the five giants Want, Disease, Squalor, Ignorance and Idleness. During the last century, the British model of the welfare state (discussed in more detail in ch. 3) exercised an influence well beyond British shores, although other models of welfare provision, especially the Bismarckian (established earlier) and the social democratic, were dominant in other parts of Europe (for discussion see ch. 3). Both the British and the Bismarckian style welfare states were predicated on the assumption that families would operate with a male breadwinner/female caregiver arrangement within the household (Crompton 1999).

Despite its universality, paid work, of course, does not have precisely the same cultural, economic or social significance across all Western societies, and the relationship between employment policy and employment status and welfare policy and eligibility for welfare support varied considerably between European countries throughout the twentieth century. Comparative analysis of different states, including that offered in this chapter, shows that there are a number of different ways of approaching work and welfare issues in different countries. Esping-Andersen's typology of different welfare 'regimes' (1990) stressed the different underlying rationales for the relationship between welfare arrangements and labour markets, and stimulated extensive discussion of different types of welfare state regime. Although review of this literature is well beyond the scope of the present chapter, it is appropriate to consider some of the ways in which labour market change and welfare policy arrangements have been theorised.

Cousins (1999: 67) has pointed out that three processes are currently affecting the economies of European countries: 'increased international competition, the shift to neo-liberal policies, and European integration'.

We have seen in the previous section some of the ways in which the latter is becoming visible in European employment policy – as Cousins notes, this development stems mainly from the Luxembourg Jobs Summit in 1997. In the remainder of this chapter we now consider neo-liberal policy development, and the development of the 'third way'.

Goodin (2001) claims that in addition to the three welfare state regimes identified by Esping-Andersen – liberal, corporatist and social democratic – a fourth, 'post-productivist', needs to be added. Goodin's argument is that the liberal ('work *not* welfare'), corporatist ('welfare *through* work') and social democratic ('welfare *and* work') regimes are all in different ways productivist. This means that they are founded upon the assumption that paid work is a central means for an economy to function and for the provision of welfare. Analysis of the trajectories of some welfare states in the late twentieth century has led, however, to identification of a fourth regime type, in which work occupies a less central role. Declining labour force participation rates in some countries, it is argued, suggest that a new welfare regime may be emerging, in which a reasonable living can be made from non-employment income sources, including social security benefits and early retirement packages.

This argument has its origins in debates associated with Giddens (1994, 1998) and with Beck (1992). Both these authors argued in the 1990s that a standardised full-time employment relationship was indeed being eroded, although Giddens especially acknowledged that this relationship had only ever applied to half the population, men. Beck put the argument that standardised full-time employment as the societal norm was being replaced by a 'system of flexible and pluralized underemployment' (1992: 140). In his view this development was bringing

a risk-fraught system of flexible, pluralized, decentralized under-employment, which, however, will no longer raise the problem of unemployment in the sense of being completely without a job. In this system, unemployment in the guise of various forms of underemployment is 'integrated' into the employment system, but in exchange for a generalization of employment insecurity that was not known in the 'old' uniform full-employment system of industrial society. (Beck 1992: 143–4)

As the discussion of EU employment policy above has indicated, however, and a review of state employment policy in a number of specific examples reveals, not all evidence supports the case that EU states are consciously pursuing such a post-productivist model.

From at least the 1960s onwards, social theorists have suggested that the Fordist model of production which dominated the first half of the twentieth century, supported by Taylorist models of scientific management, was being replaced by 'post-industrialism' (Bell 1976, Jenkins and Sherman 1979, Piore and Sabel 1984, Esping-Andersen 1993). Based on evidence about technological change, new systems of production and the rise of mass higher education, the post-industrial thesis argued that advanced societies were moving away from industrial models of production towards service economies in which most people would have far greater amounts of leisure than had ever been possible in the past. Some worried that the new developments were deskilling the working class (Braverman 1974), leaving them ultimately more vulnerable to exploitation and immiseration than had been the case through the previous century. Some predicted a more optimistic future, in which most men would be freed from the exhausting burden of demanding, physical labour. Others feared that downsized and super-efficient organisations devoted to 'lean production' would offer rewards to only a few favoured and highly skilled employees, while most of the workforce would find it increasingly difficult to find a secure place in the world of work, in which flexible systems of production would weaken job security.

The context for this, as Giddens has noted, was provided long ago by Max Weber. Work, Weber observed,

as paid employment, has been separated out in a clear-cut way from other domains of life. Work becomes a standard-bearer of moral meaning – it defines whether or not individuals feel worthwhile or socially valued; and the motivation to work is autonomous. (Giddens 1994: 175)

Furthermore, the

Autonomy of work still survives as the dominant ethos and defines what the experience of unemployment means . . . The overall number of hours worked by men in paid employment has dropped by half over the past fifty years. As yet, most men still face or expect to face a fulltime working life. But even if they should actively desire it, for many this expectation will prove unrealistic. The objective of full employment, so closely tied to the welfare state, makes little sense any more. Employment under what conditions? And, what relation should work have to other life values? (Giddens 1994: 177)

In 1991, Jessop predicted that, in the foreseeable future, a 'Schumpeterian workfare state' would succeed the Keynesian welfare state model (Lind and Møller 1999: 3). The concept of workfare emerged in the 1970s from the USA, where certain states had introduced schemes requiring claimants to work in return for social assistance benefits (Lødermel and Trickey 2001: 3–4). Jessop argued that this new workfare state would aim to sustain market forces and would deprioritise full employment, giving emphasis instead to economic competitiveness. Since the 1970s, the political reality has, of course, been that Western societies have defined unemployment as a matter of major social as well as economic concern. Nevertheless, as Lind and Møller put it

a major re-orientation of welfare policies is . . . taking place: away from redistributive concerns towards cost-saving and productivist concerns. The welfare state has added a new and stronger emphasis on its role as a disciplinary force in society to maintain the work ethic. (1999: 3)

Detailed discussion of the extent to which 'workfare' ideology has in fact influenced different states in combating unemployment and economic inactivity is beyond the scope of this book, but has been attempted elsewhere (Trickey 2001, Evans 2001, Finn 1998). Trickey stresses that 'workfare' approaches, which 'require compulsory activity from people in need of social assistance' (Trickey 2001: 255) vary both between and within countries (for example, Germany and the USA). Workfare is associated with a number of objectives: reducing costs, preventing dependence, combating exclusion and linking rights and responsibilities.

Workfare-type policy responses involve what some consider a systems shift. As Jessop's contribution suggested, the Keynesian position adopted in post-war Britain (Alcock 1999a) was in the 1990s being replaced by new arrangements. In his view, these represented a neo-liberal model, consistent with Joseph Schumpeter's economic philosophy. Part of the argument here was that unemployment insurance systems originally designed to assist the temporarily unemployed had come increasingly to have work disincentive effects, and had drifted into long-term income support. A new approach, exemplified by the USA's Personal Responsibility and Work Opportunity Reconciliation Act, was needed to impose work requirements on benefit recipients and to limit the duration of their claims (Walker 1999).

Underlying this position, as Walker explains, lie three critical, but ill-founded, assumptions: that welfare dependency is primarily a 'problem of attitude'; that poverty is to be condemned when it is found among minorities; and that welfare payments, over anything but the very short term, destroy the 'work ethic' (Walker 1999: 542–3). Among those rejecting this perspective, Walker identifies Handler and Hazenfeld (1997) and Schwartz (1998) for the USA and Donnison (1997) for the UK. These writers argue that it is shortage of jobs, low wages and growing income inequality which is driving long-term benefit claiming, not overgenerous benefit systems and moral degeneracy. Despite these critiques, variants on the USA's workfare approach continue to be widely enforced – on both sides of the Atlantic. And as Walker and others have noted, policy in the UK under Labour, with the support of statements by Tony Blair, continues to stress the need for welfare reform and the importance of 'welfare to work' (Cm 3805 1998).

There is growing evidence that a 'get tough' workfare policy is emerging, especially in some schemes in the USA, although this is 'not a sure way of creating success' (Evans 2001: 57). Evans concludes, from his review of the implementation of workfare approaches in the USA, France, Germany and the Netherlands, as well as the UK, that:

Welfare to work programmes are a complex set of policy interventions which require careful balancing of approaches and methods, and which must take into account the micro- and the macro-circumstances of their recipients ... The questions are *who* are we going to help first and most, and, second, *where* do we want them to end up? (Evans 2001: 57)

In Evans's view, British approaches to integrating people without work into employment, as through the New Deals, have tended to concentrate disproportionately on the young unemployed (18–24 year olds) and lone parents. Schemes for older people (New Deal 50 plus) and for people with disabilities (New Deal for Disabled People) have been introduced but have been resourced at a much lower level than support for the young. This point is taken up in discussion of the implications of the findings from our study in the final chapter of this book.

In an influential text published just after the Labour government came to power, Giddens stressed that the 'difficulties of the welfare state are only partly financial'. Once established, he claimed, 'benefits have their own autonomy, regardless of whether or not they meet the purpose for which they were originally designed' (1998: 115). He suggests that sickness and disability benefits in the UK (and elsewhere) have come to be used in different ways from those originally intended, in that many people who would like to work appear not in unemployment but in disability and incapacity statistics. The 'Dutch model', sometimes cited as a prime example of modernised social democracy, Giddens pointed out, looks less impressive on close examination – not least because of the extent to which claimant unemployment there has been concealed in disability statistics. Success in reducing the unemployment figures to below 1 million in the UK was officially trumpeted during 2001, yet few official voices drew attention to high levels of inactivity among older workers and those claiming sickness-related benefits.

For Giddens, the following values are central to the third way, a redefined and renewed social democracy: equality; protection of the vulnerable; freedom as autonomy; no rights without responsibilities; no authority without democracy; cosmopolitan pluralism; philosophic conservatism (1998: 66). He stresses that:

sweeping deregulation is not the answer. Welfare expenditure should remain at European rather than US levels, but be switched as far as possible towards human capital investment. Benefit systems should be reformed where they induce welfare, and a more active risk-taking attitude encouraged, wherever possible through incentives, but where necessary by legal obligations. (Giddens 1998: 122)

He emphasises that a human capital approach, along the lines advocated by Moss Kanter, may not be enough. Her claim has been that governments can move from alleviating unemployment towards job creation by focusing on support for entrepreneurial activities, an emphasis on lifelong education, public project partnerships, portability (common standards of education or portable pension rights) and family-friendly workplace policies (Moss Kanter 1990). All these remain central to the New Labour project and were reiterated loudly both during the 2001 general election campaign in the UK and after the Labour government's re-election.

Giddens doubts that these strategies are enough to deliver full employment – but argues that a shift towards 'positive welfare' would be beneficial for all members of society:

Positive welfare would replace each of Beveridge's negatives with a positive: in place of Want, autonomy; not Disease but active health; instead of Ignorance, education, as a continuing part of life; rather than Squalor, well-being; and in place of Idleness, initiative. (Giddens 1998: 127–8)

Such a radical transformation of the welfare state would involve abolishing the fixed age of retirement and redistributing employment – something which Giddens claims is already happening on a large scale. Arguably the Netherlands, and to a lesser extent the UK, are among the economies in which this redistribution has already begun to take place.

Many of the ideas referred to in this chapter have already begun to influence policy relating to labour market detachment. We have seen here that some European states have come to recognise that massaging labour supply using early retirement policies, and an excessively flexible stance on the definition of incapacity, is no longer an appropriate response. Later chapters of this book reveal that for some men, detachment from the labour market is problematic not just because of its economic impact, but also because it affects male identity. Official approaches to social security claimants have begun to move in the direction which the neo-liberal position proposes, and in the UK, the Chancellor of the Exchequer has made no secret of his view that social and welfare policy reform is taking 'work for those who can' as its defining mantra. In the next chapter, Pete Alcock looks in detail at the operation of the British social security system from the perspective of men who are detached from the labour market.

3   The benefits system

Pete Alcock

Social security and unemployment

Most commentators on social security provision agree that the protection provided by state benefits serves a number of different purposes. These include the relief or prevention of poverty, the maintenance of income in periods of labour market absence, life course investment to support retirement and the provision of extra resources to support child care or disability costs (see McKay and Rowlingson 1999, Ditch 1999). Within the UK these different purposes have also resulted in the development of different forms of protection, subject to different rules and administrative procedures. Taken as a whole, social security is complex, confusing and contradictory, as the experience of many of the respondents in this research testifies, and we cannot hope to explore all of this complexity here. However, the study was concerned primarily with men's experiences of unemployment or labour market detachment; and the way in which the social security system responds to these issues has a particular history and incorporates a number of key elements of current policy, which are explored in more detail in this chapter.

Current benefit policies on unemployment can be traced back to the nineteenth century and to the Poor Law, the legacy of which remains to some extent still with us over a century and a half later. The concern of the nineteenth-century Poor Law was with pauperism rather than poverty, with the individuals and families who could not provide for themselves. And in responding to this problem, social security protection sought to distinguish between two broad categories of dependants – the deserving and the undeserving poor (Alcock 1999b, Novak 1988). While the deserving poor were those who were the victims of social circumstances largely outside their control, the undeserving poor were those whom it was assumed were – or ought to be – in a position to do something about their plight. The unemployed largely fell into this latter category.

Unemployed people – or, rather more accurately, unemployed men, for women were assumed to move into financial dependence upon their husbands on marriage – were those of working age who were not engaged in full-time paid employment. Their need for support arose because of their absence from the labour market, and thus their route out of poverty and deprivation was assumed to be a 'return' to the world of paid work. Social security protection for these undeserving poor should therefore not seek to undermine the pressure to return to full-time employment – indeed, it should seek to encourage it.

Following the Poor Law Amendment Act of 1834 such encouragement primarily took the form of the principle of 'less eligibility'. This was the notion that the position of the unemployed dependant must be made less eligible that that of the lowest paid worker. Poor Law support should thus be minimal and punitive in order to provide a clear incentive to seek paid work; and in the nineteenth century this was achieved through the regime of the workhouse (Fraser 1973: ch. 2). Of course, workhouses are now the stuff of history (although some of the old buildings still remain), but the principle of less eligibility remains a core feature of social security protection in the UK in the twenty-first century. It is now sometimes referred to as the problem of the 'unemployment trap', the fear that unemployed claimants for whom social security entitlement is 'too generous' may be unwilling to take low paid employment and will thus remain trapped on benefits (Deacon and Bradshaw 1983: ch. 8). That social security protection should operate within competitive labour markets is, of course, an essential feature of their development in advanced industrial countries, and in this sense the unemployment trap poses an inescapable policy dilemma. However, the legacy of pauperism and the fear of creating dependency among the undeserving poor have meant that the predominant tendency within unemployment protection has been to minimise the scale of protection in order to provide an individual incentive to self-improvement. This tendency still holds sway in policy-making today, in particular within means-tested – social assistance – provision, as we shall discuss below.

The Poor Law was not the only form of protection against unemployment developed in the UK in the nineteenth century, however. Indeed, its punitive and stigmatising regime in practice provided a strong encouragement for other forms of protection to develop, initially outside the state benefits system, and these have left a rather different legacy within social security. In order to avoid the need for dependency upon the Poor Law some groups of workers began, in the latter half of the nineteenth century, to join together in voluntary organisations to provide collective protection against unemployment and other temporary causes of labour market absence. The idea behind these Friendly Societies, as they came to be called, was one of mutual self-support based upon an insurance model

(Thane 1996). Working members would pay regular contributions into the Society and then when out of work they would be able to claim benefits from it. Benefits were thus paid in return for contributions made under a collective 'contract' between the members, which required, of course, that the schemes themselves be actuarially sound.

The Friendly Societies provided a very different model of social security protection from the Poor Law. They were mutual and collective, they were based upon reciprocity (rights to benefit in return for contributions made), levels of protection were based on need rather than labour market incentives and, initially at least, they operated outside the state. This idea of mutual and collective protection – social insurance – was taken up on a national basis in Germany in the late nineteenth century by Bismarck to develop a state-run social security scheme. This established a model of public protection through the employment market that was followed in many other countries over the ensuing century, in particular in the continental European nations discussed in ch. 2. In the early part of the twentieth century this model of national provision was introduced into the UK, too. In 1911 a national scheme for unemployment and sickness benefits was established. It involved a partial nationalisation of the Friendly Societies and the provision of state benefit protection in return for contributions made by employees, their employers and the Treasury – popularly known as 'ninepence for fourpence' because the employee's contribution was only 4d (old pennies).

The new social insurance protection operated alongside continuing Poor Law protection, although the Poor Law itself was reformed following the reports from a Royal Commission in 1909, with workhouses replaced by cash payments. The insurance protection also initially covered only workers in certain industries. The result was thus the creation within public provision of two different models of social security protection – social assistance and social insurance. As mentioned above, social assistance was punitive and minimal in order to enforce labour market participation. Social insurance was based on mutual rights and obligations, and was based on a notion of income maintenance which in Germany and other continental countries meant benefit payments linked to previous wage levels. Not surprisingly, therefore, while social assistance carried the stigma of the Poor Law and was widely hated and feared by the working class, social insurance was a much more popular form of benefit support. The legacies which these distinctions created continue to structure the experience of social security support today, in particular support for unemployment and labour market absence.

The social insurance schemes developed in the UK did not follow the Bismarck model directly (Hennock 1987). Benefits for the unemployed were not earnings related (apart from a brief period from 1966–82), and, although they were extended in the 1920s to cover most workers, they never provided a comprehensive protection to replace social assistance. Furthermore, when economic recession began to lead to rapidly rising unemployment in the 1930s there were concerns about the financial viability of the schemes and their impact on a depressed labour market (Gilbert 1966). This led in 1930 to cuts in the levels of benefits paid to reduce the cost to the Exchequer, and to the introduction of more stringent conditions for entitlement to support. Of particular importance here was the introduction of a new test to distinguish the deserving from the undeserving poor. This was the requirement that claimants must be 'genuinely seeking work' in order to receive benefit (Deacon 1976), and in effect it incorporated some of the older Poor Law attitudes about labour market incentives into social insurance protection. Of course, an insurance scheme aiming to provide protection for labour market absence would need some test of whether such absence was avoidable; but this new test involved not just a requirement that claimants were actually unemployed but also imposed a duty on them to look for work. This sealed within the broader social security system a concern to combat what might now be referred to as 'scrounging', and it also made clear the distinction between unemployed claimants and those dependent upon benefits for other reasons.

In fact provision of benefit support in times of sickness or disability, although linked to the development of unemployment insurance, had something of a different history and rationale – a difference which has also left a legacy within current social security provision. In the nineteenth century the Friendly Societies, and some commercial insurance agencies, had developed insurance protection for sickness. This included financial support during labour market absence resulting from sickness, and also access to medical treatment which, in the absence of any national health service, many did not have. In 1911 this form of protection was incorporated into the new NI scheme. However, the benefits were administered through 'approved societies' who also secured access to medical services, and thus the services provided varied between different societies, although national weekly rates for benefit were set, with a lower rate for women (assumed to have lower loss of earnings) and a lower rate, too, for longer-term disability (Thane 1996: ch. 3).

Provision for income support for sickness was thus within the insurance scheme, and was linked to access to health services, establishing a popular view, which is still to a marginal extent accurate, that NI contributions were part of a welfare contract to support health as well as social security services. However, there was also a separate, and more generous, form of support developed at around the same time for those whose sickness or disability arose as a direct result of their employment, called Industrial Injuries Protection. Although this was a public benefit scheme, it drew some of its rationale from the notion of legal compensation for accidental injury; indeed, it was expected to reduce the need for legal actions arising out of accidents at work, and hence provided much more generous levels of benefit for those covered. This created a two-tier benefit provision for sickness and disability which still remains in the more generous Industrial Injuries Disablement Benefit paid to some claimants today, although entitlement to these industrial benefits is tightly controlled (McKay and Rowlingson 1999: ch. 5).

In 1942 the publication of the *Beveridge Report* provided a blueprint for the comprehensive reform of social security provision, and was largely implemented by the post-war Labour government. The main thrust of Beveridge's plan was for social insurance protection to become the predominant feature of social security provision; and the NI scheme implemented in 1948 sought to achieve this by replacing all the previous sickness, unemployment and pension provisions with one national scheme. This new scheme continued the notion of collective protection through contributions. As Beveridge commented, 'The capacity and desire of the British people to contribute for security are amongst the most certain and impressive social facts' (1942: 119). All employees and their employers were to pay into a national fund out of which benefits would be paid in times of unemployment, sickness, retirement, maternity and widowhood. The scheme was established on a 'pay-as-you-go' basis (benefit payments were met from current contributions with no invested surplus) and benefits were paid at subsistence levels (to provide only for basic needs) (Hill 1990: ch. 3).

Much has been written about the strengths and weaknesses of the Beveridge NI scheme and its operation in the decades following its introduction (see Baldwin and Falkingham 1994, Hills, Ditch and Glennerster 1994). Of particular significance in this context, however, was the fact that even at the time of its introduction the NI scheme was never a comprehensive form of protection. Because of a concern that some people in need might not have been able to meet the contribution conditions required for receipt of NI benefits, a form of social assistance protection was retained as a 'safety net' to provide for those falling through the insurance scheme. It was retitled 'National Assistance' and was operated on a means-tested basis by a separate National Assistance Board and, like the Poor Law which it replaced, it was perceived by many as a 'less eligible' form of support than NI.

The expectation among most policy-makers was that National Assistance would play a minor and declining role in post-war social security protection. However, in practice this has proved to be a gross miscalculation. From the early 1950s over 1 million were dependent upon this form of social assistance; by the 1970s this had risen to 4 million and by the 1980s to 8 million. In the mid-1990s over 10 million were reliant directly or indirectly on this basic means-tested scheme, which by then had been retitled Income Support (from 1966 to 1988 it was called Supplementary Benefit). The reasons for this growth in dependency upon assistance are complex. In part they arise from the changing nature of poverty (mainly experienced by pensioners in the early decades and later spreading to unemployed and low paid families), in part from rises in benefit rates which meant that many NI claimants were also entitled to means-tested support, and in part from the failure of the NI scheme to provide comprehensive protection for all (Deacon and Bradshaw 1983: ch. 6).

For unemployed and Sickness Benefit claimants, in particular, the overlap between social insurance and social assistance benefits became particularly complex in the last two decades of the twentieth century. The intention behind the NI scheme was that it would provide support for those experiencing periods of absence from work as a result of redundancy or sickness, with a longer-term protection for the chronically sick and long-term disabled eventually paid at a higher weekly rate (Invalidity Benefit – IVB), with continued separate provision for industrial injuries. However, support has never in practice provided for all and increasing numbers of working-age claimants have had to rely on means-tested support. There are three broad reasons for this (see Alcock 1996):

- NI benefit rates, fixed at subsistence level, were not sufficiently high to lift many claimants above the entitlement levels for means-tested benefits, especially where claimants had dependent families and significant housing costs.
- Conditions requiring NI claimants to have made the requisite contributions into the scheme excluded many unemployed people, especially after these conditions were tightened in the 1980s.
- Those unemployed for long periods of time exhausted the entitlement to NI benefits, limited to twelve months in the 1970s and 1980s and reduced to six months in 1996.

In the 1990s less than 20 per cent of the unemployed relied entirely on NI support and over 60 per cent were dependent entirely upon Income Support (Webb 1994). For Sickness and Invalidity Benefit claimants the situation was slightly different. In the 1980s Sickness Benefit was replaced for the vast majority of claimants by statutory sick pay, paid by employers under regulations. For long-term claimants IVB was paid at a higher rate than Income Support and so lifted many claimants above this, unless they had dependants or high housing costs.

The consequences of large numbers of claimants relying upon means-tested support were to introduce a number of problems into the operation of the social security system (see Deacon and Bradshaw 1983). This is not the place to discuss these in detail, but they include:

- the disjuncture between the individual entitlement base of NI benefits, so that either member of a couple may claim independently, and the family base of means-testing, which assumes that all resources are aggregated within households (Esam and Berthoud 1991);
- the problem of the unemployment trap – benefits based on the needs of a large family may be more than a claimant may be able to command in wages from the labour market (Alcock 1997: ch. 14);
- the problem of the poverty trap – to combat the unemployment trap subsidies are paid to low-wage earners, through the Working Families Tax Credit and Housing Benefit. These are withdrawn when wages rise, thus trapping workers on a net low income plateau (Field 1995, Alcock and Pearson 1999);
- the problem of the savings trap caused by the loss of means-tested benefits where income is received from pension schemes or from capital holdings, thus reducing the advantage of savings or investments for those on benefits (Alcock and Pearson 1999);
- the problem of low take up of benefit entitlement due to the complex procedures for determining entitlement to means-tested benefits and the stigma still associated with dependence upon them (McKay and Rowlingson 1999: ch. 7).

It is clear from ch. 9 later in this book that some of these problems did pose real problems for a number of our respondents, and probably therefore for many other men outside or on the margins of the labour market. They can make the claiming and receipt of benefits a process that is fraught with apprehension, frustration and confusion, no doubt compounded by the fact that alongside the increased dependency upon means-tested benefits NI provision does continue to operate for some. For short-term unemployment, chronic sickness and disability, and retirement, entitlement to NI benefits remains for those who meet the contribution conditions; and for some, particularly long-term claimants, these benefits can be higher than alternative means-tested support. Current social security provision thus continues many of the complex and contradictory problems which have dogged its development over the last century or so. Despite Beveridge's comprehensive plan, social insurance benefits continue to operate alongside social assistance support, creating problems for claimants, administrators and policy-makers and maintaining the legacies of distinction and desert on which they are both based.

Current benefit provision

Benefit provision for people of working age outside the labour market is complex. There are a number of different benefits to which individuals and families may be entitled and, as discussed above, these are based upon different traditions of funding and entitlement. Establishing the particular benefits to which particular claimants may be entitled is thus an expert task best left to benefit administrators and welfare rights workers. The administration of these benefits has also itself been undergoing significant reform in recent years. In the 1990s this took the form of the Next Steps reforms, which removed the administration of benefits from the DSS to independent quangos, primarily the Benefits Agency. The administration of provision for unemployment remained, as it had been before, with the Department for Employment (later Education and Employment (DfEE)), although here too under a separate agency, the Employment Service operating through the job centres.

In June 2001 both the DSS and DfEE were restructured. Responsibility for employment policy and support for the unemployed was removed from the DfEE, which became the Department for Education and Skills (DES), and was combined with social security policy in a new Department for Work and Pensions (DWP). Following this it is planned to merge the administrative operations of the Employment Service and Benefits Agency to create a new agency called Jobcentre Plus, administering all benefits for those of working age, with a separate agency administering pensions. This should simplify the process of claiming for many of the men covered in this study who should in the future have to deal with only one central government department and administrative office, although Housing and Council Tax Benefits will continue to be administered quite separately by local government.

This merged administrative framework results from a new government commitment to focusing more directly upon the needs of claimants, and it will almost certainly improve benefit delivery; but the benefits delivered will remain the same. Thus there will continue to be a division between social insurance and social assistance protection. The major benefits involved here remained unchanged from the mid-1990s when this research was carried out.

NI unemployment benefit was replaced in 1996 by the Jobseeker's Allowance (JSA). The change was an important symbolic shift emphasising the clear expectation that claimants were to be supported only on the condition that they were looking for paid work – a similar change to that introduced in the 1930s. It also involved a number of important technical changes. The period of entitlement was reduced from twelve to six months, claimants were required to be 'actively seeking' work and were expected to outline the steps they were taking to do this in an agreement with an Employment Service officer. They were also expected to attend for interviews with officers after fixed periods of dependency to review their efforts to secure work. This was a significant change to a more active enforcement of job search through benefit administration. It has been evaluated by a number of research projects sponsored by the DSS, which have found that claimants had experienced a clearer and more active administrative process and, to some extent, had been able to move more quickly off benefit dependency (Raynor *et al.* 2000, Smith, Youngs, Ashworth, McKay and Walker 2000). The numbers claiming the contribution-based allowance also began to decline slightly after 1996–97 from over 300,000 to under 200,000 a year, with a comparable decline from over 1.3 million to under 900,000 for the income-based scheme, although this was during a period of more general reductions in headline unemployment count (DSS 2000b).

The 1996 reforms also extended the JSA, and its attendant administrative procedures, to cover unemployed claimants on means-tested Income Support. Prior to the change, Unemployment Benefit claimants would move on to Income Support if they remained unemployed for more than twelve months. This meant a move from NI support to means-tested support, with all the related consequences outlined above. Such a move still took place after the reforms; but it now happens after six months, and the claimant remains formally on (income-related) JSA. What is more, administration remained with the Employment Service under the same regime of active work search.

This was a complex and confusing reform. Now the administrative and job search regulations (and the name of the benefit) remain the same however long claimants remain unemployed, but the benefit levels and entitlement criteria change from an NI to a means-tested basis. Not surprisingly many claimants do not fully appreciate the implications of these new regimes, and it was clear that, when our research was carried out shortly after the changes came into force, a number of our respondents were confused about which regime they were under.

As the research reported here reveals, however, significant numbers of men of working age outside the labour market are not receiving JSA but rather are dependent (in part at least) on another NI benefit, Incapacity Benefit (IB). IB was also introduced in the mid-1990s (in 1995) in this case to replace IVB. This was the support provided for those unable to work because of sickness or disability for a period of over six months. It was an NI benefit, and thus subject to contribution conditions relating to past employment; and it was paid at a higher rate than short-term Unemployment and Sickness Benefit in recognition of the accumulated costs of long-term illness or disability. For those receiving IVB, therefore, it had the advantage of long-term insurance protection without the drawback of means-testing, thus avoiding the problems of the savings trap. And, as discussed in ch. 5, the numbers claiming this benefit grew quite dramatically in the late 1980s and early 1990s (see also Rowlingson and Berthoud 1996).

The introduction of IB was a partial response to this accelerating dependency. IB is subject to stricter entitlement conditions than those operating under IVB. It is also subject to tax where appropriate. In particular, the test of incapacity was moved on to tighter medical criteria based on a scoring system derived from a questionnaire completed by claimants and assessed by 'official' doctors working for the Benefits Agency. To retain entitlement claimants must now in theory be incapable of undertaking any paid employment, not merely that for which they were previously engaged, and further cuts in earnings-related pension additions and support for dependants were also made. In its first year of operation the numbers in receipt of IB remained as high as those on IVB, but between 1995–6 and 2000–1 they declined from around 1.7 million to 1.5 million, although this was mostly owing to a reduction in the numbers of those over pension age who were no longer eligible for this benefit (DSS 2000b; Dorsett *et al.* 1998). In addition, there is a further group of around 600,000 who are deemed unfit for work but have insufficient NI contributions to qualify for IB and are mostly on Income Support, as ch. 5 explains at greater length.

Retirement pensions are the major NI benefit, paid to around 11 million people a year in the early twenty-first century. For those with earnings-related additions or individual occupational or private protection they can provide a reasonable level of support, although for those receiving only the basic NI minimum protection remains low and leaves many dependent also upon means-tested Income Support, now retitled the Minimum Income Guarantee. However, entitlement begins at the statutory pension age 65 for men. Thus state pensions were not a potential source of income for the men in this study, although, as discussed in ch. 4, a significant proportion did have access to private or occupational pension support after early retirement.

Now that unemployed claimants on means-tested benefits have been transferred on to income-related JSA, Income Support is only available to those outside the labour market for other reasons, such as lone parents and disabled people without adequate NI protection. Dependency levels here have remained high, at around 4 million a year throughout the 1990s (DSS 2000b). However, there are other means-tested benefits which are also available to unemployed men. Housing Benefit and Council Tax Benefit cover all the costs of rent and local tax payments for those on income-related JSA and provide a means-tested contribution to these for those with slightly higher income, such as IB claimants and those with private or occupational pension protection. Some Income Support claimants can also claim benefit protection to cover the cost of interest repayments on mortgages for owner-occupied houses, but this is not available during the first nine months of unemployment for mortgages taken out after 1995. Unlike Housing Benefits, those receiving mortgage interest support cannot claim it where their income, from any sources, takes them over the Income Support level. This can add to the unemployment and savings traps for some of those on the margins of the labour market and create an apparent incentive to seek basic means-tested support, although, as this research reveals, such incentives are not linked to real choices for most people.

For those in low paid employment there are a number of other important means-tested benefits. Housing Benefit and Council Tax Benefit are available to the low paid, based on a test of net income which reduces entitlement when income rises. For those with families there is now the Working Families Tax Credit, which replaced Family Credit in 1999, which is a relatively generous subsidy to low wages for workers with dependent children; and a similar subsidy, the Disabled Person's Tax Credit, is available for those with recognised disabilities. These are a key feature of the Labour government's 'welfare to work' strategy, to which we shall return shortly. In addition to them, however, are health benefits, such as free prescriptions, and a wide range of other forms of means-tested support provided by local authorities in order to support social participation and service provision among those with low incomes. Many of these are not widely understood, or in all probability widely claimed, although their effect is to contribute even further to the problem of the poverty trap (or poverty plateau) for the low paid (Alcock and Pearson 1999).

Entitlement to benefits is not the same thing as receipt of benefits, however. In order to receive benefits people must make a successful claim, and the evidence is that not all potential claimants do so. There may be many reasons for this non-take up of benefit entitlement and, of course, any estimates as to its extent can only be 'guesstimates' (see McKay and Rowlingson 1999: ch. 7). The DWP does produce estimates of the take up of major means-tested benefits on an annual basis, and the figures for 1998–9 estimate that only between 68 per cent and 82 per cent of claimants of income-based JSA actually take up entitlement (DSS 2000c).

Their estimates for Housing Benefit were 91–97 per cent and for Council Tax Benefit 75–81 per cent.

The DWP does not make estimates of take-up levels for NI and other non-means-tested benefits, and the common assumption is that levels are generally much higher here, as entitlement is based upon contingency and contribution rather than complex and confusing means-tested assessment. Nevertheless, overall concerns about non-take up of social security benefits cast some doubt over the accuracy of dependency levels as a measure of social need, or social circumstances. It also suggests that significant numbers of the men interviewed in our surveys may not in practice be receiving all the benefits to which they may be entitled. Certainly, as we discuss in ch. 9, a number were unsure about their current benefit support and potential entitlement, and many were content to rely upon Benefits Agency or Employment Services calculations of their entitlement.

Availability for work

Since the early days of the nineteenth century, therefore, social security protection in the UK has been linked to support for labour market participation. The principle of less eligibility was intended to provide a direct incentive to those in receipt of state support to seek instead (low paid) employment, and the legacy of this incentive has remained with us. In effect it means that social security protection functions also as a means of promoting a supply-side push to overall employment levels, and this supply-side approach has remained a key feature of both social security policy and employment policy over the last decade or so.

At the beginning of the twentieth century the introduction of labour exchanges in 1909 extended this on to a more proactive and supportive basis (Smith 1972). Labour exchanges were a formal means of providing information about local job vacancies to unemployed benefit claimants, so that the process of registering for benefit entitlement (signing on) could be linked to specific assistance in seeking appropriate employment. Since retitled job centres, these exchanges remained a key feature of twentieth-century employment and benefit policy, linking claiming with job search in a way that will only now be changed in the twenty-first century with the introduction of Jobcentre Plus.

As mentioned above, however, the formal requirements on unemployed claimants to seek paid employment have fluctuated over the course of the last hundred years. In the 1930s full entitlement was restricted to those who were able to demonstrate that they were 'genuinely seeking work', whereas in the 1950s and 1960s the requirement was more passive, with claimants merely having to register as available for work. In the 1980s the requirements became more stringent once again, with the expectation that claimants should be 'taking steps' to find full-time paid work; and with the introduction of the JSA came the current formal requirement that claimants be 'actively seeking work' under a personalised agreement with an Employment Service officer. It is no coincidence, furthermore, that the periods of more stringent availability testing have been associated with increased levels of Unemployment Benefit dependency resulting from economic recession (most notably in the 1930s, and 1980s and early 1990s). It is when large numbers of unemployed claimants are claiming benefits that supply-side measures to promote employment through the social security system become more draconian.

There is a curious contradiction at the heart of such policy responses, of course. Unemployed claimants are being exhorted to search more actively for full-time employment opportunities at just the times when these opportunities are at their most restrictive. As discussed in more detail below, however, at the turn of the century the new Labour government began to take up more widely proactive policies towards supply-side support for labour market participation, most significantly in the New Deal, at a time when economic performance was climbing and unemployment levels in decline. Similar developments can also be found in a number of other advanced industrial countries, and these have prompted some commentators to suggest that there may be more general changes in social and economic policy behind the new concern about labour market participation.

As we discussed in ch. 2, some have argued that this involved a paradigm shift in the nature of welfare provision in modern industrial societies from a Keynesian to a Schumpeterian model of state intervention (for instance, Jessop 1994, 2001). Under Keynesian welfare policy, economic policy focuses upon demand-side promotion of labour market growth and the primary concern of social policy is to provide a safety net of support for those dislocated as a result of this process; under Schumpeterian workfare policy, state intervention is concentrated primarily upon supply-side measures to promote economic participation within relatively liberated market economics. As a consequence of this, social security measures become linked more closely to the promotion of labour market participation, in extreme cases requiring claimants either to undertake paid employment or forfeit their right to social security support – workfare.

Such a more draconian version of workfare within social security has been developed in some areas of the US following the welfare reforms initiated by the Clinton administrations in the 1990s; and there is some evidence that these were observed closely by policy-makers in the UK and continental Europe (Waldfogel 1997, Deacon 2000). However, within continental Europe a much wider range of strategies have been developed to provide supply-side support to labour market participation, generally referred to as social activation (see Lødermel and Trickey 2001, Roche and Van Berkel 1997). Some of these programmes are similar to the 'welfare to work' strategies now operating in the UK, discussed below; but in some countries (notably in Scandinavia – see Kvist 2001) they also provide support for participation in a range of other social activities, including voluntary work and social care, with the aim of promoting social inclusion within a range of social networks beyond the traditional full-time labour market.

Thus supply-side promotion of labour market participation, and wider social inclusion, are now significant features of social and economic policy planning in a large number of advanced industrial countries. The policy focus has moved beyond the use of stricter, or more lenient, criteria for job search within the regulations and procedures for determining entitlement to unemployment benefits, to embrace a range of measures to provide proactive support for the reintegration of men, and women, outside or on the margins of the labour market. As we discuss in chs. 10 and 11, the experiences of the respondents in this research project provide some important guides to how such measures could be designed and developed. In any case, however, the policy agenda in the UK has begun to shift in this area already as a result of a number of reforms introduced by the Labour governments.

Welfare to Work in the UK

Since its initial election victory in 1997 the Labour administration has made policies on Welfare to Work one of its most high profile political commitments. This has been a key element in most of its major public documents, such as the Green Paper on welfare reform (DSS 1998a) and it has been widely discussed by critics and commentators (see Levitas 1998, Oppenheim 1999). In practice, the UK Welfare to Work strategy draws upon both US and European experience and policy debate. It has two main elements – making work pay and support for job search.

Making work pay

In order to encourage unemployed, and detached, workers back into the labour market it is necessary to ensure that the financial rewards of

full-time employment are sufficiently positive – the problem of the unemployment trap must be tackled. Of most significance here has been the
government's introduction of a national minimum wage in 1999. Prior to
this the UK had never had a statutory floor for wages, unlike a number of
other European countries, and the minimum wage had been a key campaign target of organisations like the Low Pay Unit. The change was thus
of major economic and social importance, and has since been endorsed
by the opposition parties. On its introduction the minimum was set at
£3.60 an hour, raised in 2001 to £4.10; and within the first two years over
1.5 million workers, mainly women, benefited from higher rates of pay
as a result.

Requiring employers to provide a minimum hourly rate through regulatory control is of significant importance in ensuring positive incentives for
labour market participation. However, for some workers even the statutory minimum is not sufficient to offset the impact of the unemployment
trap. This is particularly the case for workers with dependent families.
The other key policy initiative has therefore been the Working Families
Tax Credit. This is in practice an adaptation of Family Credit, a means-
tested subsidy to low wages for families; but it has been transferred from
a social security benefit to a tax credit paid through the wage packet,
following a tax credit model adopted in the US, and it has been extended
to provide more generous support for a wider range of low income families. The aim of the new credit is to ensure that all workers are better off
in low paid employment than on means-tested social security benefits,
and to some extent it has been successful in achieving this (Blundell and
Reed 2000). A similar credit is also available to disabled workers, and the
idea has been extended on a pilot basis to workers with no dependants
or special needs (see Finlayson *et al.* 2000).

In the 2000 and 2001 budgets the Chancellor, Gordon Brown, extended the tax-based support for low wage families with the introduction,
and expansion, of child tax allowances and further tax relief for child care
costs. These allowances only apply to those paying tax at the basic rate.
This extends beyond low pay, of course, but it still involves an element of
targeting within the labour force in order to make paid work more attractive to those with families to support. For those men with child support
costs identified in this research, these new forms of support would be
likely to be of some significance in helping to make work pay.

Training and job search

The second element of the welfare to work strategy is the more active pursuit of supply-side support for labour market participation, in line with

the developments under way in other countries such as the US and in Europe. The reform to the administrative arrangements for social security delivery are evidence of a general change of emphasis here – the creation of the new Jobcentre Plus, the single gateway to government benefits for all claimants and the designation of claimant advisers to work on an individual basis with each claimant (DSS and DfEE 1998). The Labour government has also continued the JSA introduced in 1996, although the evidence that it involved significant improvements on the previous unemployment benefit scheme in its early days is somewhat mixed (Trickey *et al*. 1998).

Labour has also continued the reformed IB scheme, and introduced further restrictions to entitlement to this, although these will only take effect for new claimants, thus not affecting any currently on IB in our research. The NI contribution conditions have been further restricted, the claimant adviser scheme is to be applied to those on long-term sickness and disability support, and a limited element of means-testing will also apply to most IB claimants with occupational or personal pensions where these exceed £85 a week.

It is hoped that the claimant advisers will be able to assist IB claimants who have become detached from the labour force to re-engage with the labour market. This is a key issue for many of the men interviewed in this project, and we return to discuss its potential implications in more detail below. However, the IB reforms were also motivated by a desire to reduce the costs to the Exchequer of social security benefits. Tighter NI conditions and the introduction of means-testing are likely to achieve this. These changes will not affect any of the men in our research; but for future new claimants they may reduce access to this long-term NI benefit, and so push more claimants on to Income Support or income-related JSA. They may thus be worse off; but unless the claimant advisers are able to help them move back into paid employment they are unlikely to escape benefit dependency.

The major job search initiative introduced by the government has been the much publicised New Deal. This is not in fact a new idea: similar schemes were run by the Manpower Services Commission in the 1970s and 1980s, but the form and extent of the New Deal take this much further than previous supply-side projects. The main feature of the New Deal is the scheme for young persons (aged 18–24) out of work and on benefits. With a budget of over £2.6 billion this had provided assistance for over 400,000 people by February 2000 (Millar 2000). The assistance offered is one of four options: a work placement, a course of training and education, a placement with a voluntary agency or work on an environmental task force. Participation in one of these is intended to be compulsory – there is no 'fifth option' of remaining on benefits, although the policing of attendance and commitment is in practice problematic.

It has been estimated that around a half of young people receiving New Deal support have found jobs (Millar 2000: v), and the scheme has been viewed by many politicians and policy-makers as a qualified success. Certainly the idea has been extended to other claimant groups – the long-term unemployed (for whom it is also 'compulsory'), lone parents, partners of the unemployed, disabled people and over 50s detached from the labour market. The messages about the success of the scheme with these other groups are a little more complex. Much smaller numbers are involved and in a number of cases evidence is only available from small pilot projects. However, there has been some positive assessment, in particular about the role played by claimant advisers in providing individual support to those planning job search activity, referred to as a 'work first' orientation (Millar 2000); and this is likely to be of particular importance to many of the men identified in our research.

The high political and economic profile given to the New Deal is clear evidence of the central role that supply-side support for labour market participation – welfare to work – plays in the policy-planning framework of the Labour government. As the range of options offered to the young unemployed also reveals, there is some evidence that a broader notion of activation accompanies the new programme, despite the predominant emphasis upon 'work first'. Placed alongside the other measures now supporting the welfare to work programme, the New Deal may be indicative of a new social and economic regime developing in the UK at the beginning of the twenty-first century – a Schumpeterian workfare state. If this is the case then the experiences of the men identified in this research project – carried out just as new Labour was developing its new regime – may be of significant importance in assessing both the challenges facing such a policy framework and the likely success of new measures in meeting these challenges.

Making workfare work

The biggest problem with supply-side approaches to labour market participation is that they are just that. Encouraging and supporting unemployed workers in job search will only be successful where there are jobs to be found. And it is a matter of considerable concern that, when taking the longer view, the more draconian measures inserted into social security provision to encourage labour market take up seem to be associated with periods of labour market surplus, not labour market shortage. When jobs are relatively plentiful unemployed workers need less support and assistance in finding them, of course, and this may explain the lack of extensive supply-side intervention at such times. However, the value of supply-side intervention at times of reduced demand for labour must inevitably be questioned – in whose interests is it that workers should be set up to fail in their search for jobs?

It is in this context that the current Welfare to Work programme must be assessed – or re-assessed. At present the government is promoting a wide range of measures to support Welfare to Work at a time when, arguably, economic performance is leading to relative growth in labour market demand. Is this, as the Schumpeterian model implies, evidence of a genuinely new departure in social and economic policy planning? And, if this new support for supply-side measures to promote labour market participation is genuinely directed by a concern to promote social inclusion and participation rather than the low wage discipline of 'less eligibility', to what extent are the measures adopted in the UK likely to lead to the re-attachment to the labour force of those who have become detached from it over recent years? The research reported in this book focuses upon just such a social group, and the experiences of the men identified in our survey and interviews help us to develop some preliminary answers to this big question.

For a start it is clear that the life histories and personal circumstances are each quite unique. It is hardly a social scientific breakthrough to discover that people's lives are all different; however, past social security policy planning has largely been based upon quite the opposite assumption. A mass system of income support inevitably requires general rules and regulations that can apply to all claimants; but, once the support provided moves beyond financial assistance to job availability and work search, the assumption that 'one size fits all' just cannot be sustained. Different men in different social circumstances, with different work histories, skills and qualifications, are likely to face different obstacles in securing paid employment – as our research graphically reveals. Blanket approaches to availability for work and assistance with job search will not be able to help all equally, and do not.

The claimant advisers now provided within the New Deal programmes and the new administrative arrangements for the social security gateway are thus an important, and much belated, recognition of the need to gear social security policy to the needs and circumstances of those citizens who use it. Millar's (2000) review of the initial evaluations of the New Deal programmes described this role as 'pivotal'. The absence of such user sensitivity in the past is likely to have contributed to some of the problems which a number of our respondents experienced with previous regimes of benefit administration.

The single gateway is also intended to simplify the administrative procedures associated with the claiming and receipt of social security benefits. The introduction of a single point of contact for claimants within the new Jobcentre Plus, from which all access to all central government benefits can be secured, promises to reduce considerably the complexity and confusion experienced by many claimants in the past. Different schemes for benefit support will, of course, continue, and be subject to different regulatory frameworks and entitlement conditions; but at least they will be accessed through one administrative base. Users of these services can only benefit from this, although, unfortunately, the organisational aggregation will not extend to those benefits administered by local government. Access to Housing Benefit, Council Tax Benefit and the range of other local means-tested supports will thus remain a separate, and no doubt confusing, set of processes administered by different officers within a different arm of government.

The support provided by social security benefits is obviously of critical importance in the financial survival of many of those men (and women) who are unemployed or otherwise detached from the labour market. As the research reported here reveals, this applies to many of those who perceive themselves as early retired, as well as those who are unemployed or on long-term sickness or disability support. Such early retirement is not without its cost to the Exchequer, therefore. However, as our research also shows, many of the men receiving social security benefits also have other sources of income of various kinds, including occupational pensions, savings and investments, and redundancy or other compensation packages.

Current benefit provision does not respond consistently or sensitively in situations where such other sources of income are received. Within means-tested provision, such as Income Support, other sources of income immediately reduce or remove entitlement to state benefit, with the attendant problems of the unemployment and savings traps. With NI protection other sources of income are ignored and thus can raise actual 'take-home' resources significantly. This is not necessarily a logical response in policy terms; but, more importantly, it has inconsistent and contradictory consequences for individual claimants, especially where they are receiving benefits under more than one regime – as many men in our research had discovered. If future benefit entitlement is to meet more closely the real financial needs and circumstances of men (and women) outside the labour market, then a more sensitive and more flexible form of income-related adjustment to entitlement may be needed. The recent introduction of a simplified 'means test' for new IB claimants is one example of such an approach, although it is hardly a sensitive or flexible one. Further policy planning along these lines may provide an appropriate agenda for future benefit reform in this area.

The major problem underlying the administration of social security support to working-age adults outside the labour market, however, remains the conflict between the securing of adequate financial support for unemployed workers and their families and the pressure to enforce labour market participation through availability for work and job search. This is expressed in the legacy of less eligibility and the distinction between the deserving and undeserving poor; and it is experienced in the unemployment trap and the enforcement of regulations concerning 'actively seeking work'. It is a product of the enduring attempt to utilise the administration of social security benefits as a means of enforcing supply-side measures to promote labour market participation – in particular during times of economic recession.

As the research reported here confirms, detachment from the labour market at times (and in places) of economic recession is a complex process, strongly determined by the individual life courses and life experiences of individual people. The use of blanket provisions within social security administration is unlikely to be able to assist those individuals to address their situation and respond to labour market demand. However, at the beginning of this century, there is some evidence that many advanced industrial countries are adopting more proactive and flexible programmes to promote labour force attachment and more general social activation (Lødermel and Trickey 2001). In the UK such an approach also characterises the welfare to work strategy of the current Labour government. If these programmes can combine supply-side support for labour market reintegration with a more claimant-focused delivery of social security support, then some of the major problems which have influenced the social security support for unemployment discussed in this chapter will perhaps be subject to a new challenge.

Part II

New evidence from the UK

4   The detached male workforce

Christina Beatty and Stephen Fothergill

So just who are the men who have fallen out of the world of work? What are their skills, qualifications and work experience? How did they become detached from employment? Do they still want to work? And how do they get by, in terms of income and social security benefits? This chapter tries to provide answers to these basic questions, drawing mainly on a large-scale survey carried out in seven locations around Britain.

Chapter 1 outlined in broad terms the changing nature of men's experience of work, including the decline of traditional sources of male employment and the resulting issues of unemployment and economic inactivity. Before presenting the survey findings it is useful to look a little more closely specifically at the main statistical trends in non-employment among men across the country as a whole.

Trends in detachment

Figure 4.1 shows the trends in unemployment and economic inactivity among men of working age (i.e. 16–64) across Britain. The figures cover the years from 1977 to 2000. Unemployment – in this case the ILO measure from the Labour Force Survey – has fluctuated with the trade cycle. It rose steeply during the early 1980s, fell during the Lawson boom of the late 1980s, and rose again during the early 1990s. It subsequently fell once more to levels not much above those in the 1970s. In spring 2000 the Labour Force Survey recorded 950,000 men as unemployed in Great Britain, or 5.1 per cent of the male WAP.

Economic inactivity among men of working age – that is, the number of men neither in employment nor recorded as unemployed – has been much less responsive to the trade cycle. Inactivity has risen more or less continuously since the 1970s. The number of inactive men dipped slightly during the peak of the late 1980s boom, and dipped again slightly at the very end of the 1990s, again after several years of strong economic growth. Over the 1977–2000 period as a whole, however, inactivity among working-age men more than doubled. In spring 2000 the Labour Force Survey

79

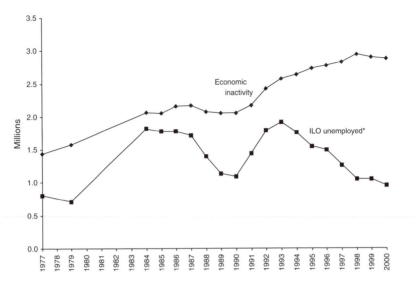

Figure 4.1   Unemployment and economic activity among men of working age, Great Britain, 1977–2000[a]
[a]Figures are for the spring quarter each year.
*Labour Force Survey unemployed for 1977, 1979, 1984.
Source: Labour Force Survey.

recorded 2,870,000 men as inactive, or 15.5 per cent of the male WAP. This was just over three times the number recorded as unemployed. Or to put it another way, at the start of the new century 'economic inactivity' had become by far the dominant form of non-employment among working-age men.

The rise in inactivity has been skewed towards older age groups. Table 4.1 shows that a large number of 16–24 year olds have always been inactive, because of extended stays in education. The big increase in the numbers staying on at school and going into higher education has had only modest impact on the scale of inactivity among this younger group, largely because so many students now work part time and are therefore classified as 'economically active'. At the other end of the age range, the number of inactive 50–64 year olds increased by over three-quarters of a million between 1977 and 2000. The number of inactive 35–49 year olds also rose by more than 350,000. By spring 2000 more than a quarter of all men aged 50–64 were inactive – i.e. neither employed nor recorded as unemployed.

By any standards these are major shifts in the nature of men's relationship to the labour market. Throughout the first three-quarters of the twentieth century the assumption of nearly all men, outside a few

Table 4.1. *Economic inactivity among men by age, Great Britain*

	Spring 1977		Spring 2000	
Age	No.	as % of age group	No.	as % of age group
16–24	750,000	21.2	819,000	26.0
25–34	91,000	2.3	266,000	6.1
35–49	110,000	2.3	464,000	7.5
50–64	490,000	10.7	1,321,000	27.5
Total (16–64)	1,440,000	8.6	2,870,000	15.5

Source: Labour Force Survey.

privileged occupations, was that they would probably need to keep on working until they were 65, the state pension age. Or at worst they would be unemployed. Now vast numbers of working age – nearly 3 million – are neither employed nor unemployed. We should not jump to the conclusion, however, that this withdrawal is all voluntary, or in particular that the increase in inactivity among older men mainly represents a surge in early retirement. Voluntary early retirement, on a comfortable pension, tends to be most closely associated with professional and white-collar occupations, which in turn draw on better-qualified workers. One of the 'alarm bells' about the real nature of the rise in economic inactivity among men is therefore its concentration among the least well qualified. Gregg and Wadsworth (1998) have shown, from Labour Force Survey data, that between 1979 and 1997 inactivity rose among all non-student men, regardless of qualifications; but the biggest percentage point increase was among those with the least educational qualifications. For those with no qualifications at all the proportion inactive rose from 5 per cent to 29 per cent. For those with only CSEs it rose from 2 per cent to 15 per cent. For those with degrees it rose from 1 per cent to 7 per cent.

That inactivity embraces far more than just early retirement or extended stays in education is confirmed by fig. 4.2, which also shows how the balance between different forms of labour market detachment varies with age. This diagram uses data from the 1991 Census of Population – regretfully still the most recent comprehensive figures available – but the contrasts are so striking that the figures are unlikely to have altered radically. It shows how non-employment among men is especially important for the under 25s and the over 50s, but the form it takes at these two ends of the age range differs. For the under 25s, extended stays in education, a place on a government scheme and unemployment are the main forms of non-employment. For those between 25 and 50, unemployment is the main form of joblessness, but the vast majority of this middle group are in

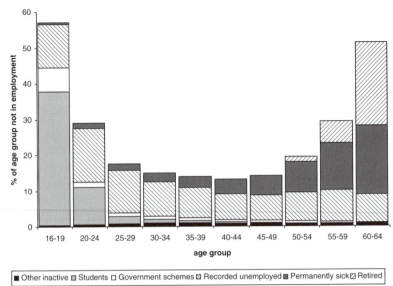

Figure 4.2   Non-employed men, Great Britain, April 1991
Source: Census of population.

work. For those over 50, unemployment is still important but 'permanent sickness' and eventually 'early retirement' become important – more important in fact than 'unemployment' itself.

What is also known about labour market detachment among men is that the incidence varies from area to area. As a general rule, inactivity is concentrated in areas where recorded unemployment is also high (see, for example, Green (1997) and Green and Owen (1998)). Many of these are urban areas, but places such as the coalfields are also badly affected. Indeed, this has prompted MacKay (1999) to formulate the general rule that 'the greater the degree of labour market disadvantage, the less appropriate is unemployment as a measure of labour market slack'.

Figures 4.3 and 4.4 present a complex indicator of labour market detachment among 25–64-year-old men for districts across the whole of Great Britain. This is the group of prime and older working-age men covered by the survey findings described later in this chapter. In excluding 16–24 year olds it leaves out the vast majority affected by extended stays in education and also by early difficulties in securing a foothold in employment. The indicator combines three sets of figures for men in the 25–64-year-old group:

• long-term (i.e. six months plus) claimant unemployed men, at April 1997;

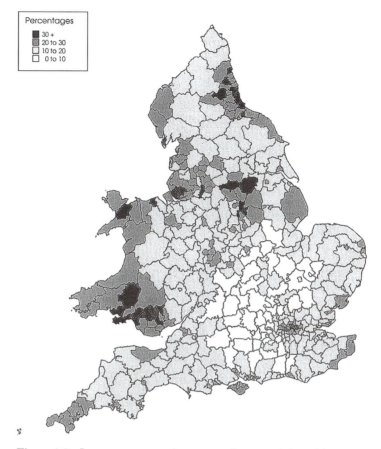

Figure 4.3   Long-term unemployment and economic inactivity among men as a proportion of males aged 25–64, by district, England and Wales, 1996–7

- men who gave their economic status as 'retired', 'student' or 'other inactive' in the 1991 Census;
- men in receipt of IB Severe Disablement Allowance or NI credits for incapacity at August 1996, i.e. men out of the labour market and recorded as sick or disabled.

In the absence of comprehensive, up-to-date Census data this is the best estimate that can be derived at the local scale of the size of this group of men who all share labour market detachment through either long-term unemployment or inactivity. In each district the total is expressed as a percentage of the male population aged 25–64, from the 1991 Census.

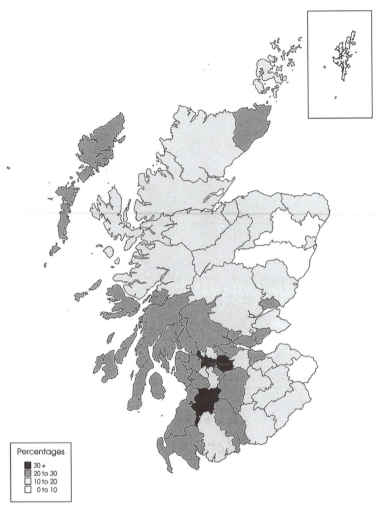

Figure 4.4   Long-term unemployment and economic inactivity among
men as a proportion of males aged 25–64, Scotland, 1996–7

These maps confirm that although labour market detachment among
men is widespread it is also skewed towards a small number of localities
where detachment is particularly prominent. On this measure there are 37
districts where 30 per cent or more of 25–64-year-old men were detached
from the labour market, and 174 districts where the level of detachment
exceeded 20 per cent. These districts are overwhelmingly concentrated
in the traditional industrial areas of Northern England, Central Scotland

Table 4.2. *Male employment rates by region, summer 2000*

	Men of working age in employment (%)	Deviation from South East attributable to:	
		Unemployment (%)	Inactivity (%)
South East	86.4	–	–
Eastern	84.3	0.6	1.5
South West	84.3	1.1	1.0
East Midlands	82.2	2.0	2.2
Yorks and Humber	79.4	3.3	3.7
West Midlands	78.3	2.9	5.2
North West	77.8	2.3	6.3
Scotland	77.4	3.3	5.7
London	77.0	3.9	5.5
Wales	74.5	2.8	9.1
North East	72.6	6.4	7.4

Source: Labour Force Survey.

and South Wales, though a few inner London boroughs also record high levels. Across much of southern and eastern England, outside London, levels of labour market detachment among men are relatively modest.

An alternative way of viewing this sort of information is to look at 'employment rates' – the share of men of working age actually in paid employment. Those who are outside paid employment include not only the official unemployed but also all the various groups of economically inactive, including any hidden unemployed. The value of this indicator is that there is little obvious reason why there should be large regional differences in the incidence of those who abstain from employment voluntarily. Employment rates should therefore be a reasonable indicator of the strength of the local labour market.

Table 4.2 combines Labour Force Survey data on employment rates in the British regions with a measure of the extent to which the deviations from the region with the highest employment rate (the South East) are attributable to excess unemployment or excess inactivity. In this instance the ILO measure of unemployment, from the Labour Force Survey, is used for consistency.

Two points are worth noting. First, there are big differences in employment rates across the British region – from 86 per cent of working-age men in the South East to 72 per cent in the North East. The regions where employment rates lag badly are mostly in the North, plus Scotland and Wales. London is the exception, where the relatively low employment rate may need to be seen in the context of the high rate in surrounding areas and the wide extent of the metropolitan labour market. The other point to note is that the substantial regional differences in male employment rates owe more to the scale of economic inactivity than to recorded unemployment. Only one region (the North East) has recorded male unemployment more than 5 percentage points higher than in the South East, whereas six regions (West Midlands, North West, Scotland, London, Wales and North East) have inactivity rates more than 5 percentage points higher. In every region except the South West the deviation from the South East's employment rate owes more to levels of inactivity than to levels of unemployment.

Arguably, employment rates are the best and most reliable measure of the scale of the regional problem in the UK. They measure the extent to which adults of working age are engaged in productive economic activity and they are unaffected by disputes about the extent of hidden unemployment which have done so much to undermine the credibility of official unemployment figures. The implications of the figures in table 4.2 would therefore appear to be that, at least so far as the male labour market is concerned, Britain has a large and continuing regional problem. This problem is also primarily reflected in the extent of economic inactivity rather than unemployment.

A new survey

The new evidence on labour market detachment presented in the remainder of this chapter (and in the next two chapters) is based on a survey managed by ourselves and colleagues at Sheffield Hallam University. This covered men aged 25–64 who were economically inactive or at the time of the survey had been unemployed for most or all of the preceding six months. It also covered part-time workers on the basis that this type of work is non-traditional for men. Taken as a whole, this is the group which we refer to here and subsequently as the 'detached male workforce'.

The uniting feature of this detached male workforce is that all these men display a substantial disconnection from full-time employment. This group excludes the short-term unemployed, for whom the detachment cannot yet be said to be substantial. It also excludes the under 25s for whom detachment is often complicated by extended stays in education or training. The detached male workforce, as defined here, comprises the prime and older working-age men for whom full-time employment was for so long the conventional aspiration if not the everyday reality.

Full details of the survey methods are set out in the appendix. At this point it needs to be noted that a total of 1,703 interviews were successfully completed, each following a tightly structured questionnaire designed to elicit basic information about skills, work history, employment aspirations and personal and household circumstances. Roughly 400 interviews were carried out in each of three towns (Barnsley, Chesterfield and Northampton) and roughly a further 125 in each of four rural areas (West Cumbria, North Yorkshire, North Norfolk and South Shropshire). The survey areas were chosen to cover a range of labour market circumstances, spread across five UK regions. Various weightings of the data from the seven areas are possible. However, no single weighting is ideal and in practice alternative weightings make only a modest difference, so here and in chs. 5 and 6 the figures presented therefore simply pool all the available data from the seven areas to provide a guide to the national picture.

A slightly fuller presentation of the results of the survey can be found elsewhere (Beatty and Fothergill 1999a). The detailed results for the four rural areas are also covered in a separate report (Beatty and Fothergill 1999b). The main features are reported below.

Who are they?

The characteristic shared by all the men covered by the survey was a significant degree of detachment from conventional employment, despite being of conventional working age. Within this broad group there is, however, considerable diversity. Table 4.3 provides a detailed breakdown of the self-declared status of the 1,703 survey respondents. Over one-third described themselves as 'long-term sick or disabled'. A quarter described themselves as 'unemployed' and nearly a fifth as 'retired from paid work altogether'. These three groups are by some margin the largest and, for the sake of convenience, we subsequently refer to them as the 'long-term

Table 4.3. *Self-declared status of detached male workforce*

	No. of interviewees	%
Long-term sick or disabled	627	36.8
Unemployed	444	26.1
Retired from paid work altogether	312	18.3
In part-time employment	155	9.1
Full-time carer	74	4.3
Full-time student	31	1.8
Looking after family or home	22	1.3
On government scheme	8	0.5
Other	30	1.8
	1,703	100.0

Source: Survey data.

Table 4.4. *Age of detached male workforce*

	All respondents (%)	Long-term sick (%)	Long-term unemployed (%)	Early retired (%)	Part-time workers (%)	Full-time carers[a] (%)
25–34	15	9	30	1	15	17
35–44	19	21	25	1	14	35
45–54	23	27	23	13	23	27
55–64	44	43	22	86	48	21
	100	100	100	100	100	100

Note: [a]In this and subsequent tables 'full-time carers' includes men describing themselves as 'looking after family or home'.
Source: Survey data.

sick', 'long-term unemployed' and 'early retired'. The remainder include those describing themselves as 'part-time workers' – making up just under 10 per cent of the total – or as 'full-time carers', who along with those saying they looked after family or home made up nearly a further 6 per cent. The rest, comprising just 4 per cent of the interviewees, comprise full-time students, men on government schemes and others.

Table 4.4 shows the age of these detached men. In this and subsequent tables, figures are presented for all respondents and for each of the five largest groups defined on the basis of self-declared status. We have already noted how official statistics show that among 25–64-year-old men the detached workforce is skewed towards the older age bands. Unsurprisingly, therefore, 55–64 year olds make up more than 40 per cent of the survey total. Also unsurprisingly, 86 per cent of the early retired in the survey fall into this older age band, though that still means that one in seven early retired men are under 55. The long-term sick – numerically the largest group – are also skewed in terms of age with more than 40 per cent in the 55–64 age group and less than 10 per cent in the 25–34 group. Part-time workers broadly share this skewed age distribution – nearly half are aged 55–64. The long-term unemployed, in contrast, are more evenly spread across the 25–64-year-old age range, with if anything a weighting towards the younger age bands.

The marital status of the detached male workforce to a large extent reflects age differences. The survey found that the long-term unemployed, being a younger group on average, are less likely to be married. Just half the long-term unemployed are married, compared to two-thirds of the long-term sick and more than four-fifths of the early retired. Overall, around two-thirds of the men making up the detached male workforce are married.

Again reflecting age, the long-term unemployed and full-time carers are the most likely to have dependent children. About 30 per cent of the long-term unemployed and about half the full-time carers have dependent children living with them, and 14 per cent of full-time carers are single parents. In contrast, only 6 per cent of the early retired have dependent children at home. The long-term unemployed are the most likely to live alone – just over 20 per cent do so – but around one in six of the long-term sick and the early retired also live alone.

Overall, half (52 per cent) of the detached male workforce are owner-occupiers, and rather more than half of all these (56 per cent) are in the privileged position of having no mortgage. But once again this disguises big differences between groups. The vast majority (87 per cent) of the early retired are owner-occupiers, and three-quarters of these have no mortgage. In contrast, half the long-term sick, and more than half of all the long-term unemployed and full-time carers, live in rented accommodation. Among these, social housing (either council or housing association) predominates.

Table 4.5 shows the differences between the five main groups in terms of social class, measured by the Registrar General's socio-economic classification of occupations. The early retired and part-time workers are distinctly more middle class than the rest – just under two-thirds of both groups previously worked in white-collar or intermediate occupations. Skilled manual workers predominate among the long-term sick and, given the absolute size of this group, among the detached male workforce as a whole. Skilled manual workers are also prominent among the long-term unemployed and among full-time carers, and both these groups also include sizeable minorities of 'unskilled' workers.

Differences in social class are reflected in the level of qualifications, shown in Table 4.6. Of early retirees 17 per cent, and no less than 21 per cent of part-time workers, are graduates, compared to just 4 per cent of the long-term sick, 4 per cent of the long-term unemployed and 3 per cent of full-time carers. These differences are especially notable because the long-term unemployed are on average the youngest group and therefore the most likely to have had the opportunity to participate in the expansion of further and higher education. At the other end of the spectrum, nearly half of all the long-term sick, the full-time carers and the long-term unemployed say they have no formal qualifications at all.

How have they become detached?

Most of the detached male workforce have been without full-time work for quite a while. This is illustrated by Table 4.7 which shows the length of

Table 4.5. *Social class of detached male workforce*

	All respondents (%)	Long-term sick (%)	Long-term unemployed (%)	Early retired (%)	Part-time workers (%)	Full-time Carers (%)
Professional	4	2	2	8	9	1
Managerial and technical	18	12	10	33	36	8
Skilled non-manual	13	11	10	20	17	11
Skilled manual	41	52	43	28	23	45
Semi-skilled manual	11	10	15	7	9	19
Unskilled[a]	13	13	20	4	6	16
	100	100	100	100	100	100

Note: [a] Includes armed forces.
Source: Survey data.

Table 4.6. *Selected qualifications of detached men*

	All respondents (%)	Long-term sick (%)	Long-term unemployed (%)	Early retired (%)	Part-time workers (%)	Long-term unemployed (%)
Degree	9	4	4	17	21	3
'O' level/CSE/GCSE	28	19	28	33	46	24
NVQ/ONC/OND/HNC/HND	15	9	17	18	24	10
Craft apprenticeship	19	21	15	22	14	18
None	40	49	44	29	24	48

Note: Columns do not add to 100 because some respondents have more than one qualification.
Source: Survey data.

Table 4.7. *Length of time since last regular full-time job*

	All respondents (%)	Long-term sick (%)	Long-term unemployed (%)	Early retired (%)	Part-time workers (%)	Full-time carers (%)
Less than 2 years	27	16	39	27	27	20
2–5 years	31	27	28	40	30	28
5–10 years	26	32	19	23	31	30
10 years or more	15	22	11	11	10	21
Never had one	2	2	2	0	2	0
	100	100	100	100	100	100

Source: Survey data.

time since the respondents' last regular full-time job. Only 2 per cent of the whole sample had never had a full-time job. But more than 40 per cent had not worked full time for at least five years, and almost three-quarters had not worked full time for at least two years. For most of these men, the degree of labour market detachment therefore appears substantial.

To some extent all the main sub-groups share this long-term detachment, but there are important differences as well. In particular, the long-term sick appear particularly distant from employment – nearly a quarter have not had a regular full-time job for at least ten years. More than half the long-term sick have not had a job for at least five years. Half the full-time carers, too, have not been in regular full-time employment for at least five years. In contrast, the duration of early retirement and unemployment is generally shorter – less than two years for nearly 40 per cent of the long-term unemployed, for example, and less than five years for two-thirds of the early retired.

Although it is generally quite a few years since most of these men worked full time, they are rarely without substantial work experience. One indicator of this is the length of time in their last job, shown in table 4.8. In nearly 30 per cent of cases this job had lasted at least twenty years. In nearly half of all cases it had lasted ten years or more. Even this understates the extent of previous stable employment. The survey enquired about the last three jobs: in 36 per cent of all cases, at least one of these jobs had lasted twenty years or more. Once more there are important differences between sub-groups. The early retired are particularly likely to have had a long period in their last job. Indeed, this sort of continuous, long-term employment with a single employer is often the pre-condition for early entitlement to substantial pension rights. In contrast, there is evidence that the long-term unemployed and full-time carers have had a more turbulent employment history – for more than half, their last job lasted less than five years.

Just as a high proportion of the detached male workforce has previously had long periods of stable full-time employment, their current detachment from employment is also mostly unusual. In a clear majority of all cases (69 per cent) there was no period out of work before starting the last job. In even more cases (76 per cent) there was no period out of work before starting the job before that. The long-term unemployed were rather more likely to have experienced a period of non-employment between jobs, but even among this group only half were affected. When gaps in employment occurred, they were also relatively short compared with the often lengthy periods of non-employment now being experienced. Well over half (57 per cent) of the men experiencing a gap between their last two jobs were without work for less than a year.

Table 4.8. *Length of time in last regular full-time job*

	All respondents (%)	Long-term sick (%)	Long-term unemployed (%)	Early retired (%)	Part-time workers (%)	Full-time carers (%)
Less than 1 year	13	11	27	0.3	7	10
1–5 years	26	25	37	5	25	46
5–10 years	13	16	12	10	12	16
10–20 years	20	25	13	22	20	15
20 years or more	29	23	12	64	37	14
	100	100	100	100	100	100

Source: Survey data.

Table 4.9 shows the principal reasons for the last job ending. Information on the causes of job loss needs to be interpreted with care. Sometimes there is a single, clear-cut reason. On other occasions a range of factors of varying importance come into play, especially where a job was left voluntarily. The difference between 'compulsory' and 'voluntary' redundancy, for example, is not always very clear when an employer is pushing hard to shed workers and staying on would involve a shift in responsibility or workplace. Ill-health and access to a pension may come into play in the same decision. The survey nevertheless asked respondents to identify the principal cause of job loss, and the table groups the responses into four broad categories – compulsory severance (where it was the employer who brought the job to an end), voluntary redundancy or retirement, other voluntary severance and illness or injury.

Despite these blurred distinctions, what is striking is how much the principal reasons for job loss vary systematically between the sub-groups. Half the long-term sick left because of illness or injury. Two-thirds of the long-term unemployed left because they were laid off. Two-thirds of the early retired took voluntary redundancy or retirement. Nearly half the full-time carers left for their own reasons, for example to take up a new role as a carer.

These differences are perhaps predictable. But what is more significant is that in each group a substantial proportion of men left for other than the 'obvious' reason. Thus nearly half the long-term sick left for reasons other than sickness. And nearly one-third of the early retired left for reasons other than voluntary retirement. More than a quarter of the men who now describe themselves as 'long-term sick' in fact left their last job because they were laid off. These discrepancies are important in interpreting the labour market status of individuals. How they describe themselves now – 'sick', 'retired' and so on – may in fact be a response to their labour market detachment rather than a reflection of the processes that detached them in the first place.

Do they want work?

That many of the detached male workforce have not lost the will to work is indicated by table 4.10. The first line of this table shows the answer to the question 'Would you like a full-time job?' to which 49 per cent said 'yes'. These include half the long-term sick and nearly 90 per cent of the long-term unemployed. The early retired are more clearly satisfied with their status – 90 per cent say they do not want a full-time job. The answers given by part-time workers and full-time carers reveal that in many cases their present labour market position is not a situation of first choice. Two

Table 4.9. *Principal reason for last job ending*

	All respondents (%)	Long-term sick (%)	Long-term unemployed (%)	Early retired (%)	Part-time workers (%)	Full-time carers (%)
Compulsory[a]	38	27	64	21	34	32
Voluntary – redundancy/retirement	23	11	8	69	32	7
Voluntary – own reasons[b]	16	8	19	3	30	54
Illness or injury	24	52	9	7	4	6
	100	100	100	100	100	100

Notes:
[a] Compulsory redundancy or retirement, dismissal, end of temporary contract.
[b] Includes leaving job to become full-time carer and miscellaneous other reasons.
Source: Survey data.

Table 4.10. *Labour market attachment*

	All respondents (%)	Long-term sick (%)	Long-term unemployed (%)	Early retired (%)	Part-time workers (%)	Full-time carers (%)
Job aspirations						
Would like a full-time job	49	49	86	7	38	40
Thinks there is a realistic chance of one[a]	20	11	46	1	20	15
Job search behaviour						
Looked after last job ended	44	27	83	21	48	35
Looking now	26	5	77	4	30	3

Note: [a] Men who say 'would like a full-time job' or 'don't know' and also 'think there is a realistic chance'.
Source: Survey data.

out of five men in both these groups say that they would like a full-time job.

Wanting a regular full-time job and expecting to get one are, of course, different things. The second line shows the answer to the question 'Do you think there is a realistic chance you will ever get one?'. This reveals that far fewer men actually think they could secure full-time employment. The long-term unemployed are more hopeful than the long-term sick or the early retired, but even among the unemployed fewer than half think there is a realistic chance.

In turn, even thinking that there is a chance of a full-time job is not the same as actually looking for work. For all the men included in the survey, the third and fourth lines of table 4.10 compare the answers to two questions – 'After your last job ended did you look for full-time work?' and 'Are you presently looking for full-time work?' These reveal both a low intensity of job search and a shift through time. Taking the sample as a whole, 44 per cent said they looked for work after their last job ended. By the time of the survey, this had fallen to 26 per cent. The notable exception are the long-term unemployed, among whom the proportion looking for full-time work – more than three-quarters – is consistently high. This may owe something to the stringent rules governing eligibility for JSA, the main social security benefit for the unemployed, which requires a claimant to demonstrate that he or she is actively looking for work.

The decline in job search activity by the long-term sick and early retired is sharp. Just 5 per cent of the long-term sick now say they are looking for work, compared to 27 per cent at the time their last job ended, and as many as half saying they would like a full-time job. One interpretation could be that individuals' health has deteriorated, making job search increasingly impossible. Alternatively, the decline in active job seeking among the retired as well as the long-term sick could be the result of growing disillusion. There is little point in continuing to look for work if the repeated experience is one of rejection or if the supply of appropriate jobs is derisory. If a man's benefit entitlement does not depend on looking for work either – as is the case with IB – there is also little pressing reason for him to keep looking. Indeed, as jobseekers give up the struggle they may at the same time redefine their status. At least some of today's 'long-term sick' and 'retired' may initially have seen themselves as 'unemployed'.

The reasons given for not looking for full-time work are shown in table 4.11. The dominant reason given is ill-health or injury – cited in more than half of all cases and by nearly all the non-jobseeking long-term sick. Half the long-term unemployed who are not looking for work also cite ill-health. Among the early retired, the decision to retire itself

Table 4.11. *Reasons for not looking for full-time work*

	All respondents (%)	Long-term sick (%)	Long-term unemployed (%)	Early retired (%)	Part-time workers (%)	Full-time carers (%)
Ill-health or injury	58	96	47	25	9	10
Decided to retire	21	5	6	65	24	2
Little chance of job due to age	12	5	32	20	0	0
Full-time carer	9	1	10	2	5	84
Don't need to work	6	1	2	18	0	0
Not enough suitable jobs	5	3	14	5	14	4
No / few jobs available	5	2	13	5	16	2
No better off	3	1	11	6	3	2
Full-time education	3	1	3	0	1	1
Other	9	1	17	6	45	19

Note: Respondents could cite more than one reason. All figures are expressed as a percentage of those in each group who are not looking for full-time work.
Source: Survey data.

Table 4.12. *Self-assessment of influence of health*

	All respondents (%)	Long-term sick (%)	Long-term unemployed (%)	Early retired (%)	Part-time workers (%)	Full-time carers (%)
Can't do any work	11	26	2	5	1	0
Some or a lot of limitation	44	71	27	34	22	31
No limitation	44	2	70	60	77	69
Don't know	1	1	1	1	0	0
	100	100	100	100	100	100

Source: Survey data.

is cited as the reason for not seeking full-time work in two-thirds of cases, though even among this group ill-health also figures prominently.

Is health an impediment?

That ill-health or injury is cited so often as a reason for not looking for full-time work deserves closer examination. The interviewers who carried out our survey were clearly not in a position to make an independent judgement so it is necessary to rely on what men themselves say about their health.

Earlier (in table 4.9) we showed that for about a quarter of the detached male workforce, ill-health or injury was the main reason why their last job had come to an end. Among the long-term sick, this proportion was half. Among the other groups ill-health accounted for less than 10 per cent. However, we noted that the reasons for job loss are often complex, sometimes with several factors of varying importance all playing a part. So although ill-health or injury was cited as the main cause of job loss by only a quarter of men overall, in 39 per cent of all cases it was cited as a factor. Among the long-term sick the proportion citing ill-health as a factor is particularly high (73 per cent). Even so, it is worth noting the converse point – that 27 per cent of those describing themselves as 'long-term sick or disabled' did not leave their last job for reasons at all connected with health.

Looking further back in men's work histories there is little evidence of health being the trigger to job loss. The survey enquired about whether health had been a factor in bringing the preceding job to an end, and the job before that. In fewer than one in ten of all cases was it cited as a factor. Even among the present-day long-term sick, the proportions citing ill-health as a factor in bringing previous jobs to an end were just 11 per cent for the last job but one, and 7 per cent for the one before that.

So the evidence suggests that the present-day ill-health which some men were experiencing was rarely something which had dogged them throughout their working lives – or at least that it was generally not the cause of earlier job loss. Since ill-health often increases with age this observation is not surprising. But what of their present-day health? Table 4.12 shows the men's own assessment. Three points are worth noting. First, a degree of self-reported ill-health is widespread among the detached male workforce – only 44 per cent say there are no health limitations on the work they can do. Second, among the long-term sick a degree of self-reported health limitation is nearly universal. Third, only a quarter of the long-term sick say that they cannot do any work at all. This sub-group among the long-term sick excepted, the problems facing men with health

Table 4.13. *Sources of financial support*[a]

	All respondents (%)	Long-term sick (%)	Long-term unemployed (%)	Early retired (%)	Part-time workers (%)	Full-time carers (%)
Regular paid part-time work	13	3	4	6	92	4
Temporary/casual/seasonal paid work	6	1	7	6	17	2
Pension income	35	31	12	86	45	6
Lump-sum redundancy money	19	14	11	45	25	5
Partner in work	24	24	16	25	44	17
Benefits system[b]	74	98	86	32	26	83

Notes:
[a] An individual may have more than one source of financial support, so columns do not add to 100.
[b] Excluding child benefit.
Source: Survey data.

limitations are about the type or quantity of work they are able to do. Thus, for example, heavy manual labour may be ruled out but not lighter clerical tasks, or time at work would need to be punctuated by time off to cope with recurring health problems.

How do they get by?

Table 4.13 is particularly important. It combines the answers to several questions in the survey in order to show the sources of financial support available to the detached male workforce. Since all these men are aged 25–64 they are all ineligible for the state retirement pension, which in the UK begins at 65 for men. This table therefore shows how so many men of working age are able to get by without apparently either working or looking for work.

The first line shows that in the absence of full-time employment, paid part-time work is not widespread, except, of course, among self-described 'part-time workers'. At the time of the survey even a small number of these (8 per cent) were not engaged in regular part-time work, presumably because their work was irregular or because they were between jobs. Of all the men who do regular, paid part-time work, 40 per cent say they are employed in their usual occupation, and just under half work fewer than 16 hours a week. The second line of the table looks at temporary, casual and seasonal paid work. Again this is not widespread and is confined to a minority within all the sub-groups.

Rather more than a third of the detached male workforce receive income from a pension – which in all cases means a company or private pension. Unsurprisingly, it is the early retired who are most likely to have pension income – 86 per cent have income from this source, though that still leaves one in seven without. However, pensions are much more widespread: 45 per cent of part-time workers, and 31 per cent of the long-term sick also have income from a pension. Even 12 per cent of the long-term unemployed have pension income.

Lump-sum redundancy money is less widespread. Again, it is the early retired who are the most likely to have this sort of payment to draw on, though the figures here are likely to be boosted by the lump-sums paid by some pension schemes on first finishing work and drawing on pension rights. A quarter of part-time workers also have access to lump-sum redundancy money.

Only a minority of the detached male workforce – 24 per cent overall – have a partner in work. Part-time workers are the most likely to have a partner in employment. The long-term unemployed are the least likely – a reflection perhaps of social security rules which reduce an unemployed

Table 4.14. *Benefits claimed*[a]

	All respondents (%)	Long-term sick (%)	Long-term unemployed (%)	Early retired (%)	Part-time workers (%)	Full-time carers (%)
Jobseeker's Allowance	17	1	58	1	8	3
Income Support	20	25	22	4	5	55
Incapacity Benefit	39	86	9	23	2	6
Severe Disablement Allowance	5	12	1	1	0	6
Housing Benefit	30	34	46	4	16	47
Council Tax Benefit	34	37	52	6	16	51
Family Credit	2	1	3	0.3	7	3
Other	11	17	4	4	2	44
No benefits[b]	26	2	14	68	74	17

Notes:
[a] An individual may be receiving more than one benefit, so columns do not add to 100.
[b] Excluding child benefits.
Source: Survey data.

man's means-tested benefit entitlement in response to his partner's earnings.

The final part of the table shows the extent of dependency on the benefits system. Overall, nearly three-quarters of all the detached male workforce rely to some extent on the benefits system, but this disguises important differences between sub-groups. Virtually all the long-term sick – 98 per cent – claim one benefit or another. Of the long-term unemployed 86 per cent are benefit claimants as well, as are 83 per cent of full-time carers. In contrast, only 32 per cent of early retirees and 26 per cent of part-time workers are benefit claimants.

Table 4.14 looks in more detail at benefits. There can sometimes be reluctance on the part of individuals to talk about the benefits they are claiming. However, in our survey just 15 out of 1,703 men declined to answer questions on their benefits and the impression of the interviewers was that the answers they did receive were remarkably frank. There can nevertheless be occasional confusion about precisely which benefits are being claimed. For example, JSA was relatively new at the time of the survey and includes both contribution-based and income-based elements, the latter having replaced more or less identical Income Support payments. Since the claimant unemployed under 60 are no longer entitled to Income Support, most of the self-declared unemployed who said they were receiving Income Support would in fact be recipients of income-based JSA, and we have adjusted the figures accordingly.

Four points are worth noting about benefit status. First, IB is the single most widespread benefit, providing support to nearly two in five of the entire detached male workforce. Adding in Severe Disablement Allowance, which is available to those with insufficient NI contributions to entitle them to IB, the proportion claiming sickness-related benefits rises to 44 per cent. Some of the 'other' benefits claimed include further sickness-related payments such as Disability Living Allowance and Industrial Injuries Benefit. The long-term sick are inevitably the main claimants of sickness-related benefits, but not exclusively. Nearly a quarter of all early retirees are IB claimants. So, too, are 9 per cent of the long-term unemployed.

IB and its relationship to joblessness are explored at length in ch. 5, and its role in the wider benefits system was described in ch. 3. At this stage it is worth noting that IB is intended for those who are unable to work through ill-health or injury. At the time of the survey it was an entirely non-means-tested benefit which increased with duration of sickness and was paid at a slightly more generous rate than the basic entitlement to JSA, the benefit intended for the unemployed, which is means-tested after six months. Men whose IB claim dates back to before April 1995, when this benefit was known as IVB, are additionally able to claim supplements for dependent adults and children, and their benefit is non-taxable. Subsequent changes in benefit rules have introduced an element of means-testing for new IB claimants with substantial pensions, but the favourable comparison with JSA remains valid.

The second notable point about benefit status is the prominence of Housing Benefit and Council Tax Benefit – claimed by around a third of detached men. Claimants of these two housing-related benefits, both of which are means tested, are especially prevalent among the long-term unemployed and full-time carers. By comparison, few early retirees draw on either benefit. Because these benefits are means tested and available to all on low income they offer some guide to the extent of financial hardship among these different groups of men.

The third point to note is that although four-fifths of the long-term unemployed receive JSA, one in five does not. Also, few others among the detached male workforce receive this particular benefit. This tightly restricted coverage of JSA probably reflects the rules governing eligibility – for example the requirement to look for work. Some long-term unemployed men who do actively look for work are still disqualified because of other household income such as a partner's earnings or a pension. The part-time workers who claim JSA are eligible because they are between jobs or because they are working fewer than 16 hours a week and their earnings do not exceed certain thresholds.

The fourth point about benefit status is the role of Income Support. As ch. 3 explained, this means-tested benefit is available to assist the poorest (with the notable exception of the claimant unemployed, for whom means-tested JSA is available) and it often provides a top-up to contribution-based benefits such as IB. A quarter of the long-term sick receive Income Support, though hardly any of the early retired do so. Full-time carers draw especially heavily on this benefit. Under the heading of 'other' benefits, full-time carers are often also claimants of Invalid Care Allowance, which is paid to individuals who look after a disabled person for at least 35 hours a week.

An assessment

At first sight the detached male workforce might be expected to be a fairly cohesive group because all these men are united by having a considerable degree of detachment from conventional full-time employment. In practice, the survey findings demonstrate diversity rather than cohesion. The five largest sub-groups, which account for 96 per cent of the total, differ in important respects from each other. A pen portrait of each illustrates the point.

The men describing themselves as 'long-term sick or disabled' are the largest single sub-group and are a predominantly older group – more than 40 per cent are 55 or over, although this group includes a number of younger men as well. They tend to be married, though only a minority have dependent children. By background this group is strongly working class, with skilled manual workers accounting for half the total. Around half live in accommodation that is rented, usually from the local council or housing association. They tend to have had a long period of detachment from the labour market, often five years or more, though many have previously had long periods of stable employment. Ill-health or injury was the principal trigger to their last job ending in only half of all cases. More than a third lost their last job as a result of compulsory redundancy. Half say they would like a full-time job but very few actually look for work and the proportion doing so declines as their period without work grows. Nearly all now see ill-health as an obstacle to returning to work. This group is heavily dependent on the benefits system, and in particular on IB, though nearly a third also have income from a private or company pension.

The 'long-term unemployed' – the second largest sub-group – are more evenly spread across the age range. They are more likely to be single – nearly a quarter live alone – but, reflecting their lower age, they are also more likely than the sick or retired to have dependent children. On average their level of skills and training is lower, too. Their work experience is also more spasmodic. Several have experienced a series of relatively short-term jobs, sometimes with periods of non-employment in between. Compulsory redundancy was the most common reason for their last job coming to an end. The long-term unemployed bear the hallmarks of being relatively poor – two-thirds are in rented accommodation and they are heavily dependent on the benefits system, notably JSA. They do, however, generally want work, and the overwhelming majority are actively looking for work.

The men describing themselves as 'early retired' – the third largest sub-group – are on average more affluent than the sick or long-term unemployed, and more comprehensively detached from the labour market. Unsurprisingly they are an older group – nearly nine out of ten are 55 or over. Relatively few have dependent children living at home and most are married. The higher social status of this group comes across in a number of ways. They are better qualified and are more likely to have worked in white-collar occupations, and more than half own their home outright. Their work experience is different, too. Often they have previously worked for one employer for a very long time, and these jobs have usually come to an end through voluntary redundancy or retirement rather than compulsory severance. Nine out of ten in this group do not now want full-time work, though a larger minority did initially seek it, suggesting that retirement was not always the first choice. The early retired draw on the benefits system markedly less than the sick or long-term unemployed but, even so, nearly a quarter are IB claimants.

The men who describe themselves as 'part-time workers' are a relatively small group. By virtue of their part-time employment they have the strongest residual attachment to the labour market but in many other respects they are similar to the early retired who, as we noted, mostly now show little desire for employment. On average, part-time workers are a relatively old group – nearly half are over 55. They are often well qualified and come from white-collar occupations. More than two-thirds are owner-occupiers, and nearly half have a pension. These indicators point strongly towards part-time working as an adjunct to early retirement for middle-class professionals, perhaps as a valuable source of additional income or perhaps just as a way of remaining active. However, there is also evidence that for a minority of part-time workers this is a second-best solution. A third say they would like a full-time job, for example, and approaching a quarter draw on means-tested benefits.

Lastly, men who say they are 'full-time carers', including those who look after family or home full time, are a small group with much in common with the long-term unemployed. They are spread across all the age bands, and like the unemployed are generally poorly qualified. They live predominantly in rented housing, and around half have dependent children. They are also heavily dependent on benefits. Where they differ from the unemployed is that they are much more likely to have left their last job voluntarily (to take up their caring role, for example), they have on average been out of work for longer (half for five years or more) and hardly any are now looking for work. In some respects, therefore, being a full-time carer takes on the appearance of a career choice for men who might otherwise have been vulnerable to unemployment or low pay. To speculate, if their earning power had been greater they might have remained in employment and bought in the caring services which they themselves now provide.

Some initial implications

The detached male workforce is now a major part of the economic landscape of the UK. Even a single component within it – the long-term sick of working age – is now larger than the entire stock of claimant unemployed. The survey findings ought therefore to offer some important pointers to labour market policy.

The key point is perhaps that the detached male workforce appears to hide vast numbers of men who have been marginalised by the labour market changes of recent decades. It is convenient to stereotype the older, economically inactive man as someone who has the means to retire early and to welcome the spread of this phenomenon as a release from the excessive years of hard labour once demanded of everybody. The stereotype is misleading. The voluntarily early retired are, in fact, a minority among the detached male workforce. A more accurate stereotype is the older manual worker, whose health is past its best, for whom there is presently no meaningful role in the labour market and for whom the benefits system now offers a preferable means of support.

The survey shows that detachment from the labour market is often forced upon men rather than actively sought. Without wishing to repeat the detailed arguments about hidden unemployment set out in ch. 5 it is important to note the high proportion of the detached male workforce who say they would like a full-time job, the substantial proportion who were compulsorily laid off, and the relatively small proportion who say they are unable to work, even among the long-term sick. But this is unemployment of a particular kind. Many of these are men who might still have been working if appropriate jobs had been available but who have now given up looking for work. In doing so, they often appear to have become reconciled to their non-employed fate.

Closely linked to the enforced detachment from employment is the very heavy dependence of the detached male workforce on the benefits system. The early retired and part-time workers are the exception to the general rule – more of them manage to be financially self-sufficient. But more than 80 per cent of the long-term unemployed and of full-time carers, and virtually all the long-term sick, are claimants. The detached male workforce is not, on the whole, dropping out of paid employment to live comfortably on private means. The detachment of these men from the world of work is a major burden on the Exchequer.

The survey also underlines the diversity within the detached male workforce. This is not really a single group. It is united by prolonged detachment from regular full-time work but by little else. Any policies which seek to promote labour market re-attachment need to come to terms with this reality. At one extreme there are affluent early retirees who do not want to work any more. If they are not benefit claimants – and most are not – there seems little reason for promoting their re-attachment, even though their skills are necessarily lost to the economy. At the other extreme there are the long-term unemployed – nearly all on benefit, nearly all wanting work, nearly all seeking work. For this group of unemployed men the obvious way forward is to ensure that there is a sufficient supply of adequately paid jobs and, where necessary, training to go with them. In between is a range of sub-groups, each with particular needs. The long-term sick are the most numerous, but also a diverse group themselves. A 50-year-old ex-miner, with only modest limitations on the work he can do, may above all need new jobs in his area. A 30-year-old with severe disabilities and no work history may need much more intensive personal training and support.

A 'one-policy-fits-all' approach will not work, in other words. If the scale of the detached male workforce is to be reduced, and the associated benefit bill curbed, policies to promote labour market attachment will need to be tailored to individual needs. Chapters 10 and 11 return to this issue to explore how this might be done.

5   Incapacity benefit and unemployment

Christina Beatty and Stephen Fothergill

'Sickness' and 'unemployment' have usually been regarded as two separate, unconnected reasons why men do not work. Some men are too ill to work; others simply cannot find work. Of course, for many men without jobs this clear-cut distinction between sickness and unemployment remains entirely valid.

In reality, however, the world is more complex. It has long been recognised, for example, that there is a feedback from unemployment to ill-health – that the stress and loss of earnings associated with unemployment sometimes leads to deteriorating health (see, for example, Bellaby and Bellaby 1999). It is also true that there are many degrees of sickness, from an inability to do any work in any circumstances through to much milder limitations which restrict only the type or quantity of work a person can undertake. Added to this is the impact of benefit rules that define exactly who is eligible to be counted as sick and who as unemployed and which shift through time and vary from country to country, as ch. 2 emphasised. Where then does 'unemployment' stop and 'sickness' start? Is it really so easy to draw a line between the two?

In this chapter we explore the relationship between recorded sickness and recorded unemployment among men of working age. Once again the evidence is drawn from aggregate figures for the UK and from the survey of non-employed men first deployed in ch. 4 and described in full in the appendix. We argue that in fact the interaction between recorded sickness and recorded unemployment is very powerful – so great indeed that it creates a massive distortion to official UK unemployment figures. This applies not only to claimant-based measures of unemployment but also to the supposedly standardised ILO measure of unemployment derived from the quarterly Labour Force Survey. Such a radical claim has major implications for perceptions of the contemporary labour market. It is best therefore to move towards our conclusion in incremental stages, beginning with the overall statistical background.

In ch. 8, we return to the role of long-term sickness in labour market detachment and deploy further evidence from in-depth interviews. In the

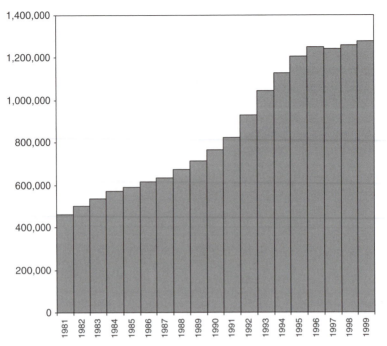

Figure 5.1   Long-term[a] Incapacity Benefit claimants, men, Great
Britain
Note: [a]For six mmonths or more (figures refer to April each year).
Source: Social security statistics.

present chapter, however, the focus is on the broader trends rather than
the experiences of individual men.

Recorded sickness among men: UK trends

Figure 5.1 shows the number of men of working age (i.e. 16–64) in Great
Britain claiming IB or its predecessor IVB for six months or more, in April
each year from 1981 to 1999. IB is the principal social security benefit
paid to men (and women) who are unable to work because of ill-health,
injury or disability. Under benefit rules, a man cannot claim both IB and
JSA – i.e. he cannot be considered 'sick' and 'unemployed' at the same
time – so all these IB claimants are excluded from the claimant measure
of unemployment based on JSA recipients.

The astonishing aspect of fig. 5.1 is the scale of the increase in the number of long-term IB/IVB claimants. In April 1981 there were 463,000 men
of working age in this category. The numbers increased every subsequent
year but one (1997) though the rate of increase did tail off following the

changeover from IVB in 1995, which introduced more demanding tests of ill-health. By April 1999 the total had reached 1,276,000. Among women of working age there has been a similar upward trend in the number of long-term IB/IVB claimants, though the level has always been lower than for men – in April 1999 710,000 women had been claiming IB for six months or more, bringing the overall total for adults of working age to just under 2 million.

These numbers refer to claimants. The number of recipients of IB is somewhat lower – 1,020,000 men and 499,000 women in April 1999, including short-term claimants. The difference between claimants and recipients – around 700,000 – reflects the intricacies of the UK benefits system, not failed claims. Some men and women have insufficient NI contributions to enable them to qualify for IB, usually because of insufficient time in recent employment. Those who fail to qualify in this way are still given NI credits for incapacity and are therefore counted as an 'incapacity claimant' in the same way that the 'claimant unemployed' include some people who fail to qualify for JSA (for example, because other household income disqualifies them from the means-tested version) but continue to claim NI credits for unemployment. In practice, most of these claimants who fail to qualify for IB then receive means-tested Income Support instead, but with a disability premium which maintains the financial incentive to keep on claiming as 'unfit for work'.

These are, however, complexities that should not distract from the central message. At the start of the new century around 2 million adults of working age, nearly two-thirds of them men, were long-term IB claimants. Even this does not tell the whole story. Adding in short-term (i.e. for less than six months) IB claimants and recipients of Severe Disablement Allowance (available to the severely handicapped who are ineligible for IB because of ineligible or non-existent employment history) brings the grand total of adults of working age in receipt of sickness-related benefits to nearly 2.5 million. All these individuals are detached from paid employment yet none of them is included in claimant unemployment figures. To put this figure into perspective, in Britain at the start of the new century the number of adults of working age claiming sickness-related benefits was more than double the number of claimant unemployed.

The increase in the number of sickness-related claimants is impossible to attribute to health factors alone at a time when the general standard of health in the population is known to be improving, albeit at the slowest rate among the most disadvantaged groups. The increase is also difficult to explain away in terms of rising awareness or admission of health problems, irrespective of shifts in the underlying reality. The General Household Survey, for example – the main nationwide survey asking regular questions about health – records an increase in self-reported

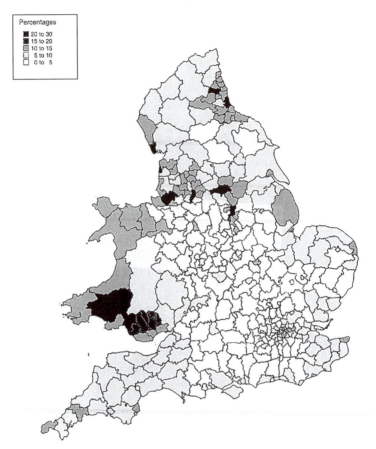

Figure 5.2   Men claiming sickness-related benefits as a proportion of working-age male population, England and Wales, August 1999
Source: DSS.

long-standing illness among adults of working age of only about a quarter between 1975 and 1995 (Berthoud 1998).

The other striking feature about sickness-related claimants is their distribution across the country, as figs. 5.2 and 5.3 show for August 1999. The data presented on these maps covers all men of working age in receipt of IB, Severe Disablement Allowance or NI credits for incapacity, expressed as a percentage of the working-age male population in each district (from the most recent population estimates, in this case for 1998). What the maps reveal is an exceptional incidence of sickness-related claimants in places such as South Wales, Merseyside, Manchester, South Yorkshire, North East England and Clydeside. In many of these areas,

Figure 5.3   Men claiming sickness-related benefits as a proportion of
working-age male population, Scotland, August 1999
Source: DSS.

sickness-related claimants accounted for more than 15 per cent of the
entire working-age male population. In a few places the proportion exceeded 20 per cent. The very highest level was in Merthyr Tydfil in
South Wales, where 26 per cent of working-age men were sickness-related
claimants. In contrast, in large parts of the South of England the proportion was below 5 per cent.

Anyone with a rudimentary knowledge of Britain's economic geography will see a familiar pattern here. There is an uncanny resemblance between the map of sickness-related claimants and the traditional maps of job loss and unemployment. Places such as North East England and South Wales have for decades suffered from above-average unemployment and were particularly badly hit by the industrial job losses of the 1980s and 1990s in industries such as coal, steel and heavy engineering. It is here that the incidence of sickness-related claimants is highest. Even within the South, the coastal unemployment blackspots of Thanet, Hastings and Brighton show up as having high levels of sickness-related claimants as well.

An explanation could be simply that areas of unemployment are also areas of ill-health. As we noted, there is certainly likely to be a link because unemployment can be a cause of ill-health. But the maps are also what might be expected if there is a diversion of unemployed men on to sickness-related benefits in the areas where jobs are hardest to find. Exactly which interpretation is correct, or to what extent, is an empirical question. Before presenting new survey data let us therefore review the existing evidence on the possible diversion from 'unemployment' to 'sickness'.

The diversion to incapacity: the existing evidence

The similarity between the maps of recorded unemployment and recorded sickness is not unusual. Turok and Webster (1998) have shown that across Britain the groups marginalised most from the workforce – the long-term unemployed, the young unemployed and single mothers on benefit, as well as the long-term sick – all tend to be concentrated in the areas where claimant unemployment is highest. An overall shortage of jobs appears to affect several different groups, they argue.

That job loss and increases in recorded sickness are linked is confirmed by local studies. The UK coalfields are a good example. Since the miners' strike of 1984–5 the UK coal industry has shed around 250,000 jobs, or about 95 per cent of its previous employment. Nearly all the jobs lost were held by men, and the losses occurred in areas where coalmining had often been the dominant source of male employment. Yet at the start of the new century, claimant unemployment among men in the coalfields is actually lower than when the pits were working in the early 1980s. This is not what would normally be expected in an area of chronic job loss. In an earlier study of the coalfields, covering both miners and other coalfield residents, we picked apart the adjustments in the local labour market (Beatty and Fothergill 1996). We found that the biggest response to the loss of coalmining jobs was a rise in economic inactivity among men. In other words, as jobs disappeared men dropped out of the labour market altogether. In turn, the biggest component of the rise in inactivity was an increase in recorded 'permanent sickness'. Other equilibrating flows were at work as well – there was net out-migration for example, and some new job creation. But it was the rise in recorded sickness that was the biggest single labour market response to mining job losses. Another study looking just at the experience of ex-miners also found that a high proportion of the men who had been employed by the coal industry in 1981 were recorded as 'permanently sick' ten years later (Fieldhouse and Hollywood 1999).

Coalmining is known to be an activity that is damaging to many men's health, so it is hardly surprising that mining areas have high rates of recorded sickness among men. But coalmining had been going on in these areas for many decades, and had generally employed far more men in the early and middle parts of the twentieth century. The striking thing is that the surge in the numbers of recorded sick in the coalfields occurred in the 1980s and 1990s, just as the pits closed. Nor can it be assumed that working in the coal industry had become more unhealthy over the years – in general, improving health and safety standards in the mines would suggest the opposite trend.

If the coalfields were alone in displaying a big rise in recorded sickness a local explanation might seem plausible. But they are not. Applying the same methods to England's most disadvantaged rural areas also reveals that a big fall in economic activity among men, and in particular a big rise in recorded sickness, has been the key factor in holding down recorded unemployment in the face of a substantial excess of labour supply over labour demand (Beatty and Fothergill 1997). A similar process is at work in Britain's largest conurbations, where employment among men has also fallen sharply. In the cities, out-migration has been particularly important in curbing labour supply but a fall in economic activity rates (of which rising sickness is one component) played a big part in absorbing job losses (Turok and Edge 1999).

The direct evidence of a diversion from recorded unemployment to recorded sickness is more patchy. Survey research for the DSS confirms that medical practitioners did at times assist their client's move on to IVB (Ritchie and Snape 1993). Sometimes they did so knowingly, sometimes unwittingly and sometimes under pressure. A detailed case study of the experience of IB claimants and their doctors in Inverclyde, in the West of Scotland, confirms this point (McCormick 2000). Other research shows that the great majority of recipients experienced only one continuous spell on sickness-related benefits (Lonsdale, Lessof and Ferris 1993).

More recent analysis of DSS data shows that on average 21,000 people a month (or 250,000 a year) move directly from JSA to IB (Edgeley and Sweeney 1998). The same DSS data show that the main reason for leaving IB after six months or more is failing the 'All Work Test' rather than going back to work (Dorsett *et al.* 1998). The rise in the overall number of IB claimants reflects the fact that once on this benefit people are staying there longer. The monthly in-flow of new IB claimants seems not to have increased and, indeed, has declined since the introduction of tighter rules in 1995.

Recorded sickness among non-employed men is higher in the UK than in all other EU countries, as ch. 2 showed. In Britain, the 2.5 million people of working age now claiming sickness-related benefits represents about 7 per cent of the entire working-age population. Among all economically inactive men aged 15 plus (including those of pensionable age) ch. 2 showed that in the UK, in 1999, 21 per cent attributed their inactivity to 'sickness or disability' compared to an EU average of just 8 per cent. In Germany, a country with an industrial heritage in many ways similar to Britain's, the figure was just 5 per cent. Indeed, Blondal and Pearson (1995) noted that between 1980 and 1993 the number of invalidity benefit recipients rose faster in the UK than in any other EU or OECD country.

Overall, Britain's hidden unemployment also appears to be larger than in most other EU states. As ch. 2 explained, Green (1999) has shown that in the UK a larger proportion of those who say they would like a job are excluded from the ILO measure of unemployment. Furthermore, the proportion excluded from the ILO figures is higher in the North, Scotland and Wales – the UK's weaker economies – than in the rest of the country. The significance of this observation is that sickness-related claimants are particularly likely to be excluded from the ILO measure, even if they would like a job, because to count as ILO unemployed a person must have looked for work in the last four weeks. Receipt of sickness-related benefits is not conditional on actively looking for work, unlike receipt of JSA, and, as we show later, most sickness-related claimants have given up looking for a job.

In a wide-ranging review of disability benefits Berthoud (1998) concluded that 'whatever the detailed pattern of change over time, a large number of people are claiming benefits on the grounds of incapacity in the mid-1990s who would not have been doing so in the mid-1970s'. The trends in the number of claimants, local labour market studies and international comparisons all point in this direction. The big question is just how many, if any, can be regarded as 'hidden unemployed'?

Table 5.1. *Key characteristics of 25–64-year-old men on benefit*

	IB claimants (%)	JSA claimants (%)
Personal attributes		
Age 50+	63	30
No formal qualifications	46	48
Manual occupation	73	81
Labour market attachment		
5 yrs or more since last full-time job	54	38
10 yrs or more in last full-time job	51	16
Would like a full-time job	47	91
Looked for full-time job after last job ended	27	88
Looking now	6	85
Health		
Some health limitations	96	23
Can't do any work	26	2

Source: Survey data.

New survey evidence

To shed light on the extent of hidden unemployment we are able to draw on our survey of the detached male workforce. The 'long-term sick' are the single largest group among these 25–64-year-old men without regular full-time jobs. The survey also covers substantial numbers of conventional long-term unemployed men, allowing comparisons between the two groups. Of the grand total of 1,703 interviewees in the seven survey areas, 668 were in receipt of IB at the time of the survey. The overwhelming majority of these (81 per cent) described themselves as 'long-term sick or disabled', while 11 per cent described themselves as 'retired' and 6 per cent as 'unemployed'. A further 353 interviewees were JSA claimants;[1] 91 per cent of JSA claimants described themselves as 'unemployed'. These IB and JSA claimants were spread across all the survey areas in large numbers.[2] A full comparison of the IB and JSA claimants in the survey can be found elsewhere (Beatty and Fothergill 1999c).

Table 5.1 summarises the main comparisons. The first part deals with three personal attributes that are likely to influence a man's chances in the

[1] This figure for JSA claimants includes 62 men who described themselves as 'unemployed' but said they were claiming Income Support, not JSA. Income Support is no longer available to unemployed claimants, having been replaced by income-based JSA in October 1996, but the two payments are effectively identical and easily confused.

[2] The numbers of interviews with IB and JSA claimants in each of the survey localities were: Barnsley (200 and 80), Chesterfield (156 and 98), Northampton (134 and 70), rural areas (178 and 105).

labour market – his age, qualifications and occupation. Generally speaking, in the contemporary UK labour market men over 50 and men with few qualifications are unattractive to many employers. Men who have worked mainly in manual occupations are further handicapped because of structural shifts in the demand for labour away from manual skills (in manufacturing and construction, for example) towards office-based activities. On all three counts, IB claimants appear vulnerable to unemployment. Nearly two-thirds are over 50, nearly half have no formal qualifications, and nearly three-quarters are from manual occupations. JSA claimants are a younger group, but in terms of qualifications and occupation at least as disadvantaged.

The second part of table 5.1 deals with the extent of labour market attachment. Here there are important differences. Compared to JSA claimants, IB claimants are likely to have been out of work longer. They are also less likely to have looked for full-time work after their last job ended, and much less likely to be looking now; 85 per cent of JSA claimants say they are active jobseekers, compared to just 6 per cent of IB claimants. This points to much greater labour market detachment among IB claimants. However, this apparently substantial detachment needs to be qualified. First, many IB claimants do have considerable previous work experience. Half had been employed in their last job for ten years or more, and a quarter for twenty years or more. These are men who have been no strangers to regular work – indeed, far fewer JSA claimants can boast such solid experience. Second, although few IB claimants now look for work many more did so when their last job ended. Their current status may therefore owe something to disillusion and failure in the job search process. Third, nearly half of all IB claimants still say they would like a full-time job.

The final part of table 5.1 deals with men's assessment of their health and the limitations it imposes on their ability to work. Again, there are important differences between IB and JSA claimants. Nearly all IB claimants report some health limitations. Just under a quarter of JSA claimants also report some limitations. However, only a quarter of IB claimants say they cannot do any work at all. For most, the problems are about just how much work they are able to do, or the type of work. Even minor health limitations can, however, act as a powerful disincentive to look for work. When IB claimants are asked why they are not looking for work, the overwhelming majority – 94 per cent – cite 'ill-health or injury'. By comparison factors such as age or shortage of suitable jobs are cited little if at all.

Turning to the causes of job loss, table 5.2 shows the main reason why IB claimants' last regular full-time job came to an end. This is one of the

Table 5.2. *Male Incapacity Benefit claimants: principal reason for last job ending*

	Barnsley (%)	Chester field (%)	Rural areas (%)	North- ampton (%)	All survey areas (%)
Compulsory[a]	46	25	24	24	31
Voluntary and other[b]	21	31	16	16	21
Ill-health or injury	33	44	60	60	48
	100	100	100	100	100

Notes:
[a] Compulsory redundancy/retirement, dismissal, end of temporary contract.
[b] Voluntary redundancy/retirement, own reasons and other.
Source: Survey data.

variables that displays systematic differences across the survey localities, which are arranged from the labour market with the highest labour market detachment (Barnsley) through to the lowest (Northampton). The four rural survey areas are grouped together because of the smaller sample sizes. On the composite indicator of labour market detachment described in ch. 4, in Barnsley 34 per cent of 25–64-year-old men are detached from the labour market. In Chesterfield the figure is 23 per cent, in the rural areas it averages 21 per cent, and in Northampton it is 14 per cent.

As we explained in ch. 4, the process by which a job comes to an end can be complex. Sometimes there is a single clear-cut reason. On other occasions a range of factors of varying importance come into play, especially when a job is left voluntarily. The survey asked respondents to identify the principal reason why their last job ended, and to simplify the picture the answers are grouped into three categories – compulsory severance (where it is the employer that brought the job to an end), voluntary severance (where the employee took the initiative) and ill-health or injury. Pooling all the survey data indicates that ill-health or injury was the principal reason for IB claimants' last job ending in just 48 per cent of cases. Compulsory severance accounted for a further 31 per cent and voluntary severance for the remaining 21 per cent. The corresponding proportions for JSA claimants were 7 per cent, 66 per cent and 27 per cent.

The proportion of IB claimants who lost their last job principally because of ill-health or injury varies with labour market conditions. In Barnsley, where the labour market is slackest, the proportion whose last job ended mainly because of ill-health is lowest, at just one-third. In Barnsley nearly half of all IB claimants lost their last job because of compulsory severance, most commonly redundancy. In Northampton, a tighter labour market, ill-health or injury was much more prominent and

Table 5.3. *Financial circumstances of 25–64-year-old men on benefit*

	IB claimants (%)	JSA claimants (%)
Income/assets		
Regular paid part-time work	2	8
Temporary/casual/seasonal paid work	1	4
Pension income	36	4
Lump-sum redundancy pay	16	6
Own home outright	24	11
Partner in work	26	11
Income Support	20	N/A
Other means-tested benefits[a]	37	65
Other non-means-tested benefits[b]	20	3
Financial commitments		
Partner not in work	46	47
Dependent children in household[c]	23	35
Mortgage or rent	73	84

Notes:
[a] Includes Housing Benefit, Council Tax Benefit and Family Credit.
[b] Includes Disability Living Allowance and Industrial Injuries Benefit but excludes Child Benefit.
[c] Defined here to include children under 18.
Source: Survey data.

compulsory severance much less so. Even adding in the cases in which ill-health or injury was cited as a factor in job loss, even if not the principal reason, does not fundamentally alter these observations. On this wider indicator, among IB claimants ill-health or injury was a factor in around three-quarters of all cases. That still leaves a quarter of IB claimants who say that ill-health or injury played no role at all in bringing their last job to an end. In Barnsley this proportion was 36 per cent, in Chesterfield 28 per cent, in the rural areas 23 per cent, and in Northampton 19 per cent – a pointer again that local labour market conditions appear to play a role.

Table 5.3 combines a range of information on the financial circumstances of IB and JSA claimants and is potentially a key to understanding why so many men are now IB claimants. By way of background it needs to be remembered that whereas JSA is means tested after six months, IB is not means tested at all except for a minority of new claimants with substantial pensions. The basic rate of IB is higher, especially for longer-term claimants, and for those who first made their current claim before April 1995 there are top ups for dependants and the benefit is also non-taxable. These differences were highlighted previously in chs. 3 and 4.

That the difference between means-tested JSA and non-means-tested IB creates financial incentives is not in dispute, but the strength of the incentive depends on personal circumstances. Generally speaking, the incentive for a non-employed man to claim IB rather than JSA is greater:

- if he has income from a company pension (since any income counts against means-tested JSA);
- if he has a partner in employment (since this household income counts more heavily against means-tested JSA);
- if he has savings above £3,000 (which reduce means-tested JSA and eliminate it entirely above £8,000);
- if he has no dependent children living with him (since they would add to means-tested JSA);
- if he owns his home outright (since mortgage or rent payments would also add to means-tested entitlements).

Part-time or casual earnings have an ambiguous role. On the one hand they count against JSA entitlement. On the other hand part-time working could prejudice the whole of IB entitlement by demonstrating a capacity for employment.

Other benefits play a complex role, too. Some IB claimants are able to claim other non-means-tested benefits as well, notably Disability Living Allowance, which provides assistance with the costs of care and/or mobility. In February 1999, 693,000 men of working age were claiming Disability Living Allowance. Also, accessing IB does not prevent an individual claiming means-tested benefits, in particular Income Support but also Housing Benefit and Council Tax Benefit. Nevertheless, it is still important to remember than non-employed men do not simply have a free choice to respond to the financial incentives and claim the benefit most favourable to them. All benefits have qualifying rules. To claim JSA, for example, a man must demonstrate that he is looking for work. To claim IB he must normally go through the 'All Work Test' which assesses his ability to carry out certain basic physical activities. Prior to 1995, IVB claimants had to secure the appropriate certification from their local doctor.

The striking feature of table 5.3 is just how much the distribution of claimants between the two benefits does conform to the financial incentives. More than a third of IB claimants have pension income, compared to just 4 per cent of JSA claimants. One in six IB claimants have lump-sum redundancy money to draw on, compared to one in sixteen JSA claimants. A quarter of IB claimants have a partner in work and a quarter own their own home outright, compared to only just over 10 per cent of JSA claimants. IB claimants are also less likely to have dependent children living at home.

Table 5.4. *Selected financial circumstances of male Incapacity Benefit claimants*

	Barnsley (%)	Chester-field (%)	Rural areas (%)	North-ampton (%)	All survey areas (%)
Pension	42	40	32	26	36
Lump-sum redundancy pay	24	21	9	8	16
Means-tested benefits	33	37	48	48	44
Own home outright	29	25	21	19	24
Partner in work	27	27	17	33	26

Source: Survey data.

Since the survey covered men who had been out of work for most or all of the preceding six months virtually all the JSA claimants will have been in receipt of the income-based variant, which is means tested. In contrast, only 20 per cent of IB claimants were also drawing on means-tested Income Support. IB claimants are in addition less likely to draw on other, mainly housing-related means-tested benefits.

Table 5.4 shows that the financial circumstances of IB claimants vary systematically between the survey localities. The table looks at five indicators. On four there is a clear progression from the slackest labour market (Barnsley) to the tightest (Northampton). In Barnsley, IB claimants are more likely to have a pension, more likely to have redundancy money, more likely to own their home outright and less likely to draw on means-tested benefits. The fifth indicator – a partner in work – shows a more variable pattern. On balance, however, IB claimants in a slack labour market appear to live in better financial circumstances than IB claimants elsewhere. This observation is especially notable because in slack labour markets, sickness-related benefit claimants are so much more numerous, as we showed earlier.

The survey provides evidence that some men do move directly from unemployment to IB. Overall, 23 per cent of IB claimants said that they were unemployed immediately prior to claiming IB. About four-fifths of these had previously been on benefit – i.e. JSA or its predecessors. In the survey localities the proportion moving directly from unemployment to IB was lowest in Northampton, the tightest labour market, at 16 per cent. There is also evidence that some JSA claimants try to move on to IB but fail and that others are removed from it against their will – 5 per cent of current JSA claimants said that they had at some time applied for IB and been refused. Twelve per cent of JSA claimants had received IB or IVB at some time in the past and, of these, half lost their entitlement because they failed the relevant medical test. Going back to work brought only one in eight of these earlier claims to an end.

Nevertheless, conformity to the expectations arising from financial incentives does not necessarily imply causality. IB claimants are on average older than JSA claimants. It is therefore to be expected that they are more likely to have pension income, less likely to have a mortgage, and less likely to have dependent children at home. The association between these variables and IB could therefore have no special significance. Added to this, age is likely to be associated with declining health and thus increased potential for claiming IB.

To try to disentangle the possible effects we carried out a range of exploratory regression analyses (see Beatty and Fothergill 1999c). These set out to measure the separate effects of a range of personal and household circumstances on the probability of receiving IB rather than JSA. The results showed consistently that health (however measured) appears to have a strong and statistically significant influence on the probability of a man claiming IB. This is to be expected, given the intended purpose of IB. Independently of health, age also appears to have a statistically significant influence. This effect is less easily explained by IB's intended role as support for those too ill to work. Older workers may be more prone to ill-health, but that age should still emerge as influential after having standardised for the effects of health points towards other factors for a full explanation of the benefit status of older workers.

Pension income also emerged as statistically significant. It is to be expected that IB claimants are more likely to have pension income than JSA claimants because some will have retired early on the grounds of ill-health and will thereby have become eligible for payments under company or private schemes. However, the regressions indicated that over and above the effects of health and age, pension income is a factor which differentiates JSA and IB claimants. In fact, pension income appears to be a more powerful predictor of who claims IB than age, but less powerful than health. Those with the most serious health problems have a high probability of being on IB anyway, but for those whose health is not fully incapacitating pension income appears to increase the likelihood of claiming IB. There is some evidence that having a partner in work also increases the probability of claiming IB, but this variable was not consistently significant. The remaining financial variables – redundancy pay, dependent children, outright home ownership – appear to have no discernible independent effects. In other words, putting aside the obvious effect of health it is pension income and to a lesser extent age that appear to be the most important factors in tipping men towards IB and away from JSA.

To what extent, therefore, does our survey evidence support the idea that there is hidden unemployment among male IB claimants? The findings which at first sight appear difficult to reconcile with this argument are that:

- Fewer than one in ten IB claimants describe themselves as 'unemployed'.
- Fewer than one in ten IB claimants are presently looking for a full-time job.
- The overwhelming majority of IB claimants give ill-health or injury as the reason for not looking for a job.
- Ill-health or injury is quoted by around three-quarters of IB claimants as a factor in bringing their last job to an end.
- Nearly all IB claimants say their health limits the work they can do.

The survey findings that appear altogether more consistent with the notion of hidden unemployment are that:

- In terms of age, skills and qualifications, IB claimants are a group that would anyway be severely exposed to unemployment.
- Ill-health or injury was the principal reason for job loss in only about half of all cases. Redundancy was often the cause.
- In about a quarter of cases, health was not even a lesser factor in bringing their last job to an end.
- In areas where IB claimants are most numerous, the proportion losing their jobs because of redundancy rather than ill-health is highest.
- Half of all IB claimants say they would like a full-time job.
- Just over a quarter looked for work after their last job ended.
- Only a quarter of IB claimants say they cannot do any work.
- For many IB claimants, their benefit entitlement is greater than if they were on JSA.
- Nearly a quarter of IB claimants moved on to this benefit straight from unemployment.

Depending on exactly how 'hidden unemployment' is defined, the balance of the survey evidence suggests that IB does hide some unemployment. Just how many might be described as hidden unemployed is not immediately obvious, however. On the other hand, the conflicting nature of the evidence is worrying and itself poses questions. Could it be that we are observing both ill-health and hidden unemployment at the same time and in the same people? Some of the evidence points to ill-health. Some of the other evidence points to hidden unemployment. Can these apparently contradictory observations be reconciled?

To make sense of this we need next to set out some ideas on how employment, unemployment and sickness do in practice interact. We can then return to look at the likely scale of hidden unemployment and some of its implications.

A model of sickness and unemployment

Our framework for understanding how employment, unemployment and sickness interact has been set out in full elsewhere (Beatty, Fothergill and Macmillan 2000). What we provide here is a summary. Figure 5.4 offers a diagrammatic illustration.

In this diagram the three groups that are the focus of our concern are arranged according to the strength of their connection to employment. On the left are those in work. This large group spans a wide range of people from those with very secure jobs through to those whose employment is highly vulnerable. On the right are the recorded sick, who for the sake of simplicity we will define as those individuals in receipt of sickness-related

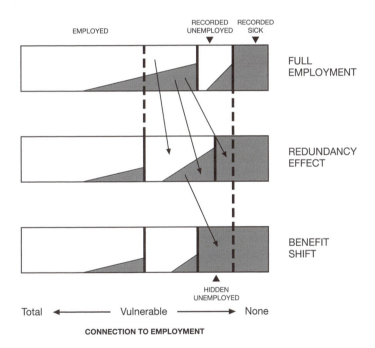

Figure 5.4 The impact of job loss on recorded unemployment and recorded sickness

benefits. By virtue of their status as sickness claimants they are usually not required to look for work (not in the UK at any rate). Some may not want work either. Their connection to employment is therefore weak. In between are the recorded unemployed, which again for simplicity we will define as those in receipt of unemployment-related benefits. To obtain unemployment-related benefits these people have to demonstrate that they are looking for work (certainly in the UK). Their connection to employment is therefore greater than for the recorded sick.

Now let us complicate the picture and introduce the concept of 'hidden sickness'. These are people who by virtue of their place in the labour market are not usually counted among the recorded sick. The real world is not divided neatly into those who are 100 per cent fit and able for work and those who cannot do any work at all because of their disabilities, even though social security systems tend to operate on the basis of such a division. There is a gradation. Some people can do some types of work but not others. Some are limited by how much they can do. Some have intermittent health problems. At the extreme, even some people with very severe disabilities continue to work. What we call 'hidden sickness' comprises those people who are in employment, and those among the recorded unemployed, who by objective standards have a significant illness or disability. In this context, let us define 'significant' as 'sufficient to enable them to qualify for sickness-related benefits should they wish to do so'. Their illness or disability may or may not impede their ability to work, depending on the job and personal circumstances, but these people continue to work or look for work. In some cases, employers prefer to keep them working, too.

The point is that an objective measure of sickness in the workforce would embrace more than just those on sickness-related benefits. The corollary is that meeting the required standard of disability to qualify for sickness-related benefits does not in itself indicate that an individual is entirely incapable of any work. In reality in the UK, for example, the assessment that acts as the gateway to IB entitlement beyond six months actually measures the ability to perform certain basic tasks (such as walking up stairs, lifting and holding), not an inability to do all work in all circumstances. Confirmation of the considerable extent of hidden sickness in the UK is provided by an analysis of Labour Force Survey data (Sly, Thair and Risdon 1999). This estimated that in the winter of 1998/9, 2.9 million people in employment had a self-reported disability. A further 0.3 million among the ILO unemployed were also estimated to have a disability. These two groups of 'hidden sick' were estimated to comprise around half of all those of working age with disabilities.

The hidden sick are particularly vulnerable to redundancy and job loss. Their health problems also place them at a disadvantage in job search. Job retention and job search are difficult because employers see health problems as an impediment to actual or potential productivity. In view of poor health, individuals may also be unwilling to hold on to a job in all circumstances. Either way, the hidden sick (like the less well qualified and those approaching retirement age) are likely to be skewed towards the most vulnerable among the employed and the least likely to find work among the unemployed. This skewed distribution is illustrated by the shaded areas in fig. 5.4.

Now let us introduce job loss into the model. The first part of fig. 5.4 shows a hypothetical 'fully employed economy'. In fact, even in this economy there is modest recorded unemployment (as there was even during the long post-war boom) and beyond this there is modest recorded sickness. The second and third parts of fig. 5.4 show the effects of a substantial loss of jobs. Two separate effects are distinguished.

The first is what we will call the 'redundancy effect' and happens fairly quickly. The job loss falls on both the healthy and the hidden sick, but disproportionately on the latter given their vulnerability. Given a choice, employers retain those they regard as fit and productive. Given a choice, many employees who are finding work difficult because of their health will be among those who volunteer for redundancy. The more fit and able who lose their jobs add to the stock of recorded unemployed. So do some of the hidden sick who lose their jobs but still hope to get back into work. Others among the hidden sick make the move directly on to sickness-related benefits and therefore increase recorded sickness. They are able to do so because their illness or disability, which was present when they were working, is such that they meet the requirements for these benefits. The extent to which this group 'seeks out' sickness-related benefits in preference to unemployment benefits, or is 'placed' there by the employment and benefit services, is unclear. Other things being equal, a differential in benefit rates (as in the UK for example) will establish financial incentives to which individuals may or may not respond. The precise balance between choice and compulsion is not important to the general argument. The point is that the redundancy effect will increase recorded sickness as well as recorded unemployment.

At this stage we need to introduce the 'queue for jobs'. Some of the people seeking work have a greater chance of obtaining it than others. Typically, those from whom employers choose – near the front of the queue – have good qualifications and experience, including recent work history, and are of prime working age (say 25–50). Those towards the back of the queue are less attractive to employers, and less likely to secure a job. Health is one of the key discriminating factors. Other things being equal, a person with health problems is likely to be further back in the queue than one without. The real world is considerably more haphazard than the organised notion of a queue suggests, but the idea that some individuals are more attractive to employers than others is a fundamental feature of the labour market which is well understood by those within it, and most people looking for work think they have a pretty good idea about their chances of finding work and therefore where they come in the queue.

But the queue for jobs is not like a conventional queue. Although the people moving into employment come overwhelmingly from near the front, new people entering the queue do not join at the back. They take their place in the queue according to their particular personal attributes. Extending the metaphor, people with employable attributes 'push in'. The net effect is that the people at the back of the queue tend to stay there. Indeed, a lengthening period without employment is actually likely to push some people further back in the queue.

The queue for jobs is central to understanding the second effect of job loss, which we will call the 'benefit shift'. This is shown in the third part of fig. 5.4. It is a diversion of workers with significant illness or disability from unemployment-related benefits to sickness-related benefits. As the number of unemployed swells, competition from the fit and healthy pushes those with illness or disability further back in the queue. Their chances of finding work declines. Their disillusion grows. The exact mechanisms diverting people on to sickness-related benefits are likely to vary from individual to individual. Some may be moved there by the employment services or by benefit administrators. Others may make a claim for sickness-related benefits if these appear to be more generous or if there seem to be fewer strings attached. Again, the precise balance between choice and compulsion is unclear but not important to the general argument. Nevertheless, so long as sickness-related benefits remain more generous there is likely to be little voluntary movement from recorded sickness back to recorded unemployment. The benefit shift may take some years to work through to its full extent. The effect is that less joblessness is recorded as unemployment and more as sickness.

This leads us to the notion of 'hidden unemployment'. This is the increase in recorded sickness above the level that would have been recorded in a fully employed economy. Again, this is illustrated in fig. 5.4. To be 'hidden unemployed', in this context, does not imply that these extra people are looking for work, or even want work. The point is simply that their labour market situation reflects job loss and the operation of the benefits system as well as their health. In a fully employed economy they would not have been recorded as sick.

Four important dimensions of this model are worth highlighting. First, it does not rely on fraudulent behaviour in order to explain the increase in the number of sickness-related benefit claimants. Indeed, in this model all those who claim these benefits are fully entitled to do so on the basis of their illness or disability.

Second, the loss of jobs leaves a residual employed workforce that is on average healthier. A large proportion of the less healthy have in effect been 'weeded out'. This actually accentuates the difficulties for those with health problems who are looking for a job, because they would stand out more in the workplace.

Third, the diversion to recorded sickness will affect the ILO measure of unemployment as well as claimant-based measures. As we explained earlier, one of the yardsticks used to define an ILO unemployed individual is that he or she must have looked for work in the preceding four weeks. If sickness-related claimants are not required to look for work (there is no requirement in the UK) and if they think that there is little point in doing so, they will accordingly not be counted as part of the stock of ILO unemployed.

Fourth, the increase in recorded sickness owes nothing to any deterioration in the health of the workforce. Indeed, the model is based on a constant 'objective' level of ill-health and disability throughout. What changes in response to job loss is that sickness which was previously hidden becomes visible. There may in practice be an overall deterioration in health, if rising joblessness causes increased ill-health, but any such effect is entirely independent of the increase in recorded sickness predicted by the model.

The key point about this model of the labour market is that there is nothing inconsistent in arguing that in the UK IB reflects both widespread ill-health and substantial hidden unemployment.

The scale of hidden unemployment

All measures of hidden unemployment incorporate specific assumptions and conceptions of 'unemployment' itself. Building on the model outlined above, the group we are seeking to identify here are those men of working age that are sickness-related claimants who might reasonably be expected to have been in work in a fully employed economy.

Table 5.5 presents a range of indicators. The first line shows the number of male IB claimants in Great Britain in April 1999. The total of 1.42 million shown here includes all those actually in receipt of IB plus those receiving NI credits for sickness disability. Of these, 1.28 million had been claimants for six months or more. Because IB normally becomes payable only after the first twenty-eight weeks of illness, virtually all the

Table 5.5. *Indicators of hidden unemployment among male Incapacity Benefit claimants, Great Britain, April 1999*

	Number	% of men of working age
IB claimants of working age	1,418,000	7.7
Statistical indicators		
Based on South East 1991 benchmark	650,000	3.5
Based on Great Britain 1981 benchmark	700,000	3.8
Survey-based indicators		
Not 'can't do any work' (74%)	1,050,000	5.7
Health not main reason for job loss (52%)	740,000	4.0
Would like a full-time job (47%)	670,000	3.6
Looked for work after last job ended (27%)	380,000	2.1
Presently looking for work (6%)	90,000	0.5

Sources: DSS, Census of Population, survey data.

claimants will not have worked for at least six months. The rest of the table presents indicators based on statistical comparisons and on the results of our survey.

The first of the statistical indicators is the one we deployed in the studies of the coalfields and of rural areas, mentioned earlier, and also in estimates of the 'real level of unemployment' published in 1997 (Beatty, Fothergill, Gore and Herrington 1997). As a benchmark it uses the rate of 'permanent sickness' among men of working age in the South East of England in April 1991, recorded by the Census of Population. At that time, the South East (in this case the old statistical region, including London) had only just emerged from a prolonged period (c. 1986–90) of virtually full employment. The South East in 1991 therefore offers a guide to what might be achievable in a fully employed economy. At that time, 3.4 per cent of the male WAP in the South East were recorded as permanently sick. Excesses above this level might therefore be regarded as a form of hidden unemployment. In the calculation shown in table 5.5 a second deduction equal to 0.8 per cent of the male WAP has also been made to allow for short-term (i.e. less than six months) IB claimants. This statistical indicator points to 650,000 hidden unemployed.

Although we have deployed this South East benchmark on a number of previous occasions its limitations need to be noted. It takes no account of regional and local variations in underlying health, in particular that in areas of heavy industry (e.g. the coalfields) ill-health is undoubtedly more widespread. The South East benchmark tends to inflate estimates of hidden unemployment in these areas. Distorting estimates in the other direction, the South East benchmark may itself include some hidden unemployment because there were parts of even this region which never reached full employment.

The second statistical indicator uses the national level of permanent sickness recorded by the 1981 Census as the benchmark. This has the advantage that it reflects prevailing levels of recorded sickness before the really big national increases in the 1980s and 1990s.[3] It is therefore likely to exclude large numbers who may have been diverted on to sickness benefits as a result of job loss and unemployment. Excesses over the 1981 level might therefore be a guide to hidden unemployment. Again, a deduction of 0.8 per cent is also made to allow for short-term IB claimants. This statistical indicator points to 700,000 hidden unemployed. The remaining lines of table 5.5 show estimates derived from the survey data. In each case the relevant percentage from the survey is applied to the total number of male IB claimants of working age, shown in the first line.

The first of the survey indicators is the share of IB claimants whose own assessment is that they are able to do some work. This points to 1,050,000 men. However, our view is that this is not a fair measure of hidden unemployment. We suspect that many men are reluctant to concede that they could not do any work at all, and this high figure disguises quite extensive limitations on what work some of these men are able to undertake. In practice, even in a fully employed economy many of them might still not have been in work.

We also have doubts about the validity of the last two survey indicators as measures of hidden unemployment. These are the modest share of IB claimants who looked for work after their last job ended (380,000) and the even smaller numbers presently looking for work (90,000). IB claimants are not required to be active jobseekers. If there are few suitable jobs available for them it is hardly surprising that so many do not bother looking or give up the search.

The most revealing figures are therefore the estimated numbers who say they would like a full-time job (670,000) and the numbers whose last job ended principally for reasons other than ill-health or injury (740,000). What is striking is that these two indicators point to a similar order of magnitude as the South East benchmark (650,000) and the 1981 benchmark (700,000). This gives weight to the view that there may be approaching three-quarters of a million men on this benefit who would have been

---

[3] A small distortion arises because of the inclusion in the 1981 Census data on permanent sickness of a small number of men aged 65 plus. The effect is to slightly reduce estimates of hidden unemployment based on this benchmark.

in work in a fully employed economy. None of these men is included in the official unemployment claimant count.

Despite pointing to similar orders of magnitude, all four of these indicators nevertheless have limitations. For example, some men may 'want work' in a generalised, aspirational way without having the health or physical ability to take up employment. Some whose last job ended for reasons other than ill-health will have subsequently become too ill to work. There will also be some unemployed men for whom a prolonged period on IB has sapped the desire to work, and some IB claimants whose health has improved since they first left work because of illness.

The overlap between the men actually counted by the alternative measures of hidden unemployment is far from complete. For example, only half of those who now say they want work also left their last job for reasons other than ill-health. In a different context, the Royal Statistical Society (1995) pointed out that though the ILO and claimant measures of unemployment were not far apart in terms of the overall totals they identified, they counted different people with only modest overlap. The fact that here four alternative measures of hidden unemployment among male IB claimants point to similar orders of magnitude should likewise not be taken to indicate that the 'hidden unemployed' are an easily identified group with clear-cut boundaries. At the level of the individual, trying to identify just who might have been in work in a fully employed economy and who would still have been on sickness-related benefits may be a fruitless task. In practice, so much depends on individual skills, limitations and opportunities, and perhaps on a measure of luck as well. Our analysis points to the overall numbers who might have been employed, but not to exactly who among the 1.4 million IB claimants would have held the jobs.

The close coincidence between statistical and survey-based estimates of hidden unemployment nevertheless gives confidence in taking the analysis one step further. The 1981 data on permanent sickness are available for all districts, from the Census, and can be used to estimate hidden unemployment among male IB claimants for local areas across the whole country. This is the method advocated by Armstrong (1999) in his study of hidden unemployment in different parts of Northern Ireland. He argues that it takes account of geographical variations in the underlying level of sickness prior to the big national increases of the 1980s and 1990s. The local 1981 benchmark should therefore be superior to the South East 1991 benchmark.

Table 5.6 summarises the results of this exercise by region. The figures are for August 1996 – subsequent district boundary changes (especially in Scotland and Wales) make comparisons with 1981 data very difficult

Table 5.6. *Estimated hidden unemployment among male sickness claimants, August 1996*

	Number	as % of resident 16–64-year-old males
Wales	76,000	8.6
North East	66,000	8.3
North West	175,000	8.2
Scotland	114,000	7.2
Yorkshire and Humber	83,000	5.4
West Midlands	77,000	4.7
London	94,000	4.3
East Midlands	50,000	3.9
South West	41,000	2.8
Eastern	39,000	2.4
South East	49,000	2.0
Great Britain	863,000	4.9

Source: Authors' estimates.

for later years. The calculation is also based on the total number of male sickness-related claimants (i.e. including Severe Disablement Allowance) and the total for Great Britain is therefore not comparable with the figures in table 5.5 earlier, which refer just to IB claimants. To be absolutely clear about the basis of this calculation, two deductions are made from the 1996 data on sickness claimants. The first is the share of the male WAP recorded as permanently sick in each district by the 1981 Census. The second is a flat-rate deduction equal to 1 per cent of the male WAP, to allow for short-term claimants. This is the share of the male WAP that in 1996 had been claiming IB for less than six months.

Across Britain as a whole this particular measure points to just over 850,000 hidden unemployed men – more than the national estimates shown earlier due to the different basis of the calculation, but broadly the same order of magnitude. The regional differences are very large. At one end of the spectrum, it is estimated that in Wales hidden unemployment among sickness-related claimants accounts for more than 8 per cent of all 16–64-year-old men. At the other end, in the South East of England the figure is just 2 per cent. Apart from Wales, all three regions covering Northern England, plus Scotland, are at the top of the table.

Table 5.7 shows the top twenty districts across Great Britain on this particular measure of hidden unemployment. The list is headed by Easington, a former mining area in County Durham, followed by Merthyr

Table 5.7. *Estimated hidden unemployment among male sickness claimants, top twenty districts, August 1996*[a]

		Number	% of men of working age
1	Easington	6,200	20.3
2	Merthyr Tydfil	3,300	18.2
3	Knowsley	8,000	17.5
4	Port Talbot	2,700	17.0
5	Glasgow	32,500	16.0
6	Monklands	5,200	16.0
7	Liverpool	20,300	14.8
8	Neath	2,900	14.3
9	Barrow-in-Furness	3,300	13.8
10	Rhondda	3,200	13.1
11	Clydebank	1,700	12.8
12	Rhymney Valley	4,200	12.8
13	Manchester	15,400	12.6
14	Blaenau Gwent	3,000	12.6
15	Cumnock and Doon Valley	1,600	11.9
16	Barnsley	8,300	11.7
17	Llanelli	2,600	11.5
18	Motherwell	5,200	11.5
19	Hamilton	3,700	10.9
20	Swansea	5,900	10.6

Note: [a] Pre-April 1996 districts.
Source: Authors' estimates.

Tydfil in South Wales (another mining area) and Knowsley in Merseyside. All the worst affected districts on this measure are in the industrial areas of Northern England, Scotland and Wales – some of them big cities like Glasgow, Liverpool and Manchester, others smaller towns with a heritage of industries such as coal or steel. In contrast, there is not a single London borough in the top twenty, nor indeed in the top fifty, despite the relatively high claimant unemployment in much of inner London. Indeed, across much of Southern and eastern England, especially outside London, this calculation points to only very modest hidden unemployment among male sickness-related claimants.

It is possible to quibble about the technical basis of these calculations. However, it is important to stress that these estimates do try to take account of underlying variations in the level of incapacitating sickness and also find support in our survey evidence. They therefore represent a serious challenge to the credibility of conventional unemployment figures and to prevailing perceptions of the scale of regional disparities in the UK.

Our figures suggest that far from waning towards the end of the 1990s, much of Britain's unemployment problem simply became hidden from view. The rules governing eligibility for unemployment benefits – these days JSA – have grown tighter over two decades, reducing the number of claimant unemployed. That much is well known. But there has also been a bigger and less-publicised shift of non-employed men from recorded unemployment to recorded sickness. What is more, the evidence shows that this shift has been geographically skewed. In Northern industrial Britain, where the job loss has often been greatest and the dole queue longest, the diversion on to sickness-related benefits has been largest. The effect is not only to mask unemployment but also to hide the true disparities between regional and local labour markets.

In what sense 'unemployed'?

It is important to be absolutely clear about this form of hidden unemployment. In particular, there is nothing fraudulent in the behaviour of these men. In order to claim IB, for example, all these men will have had to secure medical certification. In addition, it is clear from the survey evidence that the health limitations are genuine, though as the men themselves often admit, their health problems are not necessarily always fully incapacitating. These men are hidden unemployed in that in a fully employed economy they could reasonably be expected to have been in work.

However, the fact that so many of these men are not now looking for work means that they are mostly not part of the stock of unemployed workers from whom employers choose and consequently they exert no downward pressure on wage inflation. What seems to be happening is that for many the move on to IB is a one-way ticket. Detachment from the labour market grows, skills become rusty and the barriers to retrieval become formidable.

At the extreme, some men have not only given up looking for work but also wanting it as well. In local labour markets where the available jobs are scarce and generally poorly paid it can be a perfectly rational choice to opt right out of the world of work. Why endure more failed job applications and dashed hopes? Best perhaps to become reconciled to the realities of the job market and adjust your lifestyle and aspirations accordingly. This may explain why the very high number of sickness claimants rarely surfaces as a political problem except in respect of their cost to the Exchequer.

Long-term dependence on sickness benefits does not automatically mean material hardship, though it is probably rarely associated with real affluence. We noted earlier that in the survey area with the greatest number of sickness claimants – Barnsley – these men actually appear to be better off than elsewhere. A higher proportion have income from a pension, more own their homes outright and fewer draw on means-tested benefits. Importantly, more than 40 per cent of all IB claimants in the Barnsley survey area had last worked in the coal industry. One thing that is well known about this industry is that large redundancy payments (typically £15–30,000) were made to miners. This enabled many to pay off their mortgage and sometimes save a little as well. All ex-miners are entitled to a company pension from age 60, and those who left the industry after 1992 can opt to receive a pension at any age from 50 onwards. Added to this, the effect on health of working in the coal industry means that redundant miners' claims for IB are often likely to be successful. Seen in this context withdrawal from the labour market becomes easier to explain. Although many of the IB claimants in Barnsley lost their last job because of redundancy rather than ill-health, their financial circumstances and access to IB allow them to get by.

Barnsley is high on the list of towns where the incidence of non-employment among men has risen to exceptional levels. Many of the other districts recording high levels are also mining areas, and others were once dominated by steel or heavy engineering. The experience of redundancy followed by IB and effective withdrawal from the labour market is likely to be shared by many men in these places. These men may, however, represent a unique cohort – the last of a huge group of mainly manual workers shed by traditional industries during the 1980s and 1990s and given a large pay-off to leave. Now that industries such as coal and steel employ so few, the chances of their experience being repeated on a large scale have largely gone.

But to focus on job search behaviour or lack of it, or indeed on job aspirations, misses the point. Since the 1970s, when full employment came to an end, the shortage of job opportunities has pushed large sections of the workforce to the very margins of the labour market. Britain does not have a non-means-tested benefit for the long-term unemployed. A large part of the marginalised workforce has therefore wound up on the next best thing, which is non-means-tested sickness benefits. In doing so they have dropped out of the claimant unemployment figures and, because job search often seems fruitless and is not in any case a requirement of their benefit, out of the active labour market as well. Ultimately it is the absence of full employment that has driven these individuals into their present predicament. In many cases their status as IB claimants has been brought about by redundancy from employers with whom they might otherwise have continued for years. Even the coal industry had a tradition of employing less physically fit older workers in easier surface jobs. But these jobs have now gone. In so far as it is job loss and the absence of full employment that has driven IB claimants to their current status, they should be regarded as hidden unemployed.

Yet just because so many of these men can be described as 'hidden unemployed' they should not be regarded as '100 per cent able-bodied'. Our argument is not that the reported disabilities are fictitious. In reality the workforce is not divided neatly into those who can work and those who cannot, as IB rules imply. There is an extensive grey area between, which includes many men who are capable of work but with limitations on exactly what they are physically able to do. Some of these men are in employment; others are not. In the slacker labour markets that have characterised the UK since the mid-1970s, especially in Northern Britain, this intermediate group appears to have lost out badly in the scramble for jobs. Many of them are older, male manual workers, past their physical best. And a great many of them have become sickness claimants.

6   The over 50s

Christina Beatty and Stephen Fothergill

The relationship of older men to the labour market is of particular interest and importance. As we saw in ch. 4, men aged 50–64 form by far the largest group that has become detached from employment. As Campbell (1999) has documented, in the UK during the 1980s and 1990s the increase in the number of older men without jobs was especially rapid. Only a minority of men in their early 60s, approaching state pension age, now remain in employment.

The prevailing perception is undoubtedly that labour market detachment among these older men is synonymous with early retirement. It is not hard to see why this view has taken root. In many professional jobs – teaching, the civil service and local government are good examples – pension schemes set 60 as the normal retirement age many years ago. As pension schemes have gradually become the norm in other occupations, including large parts of the private sector, they, too, have often adopted 60 as the retirement age. Increasingly it is only an unfortunate minority, mainly in insecure manual jobs and outside the scope of occupational pension schemes, who are required to work on until they are 65.

Added to this, employers have often used early retirement as a means of slimming down their workforce. Men in their 50s are frequently seen as an easy target. They can be expensive to retain, because their salaries have risen with seniority and experience. They may be less flexible and adaptable than younger employees, who have less personal investment in long-established practices or responsibilities. They may not be up to speed with new technology. And they have usually already accumulated substantial pension rights, so only modest top ups are needed to make it worth their while to leave. So although the official retirement age in many occupations is now set at 60, in practice many men expect to be offered retirement in their mid-50s. Some positively seek this outcome.

Dropping out early from the labour market is therefore often seen as a voluntary move, providing relief from decades of hard work. It is something to be welcomed, rather than a trend to be resisted. Such cosy assumptions about early retirement are reinforced because it is the middle-class opinion formers, in the media, public service and elsewhere, who are usually those who are best placed to take advantage of early retirement on favourable terms. But is this the reality for the majority of older men who drop out of the labour market? Can middle-class assumptions really be generalised to older manual workers? Or are their trajectories quite different?

Within the 50–64-year-old group there are also likely to be important differences associated with age. At 63 or 64, many men might welcome leaving work behind. At 51 or 52 their attitude may be entirely different. Not so many years ago, and to some extent even now, men in their 50s expected to be at the peak of their career and earning capacity – near the top of their organisation if they had risen through white-collar jobs, or working as a foreman or supervisor if they had spent the bulk of their working life in manual jobs. Just how labour market detachment develops through time among the over 50s, and the extent to which it is embraced or resisted, is therefore an interesting question in its own right.

In this chapter we try to provide answers to these questions. Once again we draw on our survey of the detached male workforce, described in the appendix. Carried out in seven areas around Britain during 1997 and 1998, the survey covers men who were economically inactive or had been unemployed for most or all of the previous six months. It also covers men who were working only part time. All of these men were detached from regular full-time employment, for so long the norm for men of working age. The survey involved 1,703 interviews in all. Of these 973 were with men aged 50–64, and it is this sub-set of older men that provides the material for this chapter.

Self-declared status

Table 6.1 shows the self-declared status of the men making up this older detached workforce. The biggest single group, comprising nearly 40 per cent of the total, are men who describe themselves as 'long-term sick or disabled'. The next largest group – just over 30 per cent of the total – are those who say they are 'retired from paid work altogether'. Two other groups are significant. One is the self-declared 'unemployed' (15 per cent) and the other those describing themselves as 'in part-time employment' (just under 10 per cent). The remainder include full-time carers, those looking after family or home, and a range of others. In subsequent tables we group these remaining men under the 'other' label. For the sake of simplicity, we also refer to the four larger groups as the 'long-term sick', 'long-term unemployed', 'early retired' and 'part-time workers', in the same way as we did in ch. 4.

Table 6.1. *Self-declared status of older detached men*

	Number of interviewees	(%)
Long-term sick or disabled	372	38.2
Retired from paid work altogether	304	31.2
Unemployed	150	15.4
In part-time employment	91	9.4
Full-time carers	30	3.1
Looking after family or home	5	0.5
On government scheme	2	0.2
Full-time student	1	0.1
Other	18	1.8
Total	973	100.0

Source: Survey data.

What should be immediately obvious from the table is that early retirement accounts for only a minority of older men without full-time jobs. No single group dominates the picture, but on the basis of these figures the older non-employed man is more accurately characterised as one with sickness or disability rather than as an early retiree.

Unsurprisingly, the profile of the older men who are detached from full-time employment differs from the 25–49 year olds included in the survey. Among this younger group of detached workers, early retirement is virtually non-existent (only 1 per cent). Unemployment is more common (40 per cent of detached 25–49 year olds) but long-term sickness or disability is again widespread (35 per cent).

Within the 50–64-year-old group there are important differences associated with age. This is illustrated in table 6.2. Again unsurprisingly, early retirement is most prominent among 60–64 year olds, but even among this group it does not account for half of all the men without full-time jobs. Unemployment falls away with age as a reason for labour

Table 6.2. *Age breakdown of older detached men*

	Long-term sick (%)	Early retired (%)	Long-term unemployed (%)	Part-time workers (%)	Other (%)	All respondents (%)
50–54	45	16	22	8	10	100
55–59	40	27	16	12	5	100
60–64	34	43	11	8	4	100

Source: Survey data.

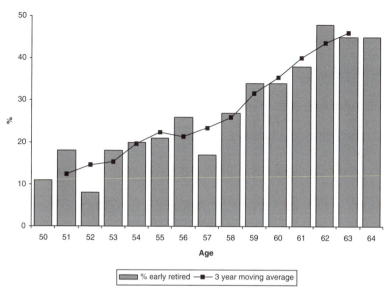

Figure 6.1   Early retirement among older detached men
Source: Survey data.

market detachment, but the share of men describing themselves as long-term sick is consistently high among men in their early 50s, late 50s and early 60s.

The share of men at different ages who describe themselves as retired is shown in fig. 6.1. To counteract the influence of the modest sample size this diagram also includes a three-year moving average. Although the share describing themselves as retired increases with age, as might be expected, there is some evidence of gentle step-changes. The proportion of self-declared retired is at a plateau of 12–15 per cent for men in their early 50s. It rises to a further plateau of 20–25 per cent for men in their mid-50s. This is followed by a further rise to a final plateau of around 45 per cent for men in their early 60s. Partly the increase with age in the share of self-declared retired will reflect the addition of extra retirees, especially around age 60. Partly, however, it may reflect shifts in the way that men see themselves. An unemployed or long-term sick man in his mid-50s may still harbour aspirations to get back to work. By his early 60s, the same man may begin to see himself as retired even if there has been no obvious change in his circumstances. Our survey failed to ask how men had first described themselves (unemployed, retired, etc.) after their last job ended – with hindsight a regrettable omission.

Table 6.3. *Social class (based on occupation) of older detached men*

	Long-term sick (%)	Early retired (%)	Long-term unemployed (%)	Part-time workers (%)	Other (%)	All respondents (%)
Professional	15	52	2	26	4	100
Managerial and technical	23	46	6	17	6	100
Skilled non-manual	29	40	14	11	6	100
Skilled manual	50	22	19	4	6	100
Semi-skilled manual	38	24	21	9	9	100
Unskilled[a]	51	16	29	3	1	100

Note: [a] Includes armed forces.
Source: Survey data.

Personal characteristics

Social class, defined in terms of usual occupation, reveals some important contrasts. Overall, the 50–64-year-old detached male workforce is
weighted towards manual workers. At 40 per cent of the total, skilled manual workers comprise the largest single group by some margin. Adding in
other manual workers brings the share to two-thirds. Professionals, who
are perhaps most closely associated in the popular mind with generous
occupational pensions and early retirement, account for only 5 per cent
of the total.

But it is the contrasts along the occupational hierarchy that are most
striking. These are illustrated in table 6.3. This shows that the early retired are far more prevalent among white-collar workers. Slightly more
than half of all professionals without full-time jobs, and just under half of
other white-collar workers, put themselves in this category. The comparable proportion for manual workers is below a quarter. Part-time working
is also more prevalent among white-collar workers, especially professionals, suggesting that it may often be an add-on to early retirement.
Long-term sickness is much more prevalent among manual workers.
Unemployment is also more widespread among manual workers, with
a clear progression along the occupational hierarchy. Among unskilled
manual workers, nearly 30 per cent describe themselves as unemployed.
This contrasts with just 2 per cent of professionals.

There is clear evidence here that occupational differences that were
undoubtedly evident when these men were working are perpetuated towards the end of their careers when they have become detached from
full-time employment. These differences are reflected in a number of
financial indicators, described later. They are also reflected in the educational qualifications of these men – nearly half the long-term sick and
half the long-term unemployed say they have no formal educational qualifications or craft apprenticeship. This contrasts with just 30 per cent of
early retirees and 20 per cent of part-time workers who say they lack any
of these qualifications.

The process of detachment

All the men in our survey were either economically inactive or had not
had a regular full-time job for most or all of the last six months. In fact,
the length of time since their last job was usually considerably longer, as
table 6.4 shows. Only 1 per cent of these 50–64-year-old men had never
had a full-time job. But nearly half had not worked full time for at least
five years, and 20 per cent had not worked for ten years or more. For

Table 6.4. *50–64-year-old detached men: length of time since last regular full-time job*

	All respondents (%)	Long-term sick (%)	Early retired (%)	Long-term unemployed (%)	Part-time workers (%)	Other (%)
Less than 2 years	20	14	25	28	23	18
2 years up to 5 years	31	25	40	28	32	25
5 years up to 10 years	28	32	23	25	32	27
10 years or more	20	28	11	19	13	29
Never had one	1	1	0	0	0	2
Total	100	100	100	100	100	100

Source: Survey data.

these men, the degree of labour market detachment therefore appears substantial. To some extent all the main sub-groups share this long-term detachment, but there are important differences as well. In particular, the detachment of the long-term sick is of greater duration – 60 per cent of the long-term sick have not had a regular full-time job for at least five years. In contrast, the duration of early retirement is generally shorter – for two-thirds it is less than five years.

Although it is generally quite a few years since most of these men worked full time they are rarely without substantial work experience. One indicator of this is the length of time in their last job. In 45 per cent of cases this job had lasted at least twenty years. In two-thirds of all cases it had lasted ten years or more. The early retired are particularly likely to have had a long period in their last job – two-thirds had held this job for at least twenty years. Indeed, as we noted in ch. 4, this sort of stable employment with a single employer is often the pre-condition for early entitlement to accumulated pension rights. The long-term unemployed have had a more turbulent employment history – for 40 per cent, their last job had lasted less than five years. Nevertheless, for most of the older men who are now detached from full-time employment, the experience of being without work is clearly unusual. In most cases, a long period of continuous employment appears to have been the previous norm.

Table 6.5 shows the reason for the last job ending. As we have explained in previous chapters, information on the causes of job loss needs to be interpreted with care. Sometimes there is a single clear-cut reason. On other occasions a range of factors of varying importance comes into play, especially when a job is left voluntarily. The survey sought to identify the principal cause of job loss and table 6.5 groups the responses into five broad categories – compulsory severance (where it is the employer that brings the job to an end), voluntary redundancy or retirement, other voluntary severance, illness or injury and other reasons.

The reasons for job loss vary strongly between the sub-groups. Half the long-term sick left because of illness or injury. Two-thirds of the long-term unemployed left because they were laid off. Two-thirds of the early retired took voluntary redundancy or retirement. These differences are predictable. But what is perhaps more significant is that within each group a substantial proportion of men left for other than the 'obvious' reason. Thus nearly one-third of the early retired left for reasons other than voluntary retirement. And nearly half the long-term sick left for reasons other than sickness. Nearly a third of the men who now describe themselves as long-term sick in fact left their last job because they were laid off. These discrepancies are important in interpreting the labour market status of individuals. How they describe themselves now – 'sick',

Table 6.5. *50–64-year-old detached men: principal reason for last full-time job coming to an end*

	All respondents (%)	Long-term sick (%)	Early retired (%)	Long-term unemployed (%)	Part-time workers (%)	Other (%)
Compulsory[a]	34	31	22	65	30	36
Voluntary – redundancy/retirement	35	13	69	15	50	22
Voluntary – own reasons[b]	7	4	3	10	12	26
Ill-health or injury	23	50	6	4	4	9
Other	2	2	0	5	3	7
Total	100	100	100	100	100	100

Notes:
[a] Compulsory redundancy or retirement, dismissal, end of temporary contract.
[b] Includes leaving a job to become a full-time carer.
Source: Survey data.

'retired' and so on – may in fact be a response to their labour market detachment and benefits status rather than a reflection of the processes that detached them in the first place.

Job aspirations

Many of the older men who are detached from the labour market have nevertheless not lost the will to work. All the men in our survey were asked 'Would you like a full-time job?' Among 50–64 year olds, 30 per cent said 'yes'. These included 36 per cent of the long-term sick and 69 per cent of the long-term unemployed. The early retired are more clearly satisfied with their status – just 7 per cent said they would like a full-time job. The response to this question also indicates that for those men who are working part time, this is usually not a second best option: just 18 per cent of part-time workers said they would like a full-time job. However, far fewer men think there is a realistic chance of actually getting a full-time job. Only 5 per cent of all the 50–64-year-old men surveyed said not only that they would like a full-time job but also that there was a realistic chance of getting one. The long-term unemployed were somewhat more hopeful than the long-term sick or the early retired, but even among the unemployed pessimism is the norm – only one in five thought there was a realistic chance of a job.

The proportion of men who say they would like a full-time job is one of those variables that declines sharply with age. This is shown in fig. 6.2. As men move nearer the state pension age of 65 and as age takes its toll on health it is hardly surprising that fewer see any point in wanting work. Moving nearer 65, the men who have been forced out of employment reluctantly are also joined by successive cohorts of men who are retiring early out of choice, thereby shifting the balance. However, the proportion who want work does not appear to fall away continuously between the ages of 50 and 64. For men in their early 50s, the share who would like a full-time job seems steady at just below 50 per cent. There is then a sharp decline, which eventually bottoms out at around 15 per cent of men in their early 60s saying they would like a full-time job.

Wanting work is not same as actually looking for work. All the 50–64-year-old men included in the survey were asked 'After your last job ended did you look for full-time work?' and 'Are you presently looking for full-time work?' Taking the sample as a whole, 32 per cent said they looked for work after their last job ended. By the time of the survey this had fallen to just 12 per cent. The notable exception are the long-term unemployed, among whom the proportion looking for full-time work is consistently high – 75 per cent looked after their last job ended, and

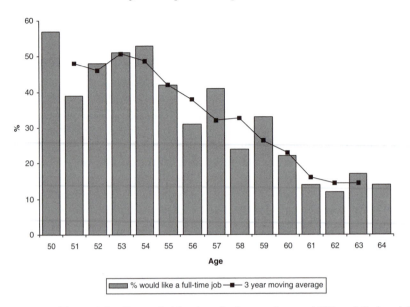

Figure 6.2   Share of older detached men who would like a full-time job
Source: Survey data.

59 per cent were still looking at the time of the survey. This may owe something to the rules governing JSA, the principal form of support for the long-term unemployed, which require claimants to demonstrate that they are looking for work. Nevertheless, even a sizeable minority of the older long-term unemployed do appear to have given up looking for work.

The decline in job search activity by the long-term sick is sharp. Just 1 per cent of the long-term sick said they were now looking for work, compared to 25 per cent at the time their last job ended – and as many as a third saying they would like a job, as we noted earlier. One interpretation could be that individuals' health has deteriorated, making job search increasingly impossible. Alternatively the decline in job-seeking among the long-term sick could be the result of growing disillusion. For the early retired there is a similar sharp decline in job search – 20 per cent said they looked for work after their last job ended, but just 3 per cent were still looking at the time of the survey.

Just as the share of older detached men who would like a job declines with age, so does the share actually looking for work, as fig. 6.3 demonstrates. Around 20 per cent of the men in their early 50s are still looking for work. But this falls away to only around 5 per cent in their early 60s.

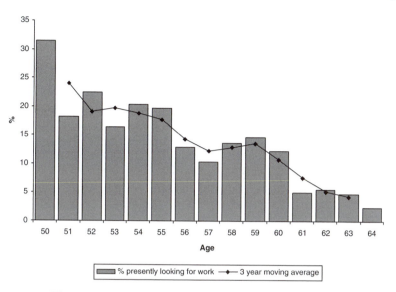

Figure 6.3   Share of older detached men looking for full-time work
Source: Survey data.

The dominant reason given by 60–64-year-old men for not seeking full-time work is ill-health or injury – cited by 54 per cent of men in the survey. The decision to retire was cited in only 30 per cent of cases. One in six men cited 'little chance of a job due to my age'. Given prevailing views about ageism in the labour market this proportion is perhaps surprisingly low but it may well reflect the importance of other factors, notably ill-health and retirement, in motivating men's decisions rather than the absence of widespread ageism.

The role of health

That ill-health or injury is mentioned so often as a reason for not looking for full-time work, and that the long-term sick make up such a large proportion of older detached men, points to the need for further scrutiny of the role of health. Although ill-health or injury was quoted as the principal reason for job loss by fewer than a quarter of the 50–64-year-old men in the survey, in as much as 40 per cent of cases it was identified as a contributory factor in bringing men's last job to an end. At least at the time of job loss the health of many of these men therefore appears to have been poor. Turning to their present state of health, fig. 6.4 shows the men's own assessment. Across the 50–64-year-old group, the share

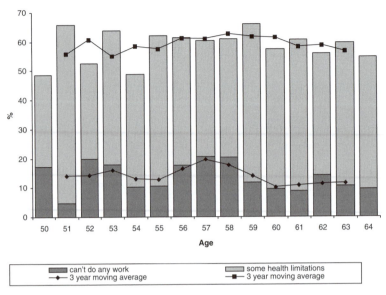

Figure 6.4   Share of older detached men reporting health limitations
on ability to work
Source: Survey data.

of the detached male workforce who report some healthy limitations is
consistently high at all ages – around 60 per cent say that there is some
limitation on the work they can do. A much lower proportion – about 15
per cent – say they cannot do any work at all, and again this proportion
is broadly stable across the whole of the age group.

The stability across the age range of both indicators of ill-health should
not be misinterpreted. Increasing age will, on the whole, be associated
with growing health problems. That much is not in dispute. Figure 6.4
reflects the net effect of two processes. One is the deteriorating health
of some individuals as they grow older. The other is the addition to
the detached male workforce of successive cohorts of men in relatively
good health who leave full-time employment because of retirement. The
63 year olds presently without full-time jobs are not the same men who,
ten years earlier, at 53, were without jobs.

At the level of the individual, health may improve or deteriorate. A proportion of the men who left their last job for reasons other than ill-health
or injury may now face considerable limitations on the work they can
do arising from their deteriorating health. More optimistically, some of
those who left through ill-health or injury may have made at least a partial

recovery. There is evidence that both these processes are at work. Of those who left their last job principally because of ill-health or injury, only 29 per cent now say they cannot do any work, though a further 52 per cent say their health limits them a lot and only 1 per cent report no limitations at all. Conversely, nearly a third of those who were compulsorily laid off now say that they are either limited a lot or cannot do any work.

Financial circumstances

Table 6.6 combines the answers to several questions in the survey in order to show the financial circumstances of detached 50–64-year-old men. The first part of the table deals with their income. The second part deals with their assets and commitments.

The first line shows that paid part-time working is not widespread, except, of course, among self-described part-timers. As we noted in ch. 4, even a small number of these were not engaged in regular part-time work at the time of the survey, presumably because their work was irregular or because they were between jobs. The second line looks at temporary, casual and seasonal paid work. Again, this is not widespread, and is confined to a minority within all the sub-groups. Given the openness of nearly all survey respondents in discussing their financial affairs there is little reason to doubt the answers to these particular questions. The responses certainly suggest that any casual work in the 'black economy' is probably quite limited in scale.

Figure 6.5 rolls part-time, temporary, casual and seasonal work together to look across the 50–64-year age range at the share of detached men who retain a connection with paid employment. Across the age range the proportion is never as high as a quarter, but it also shows little marked trend – the share is roughly 15–20 per cent of men in their early 50s and in their early 60s. There is, however, some evidence of a peak around age 57. Despite the small sample size this may not be spurious. An entirely plausible explanation would be that a sizeable proportion of men who leave full-time work in their early to mid-50s then take employment on a part-time or casual basis before finally settling into retirement. This certainly fits with what can be observed among some early retirees from professional occupations, such as teachers who return to work part time in their old jobs and senior managers who move into occasional consultancy work.

Returning to table 6.6, the third line shows unsurprisingly that it is the men who describe themselves as early retired who are most likely to have income from a pension – 86 per cent, though that still leaves one in seven early retirees who do not have pension income. Of part-time workers

Table 6.6. *Financial circumstances of 50–64-year-old detached men*

	All respondents (%)	Long-term sick (%)	Early retired (%)	Long-term unemployed (%)	Part-time workers (%)	Other (%)
Income						
Regular paid part-time work	13	2	6	4	89	18
Temporary/casual/seasonal paid work	6	1	6	10	24	9
Pension income	57	42	86	32	76	36
Partner in work	28	29	25	24	48	21
Benefits system[a]	63	98	30	74	7	59
Assets/commitments						
Lump-sum redundancy pay	30	19	45	25	40	21
Own home outright	46	32	67	39	53	41
Partner not in work	50	47	57	46	38	64
Dependent children at home[b]	9	10	4	10	10	25

Notes:
[a] Excluding Child Benefit.
[b] Defined here to include all children under 18.
Source: Survey data.

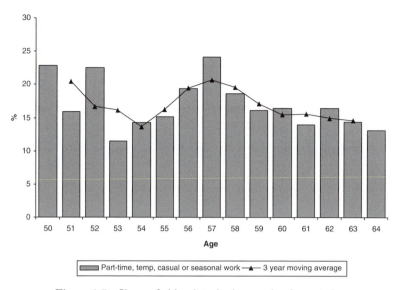

Figure 6.5   Share of older detached men who do part-time, temporary, casual or seasonal paid work
Source: Survey data.

76 per cent, and 42 per cent of the long-term sick, also have income from a pension. Even 32 per cent of the long-term unemployed have pension income.

Receipt of pension income varies by age. This is illustrated in fig. 6.6. The share of detached men with pension income rises as age 65 approaches, but there is also evidence of more than one plateau. For men in their middle and late 50s this is in the 40–50 per cent range. Around age 60 the proportion with a pension rises steeply to a new plateau around 70 per cent. No doubt this reflects the large number of private and company pension schemes which are triggered when a man reaches 60. Nevertheless, even a substantial minority of those aged 63 or 64 do not have income from a pension.

Returning again to table 6.6, the fourth line shows that only a minority of detached 50–64-year-old men – 28 per cent overall – have a partner in work. This is another variable that shows a relationship with age, as fig. 6.7 shows. Among men in their early 50s the proportion with a partner in work is nearly 40 per cent. Among men in their early 60s this proportion falls to around 20 per cent. As with part-time and casual working, the decline with age is not continuous but once more there appears to be a peak at around age 57. The two observations are quite likely to be connected. Part-time workers are the most likely to have a

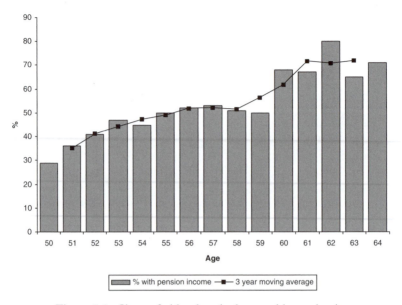

Figure 6.6   Share of older detached men with pension income
Source: Survey data.

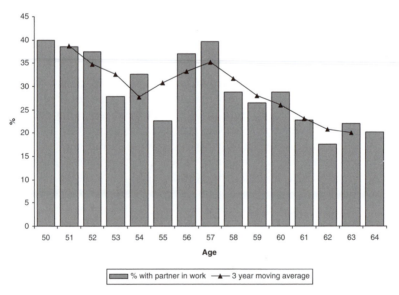

Figure 6.7   Share of older detached men with partner in employment
Source: Survey data.

partner in employment – nearly half are in this position – and part-time working peaks around age 57, as we showed earlier. That so many of these men have a partner in work (rather than a companion at home with whom they can pass their time) may help offer an explanation for their continuing engagement with the labour market.

The final line in the first section of table 6.6 shows the extent of dependency on the benefits system. The most striking feature is that nearly two-thirds of all the older detached male workforce are benefit claimants. This comprehensively demolishes the notion that early withdrawal from the labour market is relatively costless to the Exchequer. Dependence on the benefits system is highest among the long-term sick – 98 per cent of these men are claiming one benefit or another. Nearly three-quarters of the long-term unemployed also draw on the benefits system. Even 30 per cent of the early retired draw on the benefits system to some extent. The only group that make little claim on state benefits are part-time workers.

The first line of the second part of table 6.6 shows the share of men who have lump-sum redundancy money to draw on. In practice, the money referred to here will also often include the capital payments made to men when they first gained access to their pensions – 30 per cent of older detached men say they have lump-sums of this sort. They are most widely available among the early retired and part-time workers.

The next line shows that nearly half the older detached male workforce own their home outright. The proportion is highest among the early retired – two-thirds. A third of the long-term sick are also in this position. In total, only a quarter (26 per cent) of the 50–64-year-old detached men in the survey lived in rented accommodation, nearly all social housing. The long-term sick and the long-term unemployed were the most likely to be in rented property. Less than 10 per cent of the early retired lived in this form of housing.

The final two lines of table 6.6 look at other potentially dependent family members. Half of all the men surveyed had a non-employed partner. This is not simply the converse of those with a partner in work, shown earlier in the table – 22 per cent of detached older men did not have a partner, and 15 per cent lived alone. The proportion with a non-employed partner is high across all the main groups, but lowest among part-time workers. In contrast very few men – just 9 per cent overall – have dependent children living at home. This proportion is somewhat higher among the miscellaneous group of 'other' men, which includes full-time carers and some single parents.

What the aggregate figures do not reveal, however, are the important differences associated with social class. Table 6.7 therefore looks

Table 6.7. *Pension and benefits status by social class (based on occupation) of 50–64-year-old detached men*

	% with pension income	% drawing on state benefits
Professional	88	29
Managerial and technical	75	37
Skilled non-manual	74	49
Skilled manual	48	78
Semi-skilled manual	38	77
Unskilled[a]	25	87

Note: [a] Includes armed forces.
Source: Survey data.

at two key financial indicators for each occupational grouping. The first indicator is the share of men with pension income. This shows a continuous grading by social class — 88 per cent of 50–64-year-old professionals without full-time jobs have income from a pension, but this falls to just 25 per cent of the unskilled. The other financial indicator is the share of men drawing on the benefits system. This rises from 29 per cent of professionals to 87 per cent of unskilled workers. In many respects the two columns are a mirror image of each other. These occupational differences illustrate the very different nature of labour market detachment at different ends of the spectrum. For white-collar workers, detachment from employment is supported by private means; for manual workers it is supported by the state. The two forms of financial support are not mutually exclusive, but the differences are striking.

By far the most widespread benefit is IB — claimed by 43 per cent of all the 50–64-year-old men in our survey. IB is received by a significant minority of the early retired (22 per cent) and even some of the long-term unemployed (12 per cent) as well as the long-term sick, who are the obvious recipients. By comparison, JSA and Income Support were received by just 10 per cent of the older men in the survey. The other main benefits drawn on were means-tested housing-related benefits – Housing Benefit and Council Tax Benefit claimed principally by the long-term unemployed and the long-term sick. Hardly any of the early retired or the part-time workers draw on either of these housing-related benefits.

An assessment

The clear evidence is that the older detached male workforce is united by its separation from regular full-time work but by little else. It comprises a number of distinct sub-groups – the long-term sick, early retired, long-term unemployed and so on. But overlain on these differences there are pointers towards what could be described as two parallel worlds. Both are associated with detachment from the labour market but the meaning of that detachment is quite different.

The first is the middle-class world. This includes most lowly white-collar workers as well as traditionally middle-class professionals. Detachment for this group mostly takes the form of early retirement. On the whole they leave voluntarily from jobs which they have usually held for a very long time, and in doing so begin to draw on accumulated pension rights. They mostly own their home outright and they no longer have dependent children living with them. A sizeable minority maintain contact with the labour market through part-time working. Nearly all no longer want a full-time job, though a small minority do look initially for work before reconciling themselves to retirement. Overall, this group draws little if at all on the benefits system.

The other is the working-class world, which includes just about all manual workers. These men are much more likely to have fallen out of work because of redundancy or ill-health. Some are owner-occupiers, even without a mortgage, but a great many others live in rented housing. Fewer men in this world have income from a pension. Accordingly, they tend to be more dependent on the benefits system, above all on IB. Indeed, it can appear that for working-class men IB functions as the alternative to a pension when meaningful job opportunities for them have come to an end. In the working-class world, many of the men who have become detached would still like a job. But hardly any now think there is a realistic chance of finding one.

It is important to emphasise that the characteristics of the middle- and working-class worlds are not mutually exclusive. There is overlap. Quite large numbers of working-class men do have pension income, for example, although hardly any of the middle-class men are without this. IB is also widely claimed across the social spectrum, even though this is more common among working-class men. In numerical terms, it is the working-class world that is the larger. On the basis of occupational background, the middle-class/working-class split in our survey areas was approximately 40/60, though the precise balance obviously varies from place to place. Middle-class policy-makers need to take note. It is not their world of early retirement and comfortable pensions that predominates among 50–64-year-old men without jobs. A more accurate characterisation would be the manual worker, made compulsorily redundant, with physical limitations on the work he can now do and heavily reliant on the benefits system.

For the early retired white-collar worker there is generally little prospect of labour market re-attachment, since so few express a desire to return to full-time employment. Since most tend not to make a big claim on the benefits system, there is probably little reason for pursuing this objective. These men need policies which help maintain an active lifestyle and promote participation in community life. For a sizeable minority, part-time working seems to act as a bridge between their previous job and retirement. In so far as this keeps them active and makes a useful contribution to society, as well as boosting their income, part-time working of this sort appears welcome and should be encouraged.

The most appropriate intervention with regard to white-collar early retirees may be more about the timing of their retirement. It has to be questioned whether the economy as a whole can afford to lose such large numbers of experienced people at such an early age, especially in places and at times where labour markets are operating close to full capacity, as in the South East of England at the beginning of the new century. For some men in their 50s their old roles may disappear but that is no reason why they should not be redeployed or taken on by other employers. Perhaps ageism in recruitment and retention policies is the obstacle.

There is also a serious question mark against early retirement on the grounds of its cost, though this is usually an issue for pension schemes rather than the Exchequer. So far, the buoyancy of investment returns has usually meant that pension schemes have been able to meet the cost of early retirement without any reduction in benefits to members. There are signs that the limits are being reached, with more private pension funds now moving away from expensive 'final salary' schemes. The cost of early retirement becomes an issue for the taxpayer only in the case of public sector pension funds where deficits have to be made good from general taxation.

For the involuntarily detached manual worker the policy approach needs to be different. Many of these men still want and need jobs. Indeed, since so many make a claim on the benefits system there are very immediate financial reasons for seeking their re-attachment to paid employment. For those who still want work the solution is to create more jobs, including suitable and flexible jobs, especially in the industrial parts of Britain where so many of the traditional jobs for men have disappeared in recent years. These men may also need help to fill the vacancies which become available. This suggests that government initiatives such as the extension of New Deal to cover older workers, and the wider availability of in-work tax credits, are in principle steps in the right direction.

For the large group of mainly manual workers who do not want to return to employment because of declining health quite another policy approach is needed. As our data so clearly show, for these men IB provides the vital bridge between employment and retirement. Both the present and previous governments have sought to ensure that IB is not abused, but access should not become so restrictive as to force these older workers in poor health on to a labour market which has no place for them. For these men, the benefits system needs to reflect the realities of their early retirement.

7   Family, life course and labour market detachment

Sue Yeandle

For much of the twentieth century, all men were expected to work full time, to marry, to provide lifelong financial support for a wife and to maintain their dependent children. Indeed, the British welfare state was built on these expectations about men's lives, widely referred to as the 'male breadwinner model' (Land 1980, Millar 1999). When the present study began in 1997, it was already evident that these assumptions did not reflect reality for a growing segment of the male population (Haskey 1984, Cohen 1987). So far as work was concerned, lifelong full-time employment was no longer possible for many men and, in private life, there was more frequent divorce and repartnering, an increase in living alone and more widespread cohabitation outside marriage.

This chapter explores how men's family circumstances and their stage in the life course interact with their labour market experiences. From our survey data, we can sketch the parameters of how men's family and household circumstances relate to their detachment from the labour market. The follow-up interviews provide fuller information on the personal and household circumstances of a sub-sample of the men, and probe more deeply into the complexities of their situation.

The family and household circumstances of men who are detached from the labour market: evidence from the survey

Two-thirds of our sample of 'detached' men were married, almost a fifth were single and a tenth were divorced or separated. Three-quarters were aged 40 or older, and 70 per cent lived with a partner, yet only one in five was a man living with both a partner and child(ren), the household composition consistent with the male breadwinner ideology referred to above. This chapter uses analysis by household type to assemble a picture of detached men's labour market and family situation. The first part explores their situation by analysing the five types of household in which most of them lived. It then discusses all men who reported having caring

Table 7.1. *Household composition of detached men*[a]

	Number	%
Men living with a partner	1196	70
Of which couples	675	40
Of which dependent families	368	22
Other couple-based households	153	9
Men living without a partner	506	30
Of which living alone	280	16
Of which living with parent(s)	113	7
Of which lone fathers	41	2
Other household compositions	72	4
All men in survey	1702	100

Note: [a] Selected household types only. Definitions are as follows:

Couples: men living with a wife or partner but with no one else in the household.
Dependent families: men living with a wife or partner and with a dependent child or children. In this group, 87 per cent were married, 3 per cent were single, 1 per cent were divorced and 9 per cent were in 'other' categories.

Living alone: of the men living alone, 48 per cent were single, 32 per cent were divorced, 8 per cent were separated, 8 per cent were widowed, 4 per cent were married.

Living with parent(s): men living without a partner and with one or more of their parents.

Lone fathers: men living without a partner and with at least one dependent child. Some of these households may include other adults or children who are not the respondent's own children.

responsibilities (irrespective of household composition), the impact of living with a partner and the effect of age. The second part of the chapter draws on men's own accounts of their family and domestic circumstances to explore aspects of their labour market detachment in greater depth and detail.

The numbers of men living in specified household types are shown in table 7.1 (which gives the definitions used). Figures 7.1 to 7.3 show the differences between the five groups according to their self-described status, occupational social class and the main reason their last job ended. Tables 7.2 to 7.4 give further information on their job search, financial circumstances and attitudes to work.

Couples

About a third of the sample were men living as part of two-person, 'couple' households. Most of these men had held relatively good positions in the labour market at earlier stages in their lives, and they were less likely

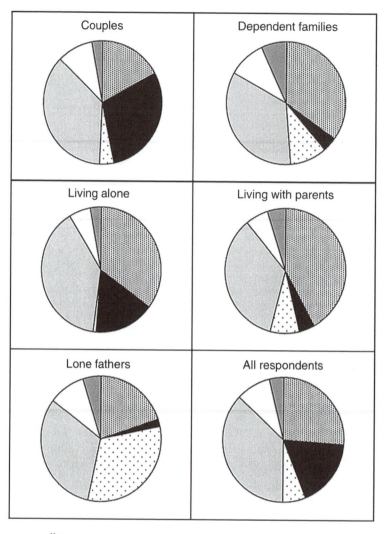

Figure 7.1   Self-described status, by household composition

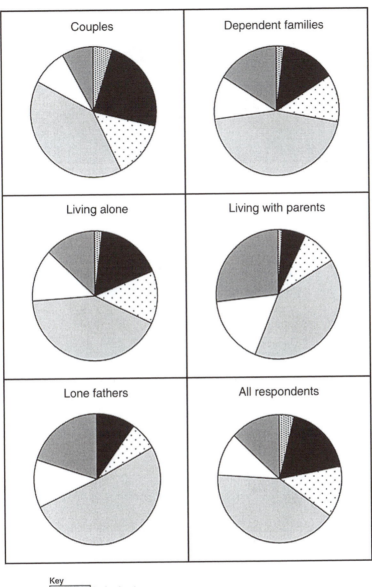

Figure 7.2 Social class based on occupation, by household composition

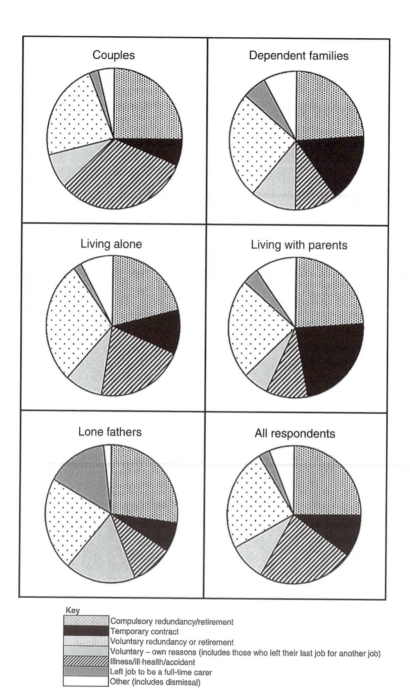

Figure 7.3 Principal reason for last job ending, by household composition

Table 7.2. *Job search, by household composition (%)*

	Looked for full-time work after last job ended	Presently looking for full-time work	Would like a full-time job
Couples	33	15	35
Dependent families	56	39	69
Living alone	49	36	56
Living with parent(s)	59	43	65
Lone fathers	42	22	68
All men in survey	44	26	49

Table 7.3. *Benefits and financial situation by household composition (%)*

	JSA	Income Support	IB	Severe Disablement Allowance	Housing Benefit	None of these benefits[a]	Pension income	Lump-sum redundancy
Couples	9	14	42	5	19	36	53	28
Dependent families	24	30	38	4	48	16	17	8
Living alone	26	19	43	5	47	18	27	12
Living with parent(s)	34	15	31	9	4	13	13	6
Lone fathers	7	66	29	7	68	5	10	2
All men in survey	17	20	39	5	30	26	35	19

Note: [a] Also not receiving Council Tax Benefit or Family Credit at the point of interview.

Table 7.4. *Do you think there is a realistic chance you will ever get a job?*[a]

	Yes (%)	No (%)	Don't know (%)
Couples	29	55	16
Dependent families	46	37	18
Living alone	38	41	21
Living with parent(s)	53	30	17
Lone fathers	41	38	21
All men in survey	38	44	18

Note: [a] This question was only asked of those respondents who responded to the previous question that they wanted a job. The figures are a percentage of this sub-group.

to be unemployed, and more likely to be retired, than other men in the sample. Although just as many had faced compulsory redundancy or retirement, or had left work for health reasons, as in the whole sample, far fewer had left their last job because a temporary contract ended and many more had taken voluntary severance. Only a third had sought other work when their last job ended, and even fewer were still looking. Since most had pension income, and more than a quarter redundancy money, only a small minority were claiming JSA or income support. This group showed a marked degree of labour market detachment related to their age, rather poor health and a relatively fortunate financial situation.

Dependent families

Another large group lived with a partner and dependent children, the classic 'male breadwinner' situation; they might have been expected to be very actively seeking work. Few were 'retired', with many more than the average unemployed or in caring roles. Comparatively few had chosen voluntary severance, while more had last worked on a temporary contract. Half those under 40 were looking for work, compared with only one in six of those aged 50 plus. Most cited health reasons for not seeking work; very few felt they would 'be no better off working'. Among the younger men, domestic roles were also important; almost a quarter were not looking for work because of care responsibilities. Many in this group, then, were in an entrenched and largely involuntary situation of economic inactivity. The high percentage who would like work, however, suggests these men are capable of re-attachment to the labour market in appropriate circumstances.

Men living alone

A number of men (280) lived alone. Three-quarters were aged 40 or older, and although only one had never had a job, almost half had been without regular full-time work for at least five years. Men living alone were more likely than others to be unemployed, or to be long-term sick, and more likely than any other group to have left their last job for health reasons. Many had held their most recent job for five years or more, however, and their orientation to work was relatively strong. They were more likely than the average man in the sample to have looked for work when their last job ended and to still be seeking work, although only a minority of those looking were confident of getting a job. Detached men living alone were often older men who had become involuntarily detached from the labour market following a prolonged spell in employment. Many qualified for sickness-related benefits, and their health was a major barrier to returning to work. Over a third were nevertheless confident of regaining employment, suggesting that this was another group for many of whom re-attachment to the labour market is a potentially achievable objective.

Unattached men living with their parents

Among this category were found some men with very serious problems of labour market detachment. Most were under 40, but a fifth were aged 50 plus. The group had the highest proportion of unemployed men, and, despite its comparative youth, contained almost as many men with health difficulties as the whole sample. Fourteen per cent had never had a job – far more than in other categories – indeed, only 2 per cent of the entire sample, and 8 per cent of all never-married men, had no work experience. Among those who had previously worked, a comparatively high proportion had left their last job when a temporary contract ended. The group was far less likely to have taken voluntary severance, but was just as affected by compulsory redundancy and poor health as the rest of the sample. Over two-thirds of the homes containing single men and their parents were workless households, and in a fifth at least one of the co-resident adults was long-term sick or disabled. Men living with their parents were more likely to receive Severe Disablement Allowance, and twice as likely to receive JSA as all men. However, comparatively few claimed IB. The group showed rather strong orientations to work, with most wanting full-time work, and greater optimism about finding it. Despite this, only two-fifths were actually looking for work, one in six giving caring responsibilities, and three-fifths their health, in explanation. This group thus contained men whose willingness to work was offset by their limited appeal to employers (through lack of work experience and lower skills), health limitations and care responsibilities.

Lone fathers

A few men were lone fathers of dependent children; the numbers here are small and need to be treated with care. Entry routes to lone parenthood varied; most men were divorced or separated, but some were single, married or widowed. Lone fathers were much more likely than other men to be full-time carers, and hardly any were retired. They were a little less likely than the average to be unemployed or long-term sick. About half the lone fathers had been without a regular, full-time job for at least five years, although all had at some time had full-time employment. They were more likely than other men to have left their last job to become full-time carers or for voluntary reasons – excluding voluntary severance, which few had taken. The incidence of compulsory redundancy and ill-health or accident was similar to that for the whole sample. This group was a little less likely than other men to have looked for work when their last job ended, or to be looking when surveyed, although their aspirations to return to work in the future were comparatively very high. More than half lone fathers not looking for work cited their caring responsibilities, while slightly fewer reported poor health or an injury; half said their health limited the work they could do. Lone fathers, then, were a group whose current spell out of the labour force had often been triggered by personal circumstances, including caring for their families. They included a large minority whose own health problems had prompted exit from employment and were making returning to work difficult. In the longer term, however, this group may have relatively good prospects of gaining employment if care responsibilities can be managed and health difficulties overcome.

As a factor in men's detachment from the labour market, caring responsibilities were not exclusively associated with lone fathers. Some men had had past spells of lone parenthood; others had care responsibilities as husbands, sons or fathers. The next section turns to the circumstances of all those men who reported having care responsibilities, irrespective of household composition.

Men who were full-time carers or looking after a family

Ninety-six men identified themselves primarily as having family and caring responsibilities; twenty-two were 'looking after a family or home' and seventy-four were 'full-time carers'. Only thirteen were included in the lone father group described above, indicating that not all lone fathers identify themselves primarily as carers. The majority of the full-time carers, and many of those looking after a family or home, lived in households where no one had a job.

Men 'looking after a family or home' were relatively young (more than half were under 40). Almost half were 'househusbands' – men with dependent child(ren) whose wife or partner was in paid employment; a few were lone parents. Of the rest, some had an employed wife or partner but no dependent children, others a non-employed wife or partner and dependent child(ren). A third had left their last job specifically to become a full-time carer. Many of the others had left employment through redundancy, illness, ill-health or an accident. Three-quarters had not looked for work when their last job ended, and hardly any were now looking for work, although two-fifths hoped to have a full-time job in the future. A quarter felt their health limited the work they could do. Those caring for a home or family thus included many men who were – for a time at least – completely detached from the labour market, with domestic responsibilities a key barrier to work, often compounded by health difficulties.

The 'full-time carers' were an older group – two-fifths were 50 plus. Most were living with a partner who was not in work; quite frequently there were also dependent children in the household. Two-fifths were in 'couple' households where the wife or partner was not in employment and there were no dependent children. Often these were men caring for a sick or disabled wife. About a fifth had no partner but lived with either dependent child(ren) or another adult. Many had left their last job because of care responsibilities, but others had faced compulsory redundancy/retirement, the end of a temporary contract, or health difficulties. Two-thirds had not looked for work when their last job ended, and only one was looking for work when interviewed, although a large minority said they would like a full-time job in the future.

Many men who had adopted caring roles, then, were rather seriously detached from the labour market. Almost all the full-time carers, and half those looking after a family or home, cited their caring responsibilities as a reason why they were not looking for work. Only one of the full-time carers and three of those looking after home and family had regular part-time work (just 4 per cent of all the carers, compared to 13 per cent of the total sample). Some of the difficulties faced by these men are explored more fully in the second part of the chapter.

The effect of living with a partner

Living with a wife or partner might be expected to have a range of effects on men's participation in the labour force. Traditional 'male breadwinner' ideology suggests that men may feel under pressure to provide for a wife, creating strong labour force attachment. By contrast, couples adhering to an egalitarian view of marriage or partnership might, more readily than others, accept that either partner could play the major role in earning income for their family. The British welfare state has an established history of disincentives for wives' employment when men are unemployed (Morris 1990, 1995), and it was argued in ch. 5 that many men are likely to be better off on non-means-tested benefits (such as IB) when their household contains a wife or partner with an income of her own. It was therefore important to explore whether having a co-resident partner was a significant factor.

Table 7.5 shows that men were more likely to be unemployed, and less likely to be retired, if they lived without a partner. However, there were no marked differences relating to other statuses. Similarly, when these groups are compared according to their main reason for leaving work, few differences emerge, although men with partners were more likely to have taken voluntary severance. Analysis of their financial circumstances shows that those without partners were more likely to be receiving JSA, but the figures for IB and Severe Disablement Allowance are very similar. Far fewer men without a partner had pension income, and fewer had redundancy money. Most of these differences relate to the relative youth of those without a partner. Contrary to expectations, logistic regression analysis showed that 'partner in work' was not a significant variable in predicting whether a non-employed man was an IB rather than a JSA claimant (Beatty and Fothergill 1999c: 37).

The above analysis by household living arrangements and responsibilities shows very clearly that detached men are not a homogeneous group. Although many are older men living with a partner, some of them relatively comfortably off (see chs. 6 and 9), substantial minorities are men with dependent children, men living alone and unattached men living with their parents. For a small minority – around one in fourteen – lone parenthood or caring responsibilities were an important aspect of their situation of labour market detachment. Many within these groups would like to return to paid work, but they face some of the most difficult barriers to regaining employment. Some of the complexities of their situation are explored in more depth in the final section of this chapter. Before turning to that discussion, drawing mainly on the in-depth follow-up interviews, we consider men's age and life course in the context of historical labour market trends.

Age, life stage and the life course as factors in labour market experience

As ch. 4 showed, age is a key factor in explaining men's detachment from the labour force. Age is important because both entry to and departure from the labour force are governed by age criteria: young people cannot leave school and start work until they are 16 (earlier, this was 15 for older men), and the statutory retirement age is set at 65. Some occupations have additional minimum age requirements, while others – including the police

Table 7.5. *Men's circumstances by partnership status*

	Men with a wife or partner (%)	Men without a wife or partner (%)	All men in survey (%)
Distribution within sample	70	30	100
Age			
25–39	21	34	25
40–49	15	23	18
50–64	64	42	57
All ages	100	100	100
Self-described status			
Unemployed	22	35	26
Retired	21	11	18
Carer	6	5	6
Long-term sick/disabled	37	38	37
In part-time work	10	7	9
Other	4	4	4
All self-described statuses	100	100	100
Social class based on occupation			
Professional	4	2	4
Managerial/technical	20	13	18
Skilled non-manual	14	12	13
Skilled manual	41	42	41
Semi-skilled manual	10	14	11
Unskilled manual	11	17	13
All occupational categories	100	100	100
Principal reason last job ended			
Compulsory redundancy/retirement	25	22	25
Temporary contract ended	9	11	10
Voluntary redundancy/retirement	24	16	23
Voluntary – own reasons	9	10	9
Illness/ill-health/accident	23	24	24
Left to become full-time carer	3	3	3
Other	6	8	6
All	100	100	100
Job search: % who			
Looked for work after last job ended	41	50	44
Are presently looking for work	23	35	26
Would like a full-time job	46	58	49
Financial circumstances: % with			
Jobseeker's Allowance	13	26	17
Income Support	19	22	20
Incapacity Benefit	40	38	39
Severe Disability Allowance	5	6	5
Housing Benefit	28	35	30
None of the above benefits[a]			26
Pension	41	21	35
Lump-sum redundancy money	23	10	19

Note: [a] Also not receiving Council Tax Benefit or Family Credit at the point of interview.

and the armed forces – have routine retirement with occupational pension at specified ages below 65. As explained in ch. 1, during the 1980s and 1990s many employers offered early retirement packages, available only to workers in specified age groups, as part of workforce restructuring policies.

If we compare the older men (described in detail in ch. 6) with a younger group – those under 40 – a range of differences emerges. Unsurprisingly, a majority of the older men had pension income, compared with just 5 per cent of those aged under 40. A third of older men were 'retired', compared with just 1 per cent of under 40s. Equally predictably, one-third of older men had left their last job through voluntary redundancy or voluntary retirement, compared with only one in twenty of the younger group. Fewer than a third of the older group, compared with almost two-thirds of the under 40s, had looked for another full-time job at this time. Only one in eight of the older men, compared with over half of the younger group, were still seeking employment. Compulsory redundancy had caused one in five of the younger, and one in four of the older men, to leave employment. However, while a fifth of the younger men had been forced to quit their last job because it was an expiring fixed term contract, this applied to only 6 per cent of the 50 plus group.

Age is also strongly associated with life and family stage. The male breadwinner model referred to at the start of this chapter, and key developments in state welfare policy, were predicated upon standardised life stages for men. This standardised pattern began with youthful entry to the labour market, and a labour market attachment phase during which young men did not have parental responsibilities (often continuing to receive daily support from their own parents). Next followed a parental stage of some twenty years or more, during which men sought job security to enable them to support a wife and children in an independent household. After this, a post-parental stage involved planning for departure from the labour force at, or near, statutory retirement age. By the 1990s, more widespread divorce, remarriage and other changes in family structure had disturbed this neat 'fit' between age and life/family stage. Thus minority groups within our sample of detached men included 41 single (never-married) men who were aged 40 or older and were living with their parents, 112 divorced or separated men who were living alone, and 77 men aged 50 or older whose household contained at least one dependent child.

Age also offers a good proxy measure for the historical point of labour market entry. This study strongly supports the argument that the timing of entry to the labour market is a key factor influencing subsequent experiences and labour market attachment. This becomes clear with further comparison of the older and younger groups. For the younger men, entry to the labour market occurred after the early 1970s, when unemployment began to rise rapidly. The older men began work during the 1950s and 1960s when there was, comparatively, full employment for men.

In our sample, four-fifths of the older men had no experience of non-employment prior to starting their last two full-time jobs, and only 1 per cent of this group had never had a job. (Men were asked if there was any spell of non-employment between their most recent job and their last job.) Almost half the older men had held their last job for at least twenty years (four-fifths had been in their last job for at least five years). By contrast, half the under 40s had already experienced spells of non-employment between their last three jobs, and a third had held their most recent job for under a year.

The survey data did not collect full work histories, so we cannot use that source for information about experience of redundancy or unemployment early in men's working lives. The qualitative follow-up interviews were able to generate fuller information. Although we cannot generalise from these data, it is worth noting what emerged. Of the twenty men aged 50 plus who were re-interviewed, only three had experienced redundancy before reaching age 40, compared with eight of the sixteen men aged 25–39. All but two of the younger men had already experienced one or more spells of unemployment, often of several years' duration or longer. In the 50 plus group, by contrast, thirteen of the twenty men had no experience of unemployment at all, or had only ever been without work for a few days.

The younger men in the sample, then, included many who had struggled to maintain a tenuous foothold in the labour market. Employment and welfare agencies had often intervened in support, offering both 'carrots' (training opportunities) and 'sticks' (control over benefit entitlement), but had been unable fully to overcome the 'risks' which poorly qualified, unlucky or unwise labour force participants encounter in negotiating a labour market pathway when they enter the workforce in a period of high unemployment.

By comparison, the older interviewees had had quite standardised labour market entries during the 1950s and 1960s, and over time had been able to exploit their various skills, personal qualities and qualifications to establish themselves and their families. This is not to argue that they had not encountered 'destabilising' factors in their life courses. However, the fact that, at this important early phase, they could establish themselves with relative ease as independent workers, capable of playing a breadwinner role for their families, seems to have affected both their attitudes and their behaviour. It was not in youth, but in middle age, that these older men had encountered the risks and destabilising factors which upset their normative expectations of lifetime employment. In some cases, life had become 'destandardised' as they aged, both in the sphere of marriage and family life and in working life. For some, occupational pension income from their previous employment and/or the fact that their wives were in employment, helped to absorb the shocks they experienced as labour market insecurity and detachment occurred, often in the wake of industrial restructuring. Others, lacking such advantages, had been thrown back on their own personal and financial resources, and on to dependency on welfare state support. These men saw the state benefits they received as well-earned compensations, whether for the failure of the labour market to provide jobs or for their poor health, in some way related to their earlier working life, which made it difficult or impossible for them to continue working, or for other health problems which had affected them or their family. Poor health and disability as barriers to employment are considered in further detail in ch. 8.

Evidence from the in-depth interviews

The final section of this chapter uses data from the qualitative follow-up interviews to gain greater understanding of the circumstances in which men come to be detached from the labour market. (Full information about the qualitative data is given in the appendix.) This material forms an important source for chs. 7 to 10, and can be summarised as depth interview data from follow-up interviews with eighty-seven men who had participated in the survey. The men were drawn from the three urban localities (Barnsley, Chesterfield and Northampton) only. The interviews were used to collect work history information, clarify financial and personal circumstances, explore job search behaviour and attitudes, gather data on health and disability and examine the impact of family responsibilities. The data were characterised by the complexity of the situations encountered. One set of events or experiences followed on another in ways which could not have been predicted, suggesting that attempts to assist detached men back into work need to be personalised and to go beyond helping men upgrade skills or search for work. Many men need the support of other public services, and some face situations where flexible, reduced hours or 'family-friendly' employment may be essential if they are to return to work. This raises important issues about the relationship between earnings and benefits. To open this section, and to illustrate the complex relationship between individual, family, employment and social security circumstances, is 'Steve's story'.

Steve, aged 43

Steve is a divorced lone parent with the care of his 13-year-old son Matt. Matt has recently been excluded from school and needs support and supervision. Steve receives Income Support, Child Benefit, Housing Benefit and full Council Tax Benefit. Until he was made redundant – along with a hundred other workers – in 1991, Steve had worked for most of his life since leaving school. At 16, he took a welding apprenticeship, and then he served in the Royal Navy for ten years. After leaving the Navy he was employed by a number of firms as a plant operator, an engineering instructor and a welder, as well as experiencing two longer periods out of work during the 1980s.

By early 1998, Steve had been without a regular full-time job for more than three years. About a year after being made redundant in 1991, he separated from his wife and moved into separate accommodation. At this stage his two children remained with their mother. After a while, Steve, who had been 'signing on and looking for work', stopped trying to find a job:

I decided I wasn't going to look for work after a while, because of the maintenance [child support] thing. You know, I'd be working for next to nothing. I mean, I didn't disagree with maintenance, but the figure that they kept turning out was ridiculous. I was paying maintenance off me dole – they stopped it out of my Income Support. She never got it – they just took it off mine! If I earned £150, they'd take half of it – and I'm trying to get on my feet! I started off in a bedsit – I hadn't got a thing. If I'd have gone to work, I'd be going for nothing – so I decided, 'no'.

Steve did, however, get the chance of a few unofficial jobs 'on the side', doing general odd jobs and a little security guard work. After a while, his ex-wife found it difficult to look after Matt, and in 1996 Matt moved in with Steve. Although Steve now wanted to return to a regular job, Matt's behaviour made this difficult:

I mean, I want to work. Even now, I'd like to work – but with him being excluded from school, time and time and time again, I couldn't take the risk of taking a job because of them phoning up. I've told Matt before, 'If you were to behave and stay at school, I could go out and get a job.' But I cannot, because of the way his behaviour's been at school. He's been sent home three days now – now he's fully expelled and got to wait for the six weeks' holiday coming up ... There's nothing worse than sitting around at home all day. I've always worked, I'd sooner be out there working, than having to worry about him all day. They keep talking about getting people back to work, you know – single parents back to work. Well, how does a person go on when there's a six weeks' holiday? He's too old for a nursery. So what do you do? I mean, I'm on my own, I don't know anybody round here to help me look after him. I've got to think of all these things – and I haven't got an answer.

Family responsibilities

As Steve's case illustrates, for some men family responsibilities played an important part in their detachment from the labour force. These men were in a variety of different household types, although those living without a wife or partner in good health were perhaps facing the greatest difficulties. Examples included men who had given up work to care for sick wives, to manage their responsibilities as lone parents, or to provide support with child care in large families or where there was a disabled child. Some had struggled in difficult circumstances before reluctantly having to give up work, while others' stories showed that redundancy or unemployment had preceded developments at home which later developed into barriers to work.

For lone fathers, as Steve's case shows, child care responsibilities could be a key barrier to work. Mark was in his mid-30s and lived alone with his two children aged 6 and 8:

I feel it's difficult to see [returning to] full-time employment, with the children so young. I've got to get them up for school in the morning, get their uniforms ready. Wash and iron the clothes and tidy up after them, make meals for them . . . At the moment, it's just looking after the kids on me own, really. Being a single parent. That's the main barrier, really . . . I haven't got any close relatives to help me out . . . So I would have to get a carer, or find work between 9 and 3 . . . There are school holidays to consider as well. Not many firms would be too happy with me taking six weeks off in the summer.

Some lone fathers looked forward to their children completing school as a time when participation in employment might be easier, although they recognised that difficulties could continue. Steve pointed out that this did not solve all problems:

Regarding looking for a job – wouldn't it be smashing if when he leaves school he just walks into a job. Because then, I'm just free. I can just go. But if he hasn't, then I've got to look at what's going to be the situation with him, at that time. Can I still go to work and trust him not to have all his mates round here?

Men caring for a sick or disabled wife explained how their circumstances affected their participation in the labour force. Jack, 54, was a former long-distance lorry driver who had left his job six years ago to care for his wife, diagnosed two years before with multiple sclerosis:

Straightforward really – she couldn't manage, so . . . I had to give up work to look after her . . . It's 24 hours a day, seven days a week, no overtime, no holidays, you know . . . If I take a job, if it's only part-time even, if I only work four hours a day, what's going to happen in the four hours that I'm not here? Plus the fact that I wouldn't gain anything by doing that, I'd probably be worse off.

Barry, 36, had also been forced to give up his job to care for his wife (suffering from severe mental illness) and their two children. When this happened, four years before, he had over fifteen years' service as a milk-man, and at first his job was 'kept open' for him (for four months). Later, he accepted the long-term nature of the situation, and realised he would be unable to return to work in the short term. This led to a range of financial problems and complex negotiations about social security bene-fits. The unpredictability of his wife's condition was still making a return to employment impossible when he was interviewed.

Similar problems could affect the self-employed. John, 55, had ceased trading in 1991 so that he could care for his young son and his wife Anne (suffering from serious psychiatric illness). When Anne first became ill he had kept his business going, with her parents and his stepfather helping out at home. But when his parents-in-law died and his stepfather reached 70,

I was left high and dry . . . I thought, 'What the hell do I do?' So I went to see social services. They said the only thing they could do was take my son into care . . . I tried every possible way to get some sort of help and sympathy and understanding, and I couldn't: it were like talking to a brick wall . . . I thought, 'Well, bugger this – you're struggling to make a living'. . . [wife] is finding it more difficult to cope. There's our [son] to consider. He was by this time about 8 or 9-years-old . . . I've got to do what, I thought, were the right thing.

Care responsibilities could also interact with other health factors. Harry had cared full time for his wife June for six years, until her death a year before the survey. In the past he had worked for long spells, first as a miner on leaving school, and then as a bus driver. He gave up work to care for June after she had a heart attack and was diagnosed with lung cancer, but did not expect this to lead to permanent detachment. Harry's comments show how in such circumstances, and with a long history of previous employment, men may nevertheless come to accept detachment:

When I left to be a carer, I thought, well, 'I'm going back to work' [eventually]. I had a two year spell [of that], before I started degenerating myself, where I felt I could have gone and done a part-time job and still coped. But the doctors said ... 'No, she wants somebody 24 hours a day.' Then, in 1991, [I had] a small heart attack, and then [another] in April 1992, and I was diagnosed as having osteoporosis. I was in enough pain that I went [to the doctor] and he said, 'You've had it. I don't think you'll work any more.' They were his exact words. So, I accepted it.

Men's attitudes to labour market detachment in such circumstances are discussed further in ch. 10.

Men's participation in the labour market could also be affected by responsibility for the care of other relatives. Martin was a 41-year-old single man living with his elderly parents and caring for his mother, disabled for nearly a decade with Parkinson's disease. He had been claiming Invalid Care Allowance for the past three years. This benefit was topped up with Income Support, but was significant for the household because it reduced the pressure Martin felt to look for work. Prior to this, when he was receiving Unemployment Benefits, he explained:

I got hassle from them, like. Getting on your back – if you don't find a job you got so much dole money stopped ... And I thought, 'Well, I'm not having all this aggro.' So I decided to help me Mam ... And I like it. No problem.

Martin's mother indicated that having him care for her was what she preferred:

He's got a job looking after me. I wouldn't want anybody else, to be honest. He knows us, he does all the shopping, cleans up ... If he did get a job, and we had to get a home help in, it wouldn't be any use to us, cos they wouldn't be able to do the jobs that he does.

Other men had become detached from the labour market through a combination of factors including care responsibilities. Colin, 45, had been out of work for fifteen years, and described himself as long-term sick (suffering from severe migraines and kidney problems). He was married, with a much younger wife and five children, including one severely disabled child for whom the family received Disability Living Allowance, and another child suffering from severe eczema. His situation was shaped by a range of factors: his poor basic skills, his own poor health (he had been receiving IB for the past year), his youthful criminal record and his family care responsibilities. Colin explained that, after a period on unemployment benefit, he had been transferred to Income Support shortly after his disabled child was born:

That's to do with the baby – [who]'s handicapped. One of us has to go to hospital, and one of us has to be at home, to look after the kids ... So it got a bit hard. I went to see Dole office – see if I could get a book [because] we've got all these problems. And ... then I've been on that, ever since.

Other men emphasised the extensive care responsibilities they carried as fathers of children with disabilities. For Darren, 30, everything had changed when his youngest child was born with complications including epilepsy and pneumonia, particularly since they had two other children and his wife Marie was epileptic. Marie explained: 'He cannot find a job because he's needed (here). He works (part time, four or five hours a week), just to give some sanity for himself.' Darren commented:

You can't just walk away from kids with special needs – you can't just let them play in a corner on their own. You have to be there with them all the time. You have to watch them 24 hours a day. You have to be their eyes and their ears. Virtually everything you have to do for them. Marie and I work in shifts. You just get on with it, but you need two people. You can't do it on your own. A single parent would go nuts. It's impossible for you to do it on your own.

A changing sexual division of labour

It was not only men in the relatively unusual situation of having severely disabled wives or other relatives, the sole care of children, or a disabled child in the family who were carrying out unpaid domestic work. For some men a male breadwinner and female homemaker arrangement was simply no longer appropriate or desirable, and had been replaced by sharing both paid and unpaid work. Evidence about this came mainly from men living in dependent family households or living as part of a couple without children in the home.

Geoff was 57, married with two teenage children. He had taken an early retirement package from teaching three years before and liked his current situation, working part time, because it enabled him to give domestic support to his wife, who had a full-time job and was no longer in the best of health:

She is the breadwinner at the moment. I don't want to put too much pressure on her. Physically her health is not very good: she can get to work and can work, but when she gets home she is exhausted. Therefore I do need to do as much at home as possible. She was very happy when I said I would give up work and work part time. I used to work mornings 8.30–12.30, then I would be around the house to do the hoovering, the ironing and get the dinner prepared.

Kevin was now divorced and living alone, but explained that he had given up his work in the construction trade when his daughter was born in 1983:

Because [my wife] could earn more than me – basically I became a househusband. That's when we swapped places. She went to work and … I looked after my daughter for approximately four years.

For some, family responsibilities were a permanent part of their lives, with both partners playing a role. Phil, 39, explained that his wife Stella was continuing to work full time although he had recently managed to get back into unskilled factory work. Stella's employers had been 'brilliant', letting her take time off to take and fetch the children from school on the day his job started, but his employers offered only set shifts. He had taken afternoon shift, 2–10 pm, to be able to take the children to school, as he had done while out of work:

We had to ask Stella's mum if she would help us out, otherwise it would have been a no-go. We'd have had to get help with the children fetching them down from school. I've settled in well. It's a low paid job. But with Stella working and me working, it puts it together and it is a little bit better than being on the dole. It opened my eyes – housework is not as easy as people – us men – think it is. You know what I mean? You're at it all day. Those who say you can do housework in an hour are liars – it's not that easy, especially when you've got three children. Now, instead of Stella doing it all, we share it.

Decision-making in the household

Decisions about leaving or re-entering employment were often arrived at following extensive discussion and negotiation between couples. Frank, unemployed and aged 60, commented:

You're always in doubt as to whether you're doing the right thing. Obviously the financial side of it is a worry. You think, 'I can't go out and get a job without coming back and conferring with the wife.' See what she feels about it . . . seeing what's what.

More positively perhaps, Alan, 55, explained 'Everything that's done in my household is a joint decision – my wife tells me what to do! [Laughing]. No, we always discuss everything. We do everything jointly.'

Men stressed that they had consulted their wives before taking critical decisions. After thirty-eight years with the same firm Len, 56, had opted for voluntary redundancy from his job in the steel industry, rather than redeployment to another location:

I rang my wife when [the redundancy package] came about. [She] thought I should not accept the offer of redeployment – and should take the redundancy. Subsequently she has said that she thinks we made the right decision.

This family considered its financial circumstances carefully. Len and his wife Linda are owner-occupiers with no mortgage; their daughter who lives with them works full time. Linda earns £11,500 pa and Len's re-dundancy package produced investments of about £37,000, 'growing at about £5,500 a year', and an occupational pension of £6,000 pa. As Len remarked, 'At the moment, I'm in a position where I can pick and choose.'

Other early retirees had wives who were working part time and felt their situation was 'comfortable'. After years of being the main earner, Bob, now 53, had taken early retirement from the bank where he had always worked. Although they still had a teenage son at home, Bob commented, '(My wife) has said to me that I couldn't do much more for (the family) – I've done all I could.'

Labour market detachment and stress within the family

Family breakdown or difficulties emerged as factors which sometimes led to detachment. Such circumstances imposed stress affecting men's health and also triggered practical problems, which interfered with work or with looking for work.

Peter had been sacked after taking time off during a 'messy' divorce, which ended in his two children going to live with his ex-wife:

I went down to the Unemployment Office to try and claim Unemployment Benefit. I was not eligible for Unemployment Benefit for twenty-six weeks because I'd got sacked, and they asked me if I'd got an illness so I could go on to Sickness Benefit, so I could get a little bit of money. I then went to see my doctor. She realised I was suffering from depression, and after a year, two years, I was then referred to mental health for my depression – I was getting suicidal. Basically I've been on Incapacity Benefit ever since.

By the time of the interview, Peter was living with a new partner and child and felt this diagnosis had become a barrier to employment: 'Well, I'm fit – I'm healthy. I just suffer with depression. There's no major illness or anything that can stop me from working. It's just getting employers to give me a chance.'

Mark, a 37-year-old former miner, had also experienced a painful family breakdown. Following the intervention of the court he now had care of his two children. He described himself as 'looking after a family or home' and as 'unemployed', rather than long-term sick, although he, too, was in receipt of IB:

Things were a bit messy, we were splitting up and there were difficulties with the children. I changed from Unemployment Benefit because I was under the doctor through stress and migraine and things like that – because of the difficulty I had with my ex-girlfriend and children. So I actually came off Unemployment Benefit and went on to Invalidity Benefit, through my doctor.

Another formerly steady worker explained how losing his job had affected his family life. After working in the coal industry most of his life, Ian, 42, had left mining in 1991 following an accident and taken a plastering course which led to building work. This new start faltered when his firm went bankrupt, and when, just after, he was diagnosed as suffering from a degenerative muscle wasting disease and had to give up work. These developments began to affect his mental health and put strain on relationships with his wife, Carol:

Carol was getting on at me – 'You're just sitting around.' But it wasn't registering. I used to sit in the kitchen for five hours – just sit, not move...And next thing I knew, I was in hospital, I just cracked up... I don't think Carol actually understood it...I take approximately 184 tablets a month. For depression, etc. 'Cause you do go down a bit – I mean, my wife'll go out to work, my daughter'll go out to work, my son's at school – and then you're here. With four walls to look at. You know what I mean?

Older men also reported that being out of work led to family problems. After working in the mining industry most of his life, Joe, 60 and with a non-employed wife, had taken voluntary redundancy and worked as a lorry driver until he injured his back in a traffic accident. He now suffered from angina and depression and was receiving IB: 'She'd love me to get a job, to get out of the house. Because it's the first thing that we noticed when I got made redundant – I was invading her space. And she didn't like it.'

Detachment, retirement and 'work ending'

Older men sometimes expressed ambiguity about their status in relation to retirement and the ending of a long phase of their life in which they had expected to work full time. It was striking that some men, despite having a pension or going through a formal 'early retirement' process, did not describe themselves as 'retired'. By contrast, others whose poor health made managing a full-time job impossible, and who might have been expected to emphasise the role of disability or illness in their situation, preferred to see themselves as 'retired' rather than 'sick'. Employment status is intimately bound up with male identity, and consequently this ambiguity may be unsurprising. It nevertheless contributes to the difficulty of measuring unemployment and other aspects of detachment when compiling official statistics. The situation was both experienced and described as complex and continually changing.

Fred, 59, had 'retired' from his work as a self-employed fitter. He had pension income of £400 per month, and also received IB. He remarked:

I prefer to see myself as sick, to be honest . . . What really upsets me, two friends of ours have retired, and from the day they've retired, they've become old people . . . I don't want to think of myself as in that kind of category. Maybe I should, I don't know. I would rather think there's hope.

Concluding remarks

Labour market detachment, then, was often a gradual and complex process over which men had little personal influence, and in which labour market, health and family factors all played their part. Traditionally, men's role as breadwinners for their families has been seen as important in establishing their attachment to the labour market. Even in periods of 'full employment', young unmarried men changed jobs frequently and had short periods of unemployment. Marriage, and especially the responsibilities of parenthood, tended to strengthen attachment to jobs, with being a reliable worker a key feature of adult masculine identity (Allatt and Yeandle 1992).

In this research, a minority of men cited family or care responsibilities as reasons for not seeking work, and the evidence from the qualitative interviews shows that while breadwinning remains important in men's family role, family responsibilities can lead to detachment. In 1997, when our research began, there were 179,000 lone fathers in Great Britain. Their full-time employment rate stood at 40 per cent for those with a child under five, 56 per cent for those with a child aged 10–15 and 42 per cent for those with a child aged 16–18. The gap between these rates and those for married fathers was around 40 percentage points (Holtermann, quoted Dex 1999). While 'family-friendly' employment practices are slowly increasing, there remains a gap between policy and implementation and wide variation between employment sectors. Employers also tend to expect workers requiring flexible working conditions to be women. This means that men with care responsibilities may face particular difficulties in managing to remain in employment when they take on onerous care duties.

The examples given here show how fragile some men's connection to the labour market may be. Men who experience relationship breakdown, widowerhood and sickness or disability within the household appear to be especially vulnerable to detachment. Such men need employers to be responsive to their circumstances just as much as women, and this area of policy, to which new attention is being given at both European and national level, needs development. It will never be possible to maintain labour market attachment in all circumstances. Nevertheless, attention needs to be given to how those who need to withdraw from employment for a spell, to care for a terminally ill wife or to readjust to a change in family circumstances, can be helped to regain employment when their situation eases. Possible responses might include measures to enhance their employability, such as better access to flexible respite facilities, improved support services for carers, and the introduction of 'carer's breaks' from employment as an alternative to detachment. The needs of lone fathers also need to be recognised: provisions introduced via the Employment Relations Act 1999 may help, but far more support and employment protection will be needed by those with demanding responsibilities for dependent children.

The complexity of individuals' circumstances has been one of the most striking findings of this analysis. We can observe that the initial trigger which leads to labour market exit is often different from the circumstance which prevents labour market re-entry. Few detached men can attribute their situation to a single cause: rather it is the interaction of family situation, health, labour market conditions and welfare benefit arrangements that determines outcomes – and which must determine policy response if detachment is not to become entrenched and permanent.

A final concern relates to how younger men, who entered the labour market during difficult times, will approach their own later life, from beginnings so different from those of older men. Younger men's expectations of marriage, work and the welfare state will inevitably be shaped by their experiences at the point of labour market entry and by the difficulties they have faced. Many older men, with long decades of employment security in their past, have been able to leave the labour market feeling that they have 'done their bit' in terms of labour market participation, and that the pensions, redundancy payments and welfare benefits they receive have been 'earned'. Younger men, with less security of employment in their 30s and 40s, may be unable to acquire either the pension or the redundancy entitlements which have cushioned the labour market exit of older men. The destandardisation of retirement, of family structures and of working life as a whole presents a complexity of social risks and differentiated needs which defy simple welfare solutions. We return to some of these issues again later in the final chapter of this book.

8 The role of health in labour market detachment

Sue Yeandle and Rob Macmillan

Earlier chapters have already described some of the ways in which men's labour market behaviour has altered in recent decades in response to a variety of changes in the occupational and industrial structure, family roles, access to welfare, pensions and education and new forms of work organisation. We have seen that for many men, especially, but not exclusively, those in the older age groups described in detail in ch. 6, detachment from the labour force has arisen through redundancy, early retirement or ill-health. Throughout the book, we have been exploring what 'detachment from the labour market' means. Chapter 1 outlined issues about measuring unemployment, noting that in the past standardised patterns of male employment partly disguised the measurement problems which are now so evident. Chapter 5 considered the extent to which men who would prefer to be working have disappeared from unemployment statistics because they have been recorded as economically inactive. Most commonly they have instead been defined as incapacitated (because they are claimants of IB) or as early retired (in some cases claiming no state benefits at all).

This chapter focuses specifically on the relationship between health and labour force detachment. It opens with discussion of some possible reasons for the increased claiming of sickness and disability benefits in recent decades. By 1999, when we conducted our last interviews, around 1.3 million men had been claiming Sickness Benefit or IB for six months or more, and 463,000 men gave 'long-term sickness' as their reason for not looking for work in the previous four weeks (1999 Labour Force Survey, spring). The second part of the chapter, which draws on both the survey data and the follow-up interviews, then looks at how men's own health difficulties have contributed to detachment and continue to make re-entry to employment difficult or impossible.

Ill-health and disability as a factor in men's labour market detachment

That ill-health and disability are important issues in contemporary policy debate about labour market detachment is hardly surprising given the rapid rise in the number of men claiming sickness-related benefits during the 1980s and 1990s. This increase was discussed in ch. 5, and has been the subject of a range of studies (Beatty and Fothergill 1996, Gregg and Wadsworth 1998, Walker and Howard 2000). After 1997, the incoming Labour government quickly set 'reduction in spending on Incapacity Benefit' as a key target guiding its welfare reforms (DSS 1998a: 83). In 1999 it responded to the level of claims for sickness and disability benefits by enacting controversial changes to the law governing access to IB in the face of strong opposition in both Houses of Parliament, and further proposals relating to this benefit were announced shortly after the June 2001 general election (Hansard, 4 July 2001: col. 859).

In theory, there are at least four sets of possible factors underlying increased claiming of sickness and disability benefits. These can be summarised as: (1) actual increases in the numbers of men who are sick or disabled; (2) changes in the rules governing access to sickness/disability benefits; (3) inappropriate or fraudulent claiming by men who are not in employment for other reasons, but who are erroneously placed on sickness/disability benefits by an inefficient or flawed system for processing claims; (4) benefit claims by men whose poor health has previously been concealed – either by their employer's willingness to 'carry' workers unable to perform to their full potential when fully fit and healthy, or by their own reluctance to recognise their health difficulties.

More sickness?

The first explanation is frequently dismissed out of hand as implausible given rising expenditure on health, improvements in health care and related technology, and increased longevity. However, 'the number of people of working age in Great Britain reporting a health problem or disability has increased by about 4 per cent a year since 1984' (Cousins, Jenkins and Laux 1998: 321), in part reflecting 'changing awareness' of disability. Furthermore, ill-health and disability are unequally distributed across the population, with huge regional, social class and age variations (Sly, Thair and Risdon 1999), and life expectancy among disabled people has increased (DSS 1998a: 14).

The proportion of UK men of working age who are disabled (i.e. have a current long-term disability covered by the Disability Discrimination Act or a work-limiting disability or both) varies both by age and by region (nationally, 32 per cent of men aged 55–59 compared with 10 per cent of men aged 25–29, and 24 per cent of people in South Yorkshire, compared with 15 per cent in the South East). The 1999 Labour Force Survey showed an ILO unemployment rate among people with disabilities of 11 per cent (compared with 6 per cent for people without disabilities). This figure disguised quite large regional variations, from 16 per cent in the North East, to 7 per cent in the South East. The Labour Force Survey 1999 also revealed a 33-point gap between the economic activity rates of disabled and non-disabled people in the UK. This gap stretched to over 40 points in the North East, North West, Wales and Northern Ireland, but narrowed to under 25 points in the South East and the South West.

It is also possible that new sources of ill-health and disability (including new sources of stress contributing to mental ill-health) have developed, or that some ill-health is a consequence of some other factor, such as unemployment or redundancy. A key issue here concerns who defines when a given person can appropriately be labelled 'sick' or 'disabled', and in what context. It is clear that there is no single definition, which is stable across time and culture.

Different rules?

The second explanation recognises that the way in which qualifying criteria are defined necessarily shapes the number of sickness and disability benefit claimants. During the 1990s such rules were in fact tightened, rather than loosened, making it more rather than less difficult to make a successful claim (Walker and Howard 2000: 115). Reducing the number of disability benefits claimants was a specific aim of the (Conservative) government in the mid-1990s. In April 1995, a new medical test governing access to sickness benefits was introduced, and claimants became subject to an assessment process independent of their own family doctor, which was periodically reviewed. (The 'All Work Test' and related arrangements were introduced at this time. The frequency of reviews was at the discretion of Benefits Agency staff and normally took into account the likely prognosis for the claimant's condition. In April 2000 the 'All Work Test' was replaced by the personal capability assessment (DSS 2000d)). As already noted in ch. 5, the numbers of male IB claimants of working age stabilised between 1996 and 1998, after a period of rapid increase in the early 1990s. It is likely that this can be at least partly attributed to the new test, although the government itself argued that the All Work Test had some 'perverse effects' (DSS 1998a: 12). It has been shown that the replacement of IVB with IB in 1995 had a greater impact on on-flows to the benefit than on off-flows from it (Berthoud 1998).

Inappropriate claiming?

This third explanation is related to, but different from, the previous one. It is sometimes suggested that some unemployed or inactive men claim to have health problems when they do not, or claim to be affected by their health problems more severely, or for longer periods, than is in fact the case. Particular attention has focused on localities affected by persistent high unemployment. In these areas, it has been suggested, discretion in the system of allocating people to benefits has been used to place some men on non-means-tested (and higher rate) benefits, rather than on Income Support/JSA (Ritchie, Ward and Duldig 1993, White and Lakey 1992, BBC Television 1998, *Observer*, 22 July 2001). There is, indeed, some evidence of this happening in the past, with the government itself stating that 'Incapacity Benefit has proved a simple but costly escape route for government to keep the unemployment figures down' (DSS 1998a: 54). However, the tightening up of rules governing access to sickness benefits, particularly IB, would seem to have reduced the scope for this to occur from the mid-1990s onwards. The inherent complexities of implementing policy in this area are obvious. The administration of any benefits system is likely to contain inefficiencies. These could include genuine mistakes, systematic errors or inappropriate use of discretion by administrators, and flaws in the design of the system which create inappropriate opportunities for claiming or have unintended consequences (Benefit Fraud Inspectorate 1999). Recent changes to the law, and official statements (DSS 1998a, 1998b), imply that the government considers design flaws to be one source of the problem of rising claims.

Hidden sickness?

Finally, there is the 'hidden sickness' explanation, outlined in some detail in ch. 5. Employers' acceptance of 'hidden sickness' may arise for a variety of reasons, including paternalism, collective agreements, a culture of providing employment until retirement or a period of high profitability. In traditionally male industries such as coalmining, construction and heavy engineering, as workers aged they were frequently taken off duties requiring strength and stamina, and placed in less demanding roles. Thus the coalface worker might in his 50s be al-located to surface work, or possibly unskilled work in offices or sup-port departments. Part of the importance of this explanation lies in the pressures which, over recent decades, have eroded such practices, particularly those pressures which have involved achieving greater busi-ness efficiency, including 'downsizing' operations. Some argue that some recent policy measures, for example good practice advice given to em-ployers relating to ageism (DfEE 1999), the Disability Discrimination Act 1995 and the EU directive on parental leave, seek to counter such pressures.

In addition, social and individual responses to disability and poor health have changed significantly over the past forty or so years. Walker and Howard (2000) have recently summarised many of the social and ideo-logical changes affecting policy on disability. There is also the question of changes in male identity. Studies of masculinity have emphasised that heavy manual labour, in which male workers have historically been con-centrated,

calls for strength, endurance, a degree of insensitivity and toughness . . . [W]orking men's bodily capacities *are* their economic asset, are what they put on the labour market. Industrial labour . . . uses up the workers' bodies, through fatigue, injury and mechanical wear and tear. (Connell 1995: 55)

In the past, this situation led to a strong connection between phys-ical fitness, resistance to bodily weakness and masculine identity. Men frequently responded to poor health or physical limitations with denial. As the link between physical strength and a man's value on the labour market has declined, however, men's willingness to 'admit to' frailties has increased. It seems entirely plausible that this is another factor in the trend towards rising levels of male sickness and disability.

In emphasising that the statistics on sickness and disability conceal 'hidden unemployment', ch. 5 has already stressed that the behaviour of the men counted in these figures is not fraudulent. Indeed, our detailed research interviews found nothing to contradict Walker and Howard's assertion (2000: 121) that there is no evidence for 'a deliberate choice by individuals to positively choose a life on benefit'. The 'hidden unemploy-ment' thesis, for which this study offers important confirmation, calls for much more effort to be put into the creation of employment opportuni-ties in areas where job losses have been concentrated. But there remains a further important policy concern. With so many men experiencing health problems, what can be learned in this situation about the causes of their poor health, and about the barriers which prevent them from returning to employment?

To explore incidences of sickness-related forms of labour force detachment, both the survey results and the qualitative data have been examined. The evidence presented in this chapter shows that health-related problems are indeed widespread among inactive and unemployed men. When
added to the impact which poor health or disability within men's families
can also have (as discussed in ch. 7), health factors thus play a key role in
labour force detachment. Some of men's own poor health can be linked
to their previous jobs (highlighting the continuing need for attention to
poor working conditions). Poor health or disability has demonstrably led
a large group of men to withdraw from the labour force. In addition,
sick or disabled men believe they face exclusion from the labour market,
and that they are at a serious disadvantage if they attempt to re-enter it.
Finally, some men blame redundancy, unemployment and their consequences for damage to their health.

The rest of this chapter focuses on three aspects of the relationship
between health and labour force detachment: health problems related to
occupation, non-occupational health and disability and mental health.
Some of these categories, along with the role of family responsibilities,
discussed in ch. 7, overlap. To set the scene, the next section briefly reviews the relevant evidence from our survey of detached men.

Survey data on the role of health in labour market detachment

Men who described themselves as 'long-term sick or disabled' formed
the largest single group among our respondents, itself suggesting an important relationship between health problems and economic inactivity
(table 4.3). Our survey also explored the part played by poor health,
disability and accidents in the processes through which men had become
detached from the labour force. Table 8.1 summarises the extent to which
men reported health or injury as either the principal reason, or a contributory factor, in their leaving the labour market. As would be expected, men
who described themselves as long-term sick or disabled gave this explanation much more frequently than other groups, more than half saying it
was the principal reason for their last job ending, and three-quarters citing
it as a factor. While other men were far less likely to cite health as a factor
in their quitting the labour force, nevertheless, over a quarter of 'retired'
men gave health as a contributory factor, and around one in seven of men
in other groups. Overall, nearly 40 per cent of all detached men said that
illness, ill-health or an accident had been a factor in their last job ending.

About three-quarters of our survey respondents (1,253 men) said they
were not looking for work. Table 4.11 has already shown the reasons they
gave, broken down by their own definition of their current status. Overall,

Table 8.1. *The role of illness, ill-health and accidents in departure from the labour market*[a]

	Long-term sick/disabled	Unemployed	Retired	Part-time employed	Full-time carers	All respondents
Number of men in self-defined category	604	425	308	151	73	1,648
% citing illness, ill-health or accident as the principal reason for their last job ending	52	9	7	4	6	24
% citing illness, ill-health or accident as a factor in their last job ending	73	15	27	13	15	39

Note: [a] Columns should not be added as these were asked as separate questions.

58 per cent of men gave ill-health or injury as a reason why they were not seeking a job; this included almost all the 'long-term sick or disabled' (96 per cent), almost half the 'unemployed' (47 per cent) and a quarter of the 'early retired'. Some fifteen years previously, White's study also reported widespread health problems among, in his case, long-term unemployed men: 69 per cent reported chronic health problems, and 19 per cent were registered disabled (White 1983: 215–16). Writing about the situation in the early 1980s, White conjectured,

A lot of older manual workers will inevitably be troubled by ill health and feel incapable of continuing with jobs which they have coped with previously for many years. The question is: why do such workers *now become long-term unemployed*, when in the past many of them must have been retained in the labour force? The most plausible general explanation [is] that, in a period of business recession when employers seek means of rationalising their workforce, many of the relatively marginal ancillary jobs may be pruned. These may be just the type of 'light' or less stressful work which the worker in declining health would hope to get. If it is true that such jobs have been disappearing, that could account for many people appearing among the long-term unemployed, who would previously have been able to continue in work in some capacity. (White 1983: 87–8)

White's focus, at that time, on the need to explain sickness among the unemployed makes an interesting comparison with this study's exploration of hidden unemployment among men who are economically inactive on grounds of sickness or disability. It reinforces the point that we are dealing here with a very 'fuzzy' boundary between statuses.

As expected, almost all the 'long-term sick or disabled' men in our survey felt that their health prevented them from doing any work or limited the work they could do (97 per cent) (table 4.12). A large minority of the other men also said health limited them in this way – 29 per cent of the 'unemployed', 39 per cent of the 'retired', 23 per cent of those working part time and 31 per cent of the full-time carers. Overall, 55 per cent of all the men surveyed said health limited the work they could do, or prevented them from working. Of these men, about half the 'unemployed' and 'part-time employed' were restricted by their health 'a lot' or 'quite a bit', while the comparable figure was 68 per cent for 'full-time carers' and 72 per cent for the 'early retired'.

The survey thus showed that health factors played an important, but uneven, role in men's labour force detachment. We move on now to explore qualitative data from our study, which gives further insight into the processes involved.

Understanding the role of health factors in labour market detachment

As already explained in ch. 7, the follow-up interviews provided an opportunity to explore some of the complexity of men's experiences. We encountered many men who believed their health problems were linked in some way to their previous occupations, some with serious and disabling chronic complaints and diseases, and some suffering from mental ill-health. All those claiming sickness and incapacity benefits described a health problem, often serious in nature. Some expressed the hope that they would recover and return to employment in the future, although others could see no prospect of recovery. A few men had received sickness-related benefits in the past but were now unemployed, or in other economic inactivity statuses, and a few had managed to return to work. Table 8.2 summarises the health difficulties reported by the men included in the follow-up interviews.

It was evident that occupational illness and injury had played an important role in labour force detachment. Other studies which have explored health and safety at work have shown that non-fatal major injury rates vary according to industrial sector, with rates in construction, for example, more than three times those in all industries (Health and Safety Executive 2000). When describing their own situation, our respondents frequently referred to either chronic or acute complaints, and in some cases disablement, which they attributed to their previous working conditions or to incidents which had occurred at work.

Table 8.2. *The variety of health difficulties reported (men in follow-up sample only)*

Age	Occupational injuries/disease	Non-occupational ill-health	Non-work injuries	Mental health problems
25–44	Attacked at work Back injury Knuckle injury Pit accident Severed finger Slipped disc Stress Wrist injury	Brain tumour Cerebral abcess Epilepsy Muscle-wasting disease Stomach surgery	Car accident Motorcycle accident	Anxiety Breakdowns Depression Hyperactivity
45–54	Back injury Bronchial asthma Car accident COAD[b] Fractures Hearing loss Industrial asthma Knee injury Motorcycle accident Spinal injury Stabbing Vibration white finger	Angina Deafness Diabetes Eye disease Glaucoma Heart bypass High blood pressure Kidney/stomach disorders Osteoarthritis Rheumatoid arthritis Sciatica Spinal narrowing Ulcers	Broken spine Car accident Damaged Achilles tendon Motorcycle accident	Depression Drifting/disappeared (5 years)
55–64	Back injury	Arthritis	Car accident	Depression

Table 8.2. (cont.)

Age	Occupational injuries/disease	Non-occupational ill-health	Non-work injuries	Mental health problems
	Knee injuries	Cancer	Childhood polio	Stress
	Mining accident injuries	Heart disease		
		High blood pressure		
		Osteoporosis (spine)		
		Partial sight		
		Stroke		

Notes:

[a] Some of the above conditions were reported by more than one man. Some men reported more than one condition. Men were not selected for follow-up interview exclusively on the basis of their health (see appendix). The numbers of men in each of the age groups were:

25–44 yrs: 28 men – of these, 8 described themselves as long-term sick or disabled;
45–54 yrs: 31 men – of these, 15 described themselves as long-term sick or disabled;
55–64 yrs: 28 men – of these, 8 described themselves as long-term sick or disabled.

[b] Chronic obstructed airway disease.

We found cases where ill-health had arisen from working conditions, workplace accidents and dangerous or physically demanding work. Some men had suffered attacks at work or had been injured in a violent situation (e.g. police officers, security guards). Others had contracted industrial diseases. A number had sustained accidental injuries while working (e.g. vehicle accidents while driving on work duties, accidents on building sites or involving machinery and falls). Finally, some men had health problems linked to generally debilitating working conditions (e.g. back problems, some types of arthritis, knee and shoulder complaints, heart disease and stress-related mental health problems). As the accounts given below show, some of the working practices described had contributed to ill-health, and some working conditions had been very physically demanding.

Alf, 50, was still attempting to keep a foothold in the labour market despite having very poor health. At the time of our survey he was receiving IB, but when re-interviewed a few months later he had gone back to fixed term contract shift work at a large industrial plant, on light duties (describing himself as a 'tea-boy'). Over the years Alf had worked in a range of jobs, in factories, workshops and, for most of the past twenty years, in opencast mining. He had numerous health problems (spinal deterioration, rheumatoid and osteoarthritis affecting his feet, knees, hips, hands, shoulders, neck and spine), and suffered considerable pain. His doctor had advised him to refrain from work entirely because of his health, but, as a single man living alone, Alf was worried about the financial consequences of not working. He attributed his health problems, at least in part, to his past working conditions:

I think health-wise it's contributed – working on opencast [mines] – to the condition I'm in now. Working outside all the time – even wearing waterproof outfits – you sweat a lot. Even when I worked at [the chicken factory], when I used to hang birds on the line – the chains were wet, therefore it runs down your arms and on your shoulders. And then, moving to foreman, inside, it was my job, over the top of this deep tank – 200°, and steam off it – hooking the birds out and making sure the birds that kept dropping off the shackles weren't blocking it up. And in a certain period of time, I lost so many stone in weight. I was absolutely gone down the nick with losing weight through steam.

Stan, aged 54, was receiving IB at the time of the survey and had not worked for over five years. For about ten years he had suffered from back pain, which he attributed to 'heavy lifting' in his previous jobs as a labourer: 'I've had that a long time now, that back. The building trade – it's covered with blokes with bad back problems.' His doctor had once asked Stan if he was lifting 'properly' and showed him how to lift with a straight back. Stan commented, 'You'd look a right pillock, doing that.' Three weeks prior to his follow-up interview, Stan had nevertheless returned to work, delivering parcels, via an employment agency. He explained that while most employers required medical tests before taking on new employees – tests he knew he would 'fail' – employment agencies 'rarely ask' for such tests. In consultation with his 34-year-old wife (suffering from cancer 'in remission'), he had decided he should try to 'get out of a rut' to earn a 'bit extra for the kids' (three children, all at school). Looking back, Stan recalled how he had come to transfer to sickness benefits some years ago during a period of unemployment:

I was getting that much hassle. So I cut that out – I went on the sick. I told them down there, 'I don't have to be signing on here, I can go on the sick', which I can – I mean, I have genuine complaints. With my back, I've had x-rays and everything. They know my back's genuine. It got rid of the hassle, anyway. It got rid of the running down and bloody signing on every week. It got rid of me always having to tell lies all the time. All these jobs I've not been trying to get! Selling me soul to hell!

Stan's recent return to work was proving difficult. He was concerned about the temporary and insecure nature of his work, and was worried about his health:

I know it is draining me. I'm doing work, which is nothing to me, but it is draining me. I've always been used to heavy work – very heavy work. This job I'm on now, it's taking it out of me, I know that. I'm on my feet too long. You're rushing. It's speedy work. You're rushing about with parcels and on these barrows. There's nothing heavy about it, it's just you're in a rush. And I'm drained at the end of the eight hours. I can feel it. It's affecting my health.

Bill, who lives alone, is an ex-miner who last worked in 1992. In the past, Bill, now 51, has had several spells receiving IVB and when interviewed was receiving IB. His rather complex benefits history included failing a medical test and subsequent appeal for IVB in 1994, and then a spell on Unemployment Benefit. This was followed by several years during which Bill cared for his terminally ill elderly mother and received Invalid Care Allowance.

Bill's own health became a problem in 1992 when pain in his neck caused difficulty in turning his head. After some time off sick, an x-ray indicated that he was suffering from 'degenerative arthritis in the neck'. Bill was told:

not to do any more shovelling or lifting. So that was it. What manual work would I do where I haven't to do any shovelling or lifting? There wasn't a single job round here that I was capable of doing, or qualified to do, so what could I do? That was it. I knew I had to look for one, but basically it was just a waste of time. I did [look], but none came up. And no other training was offered. As I say, I'm not qualified for a thing. Left school stupid!

British Coal had agreed to 'finish' Bill on health grounds in 1992, at which point he had gone directly 'on to sick'. After about eighteen months he was 'thrown off' and required to sign on. Subsequently he had been diagnosed diabetic (1997) and as suffering from vibration white finger. In his most recent spell on IB he had been medically tested several times, but had been allowed to continue on the benefit.

Bill now saw his health as a serious barrier to future employment:

Who will employ me when I explain what is wrong with me? As I say, the arthritis, white finger, bad circulation, high blood pressure, diabetes. Who will set me on? Nobody. They may say, 'Oh, we'll set you on. Oh, we know you've got problems, but we'll set you on.' But – I start work. Three months later, neck starts, and I'm off work for three months. Are they going to keep me? No – they're going to sack me. They'll get rid of me. Nobody would set me on. That's the problem now.

This aspect of his situation was compounded by other factors. Since Bill was made redundant from one of the last pits to close in his region, he had joined the unemployment 'queue' at a time when many others were also looking for work – 'capable, fit men', as Bill put it:

I've never had any other job except as a miner. I'm not trained for anything. The only thing you're fit for when you've been in the mines so long is labouring jobs – and the conditions I've got, that rules them out completely. Now, what other jobs is there available for somebody who's only qualified for a labourer, who can't do labouring jobs? There is none.

Bill's frustration with his experiences was summed up in his comments on employment and social policy over the previous decade. In his view, the Conservative government's attitude had been:

Put 'em on the sick, and then they're not counted as unemployed. Now [Labour] are going to try and do it the other way. Get 'em off the sick. They don't want them on the sick and incapacity, yet they don't want them on unemployment. What do they do with them? There's no jobs available!

Howard was a former police officer who had sustained back injuries on police duties and, linked to this, had suffered a pulmonary embolism. He was 'pensioned out' of the force in 1986, at which time a criminal injuries compensation case, still unresolved in 1998, was started. Howard had been through a variety of tests and appeals associated with his police pension and industrial injuries compensation claim. He explained, 'The surgeons said . . . this was never going to get any better – it's a lifetime thing. Then I got a letter from DSS . . . and they said, they accepted now that I was unemployable.' Howard had tried to work again, setting up briefly as a hotelier with his wife, but found his poor health prevented him from coping with the duties involved. There were days when he was capable of some work, but on many days, he knew he was not. He considered that his work injury had robbed him of his career. Consequently, he felt, 'I mean, I've worked all my life. I was doing a job I enjoyed. I was injured on that job. I lost a job which was really, really good money. Good money. And it would have been even better now. I think the government should pay.'

Not all of the ill-health reported in the interviews was linked to occupation. Among men of all ages, as shown in table 8.2, a variety of health conditions were acting as barriers to employment. The illness reported included heart disease, diabetes, rheumatoid and osteoarthritis, childhood polio, tuberculosis, eye disease, and various problems associated with car, motorbike and other accidents. For some men, conditions had developed and became incompatible with employment. Others had experienced acute or sudden onset conditions which meant they were initially 'off sick' (in employment) and then able to return to work, but found later that they could not continue working following either additional health problems or losing a job through redundancy. In some cases, men had negotiated alternative working arrangements or roles with their employers, enabling their sickness to remain 'hidden' for months or years, before leaving their jobs.

Malik (aged 54) was diagnosed diabetic in his mid-20s but had been able to manage his condition through dietary measures. In his 30s his diabetes worsened and he eventually became insulin dependent. At this time Malik was in secure employment, working for a multinational computer company. He moved through a variety of different work roles as his career developed and he was promoted. His work included a spell in his mid-40s when he was required to travel extensively on a daily basis, working very long hours. It was during this period that he suffered a serious car accident while driving on business, sustaining facial injuries followed by complications. While he was recovering, a heart condition also became apparent, and following heart valve replacement surgery Malik was hospitalised for an extended period. His company 'kept him on' throughout these problems, and arranged for him to return to work in a different role, developing software from his home. He was no longer required to attend the office or to travel. This arrangement worked well for several years. However, his employer embarked on a global restructuring exercise at around the time of his accident, and closed several of its UK operations. This was not a problem at first, as Malik's home-based working arrangement involved reporting directly to the firm's US headquarters. However, in 1992 the company 'folded up', and Malik was made redundant:

They sent me to a re-employment training place, where people in higher level jobs are retrained. The brain was fine, but the body wouldn't take it any more, you see, that was the problem. I have no complaint about the way they handled the shut-down. I mean, if some [other company] gave me a job at home, after I left, I would have done it. But obviously most companies want to do it differently – and they prefer younger guys, because they don't have to pay all the salaries and benefits and perks of older ones – that is a problem. One day you get a phone call saying, 'This is it. Your number is up.' That was it. In fact I didn't even go back to the office. Even when I was notified, they did everything by post or telephone – my cheques and everything just turned up. They helped me as well as they can. I've no complaints about that. A lot of companies, you wouldn't even have got a week's salary out of them. I got about 25 months' worth of salary, which wasn't that bad.

Malik was advised by the firm's personnel department to sign on as unemployed immediately after his redundancy, but on going to register was placed directly on Disability Benefit:

The doctor decided that I wasn't fit enough for work. So he signed me off for a year. That went on for two or three years, and then I had the DHSS examination – their own doctor, to prove whether I was fit. They said I wasn't, so I didn't have to get any more sick notes.

Malik's case exposes the way health problems, redundancy and limited work capacity interact. Some aspects of his poor health were unrelated to his job, although things deteriorated rapidly after his car accident, which occurred when he was travelling on business. His company responded flexibly to his circumstances and enabled him to continue working, but once made redundant, for reasons unrelated to his health, Malik's health restrictions made him very unattractive to other employers. By the time he told us his story, he had accepted that – more than ten years from statutory retirement age – his working life was, effectively, over, even though his mental capacity for work was unimpaired.

Hugh was a former engineering foreman (aged 64) who had suffered his first stroke in 1996, and two further strokes in 1997 and 1998. This condition had left him with a slight speech impediment, and partial paralysis in his left arm and leg. Hugh was a widower living alone and when interviewed was receiving IB. Despite his circumstances, Hugh said he would like, but did not expect to get, full-time work again. He had recently been re-assessed for IB, and told that, on the basis of doctors' reports, the Benefits Agency considered further investigation of his case unnecessary. Before his stroke, Hugh had worked for the same employer for ten years. He was then 'finished', as his employer considered him unfit to return to work. Subsequently, he had approached this same employer about returning to work in any suitable positions, but had not been offered anything. Hugh's previous work history included twenty years as a welder and foreman at another engineering company, from which he was made redundant in 1986. He had also experienced redundancy once before (in 1966) when his firm had lost a major contract. A striking feature of Hugh's situation was that despite a long record of steady employment, broken only by involuntary redundancies and finally ill-health, he had no work-based income to cushion his dependency on benefits.

A number of men had suffered mental health problems, which had affected their working life. This was not unexpected, given the prevalence of such problems. Nationally, almost a fifth of men aged 45–64 years suffer from 'anxiety or depression' affecting the activities of daily life, and in a recent study of work-related stress, more than one in seven reported suffering from stress, anxiety, depression or a stress-ascribed illness (Office for National Statistics 1999). In the general population, the economic activity rate of men suffering from mental illness is low (22 per cent) and there is a 25 per cent ILO unemployment rate among this group (Sly, Thair and Risdon 1999).

Some men whose wives' mental health contributed to their detachment from the labour market were also interviewed (see ch. 7). Men linked their mental health problems to stress at work, business failure and financial problems, marital and family problems of various kinds, and other illnesses and diseases. For some, mental health seemed to have deteriorated following redundancy or the realisation that it was not going to be possible for them to return to work. It is likely that some of the sources of the mental ill-health disclosed were unknown or unclear to the men themselves, or were withheld from the interviewers. However, interviewees were surprisingly frank about their condition, and made extensive comments about the way in which mental health problems affected their participation in the labour force.

Joe, a 60-year-old former pit deputy, now receiving IB, had taken voluntary redundancy from the coal industry when he was 55. He had subsequently obtained an HGV licence and worked briefly as a haulage driver, before injuring his back in a road accident, to the extent that he could not climb into the cab of his vehicle. In the aftermath of this, Joe was diagnosed with angina and depression. He had recently had a heart bypass operation, which he hoped had taken care of the angina, but the depression still troubled him:

I do get depressed, when I think I could be out working and enjoying myself, and yet here I am, thinking 'I wonder what she thinks about me?' and 'I wonder what he thinks of me?' Because they can see you walk, but there isn't like a neon sign, saying 'I'm having an angina attack.' I do get these really, really black times. I used to laugh at depressives, I used to think there was no such thing as depression. But now, I know it, and I can remember it happening to me. I think, 'Well, what's tha living for? Tha hasn't got a job, tha's never gonna have a new car.' I'm virtually now a second class citizen. 'Tha's going nowhere.'

Whereas Joe saw his depression as arising from being out of work, Roger, a 38-year-old former nurse, had been forced to quit work through mental illness. Married with teenage children, Roger was receiving IB and his wife was in full-time employment. Roger had not worked since 1993, when he retired from the NHS on health grounds (diagnosis of anxiety and depression) after approximately sixteen years' service. The depression had deepened after he finished work, and he had struggled to recover from it, remaining on medication. A variety of public services were involved in supporting Roger's recovery. Initially he attended a day centre and took self-esteem and assertiveness courses and psychotherapy. Later, he was supported by a disability employment adviser, and had meetings at the job centre which he found helpful. He had moved into voluntary work, and taken a two-year access course at college, with a view to 'getting himself fit for work'. By the time of the interview, Roger was hoping to resume employment in 'office administration'. He was on a 21 hours per week job placement scheme, receiving £10 training allowance in addition to his IB, and explained:

I think the main barrier [to work] is just myself, really. Loss of confidence, loss of – er – any sort of drive. I don't think there's any other sort of physical barriers from anywhere else. I mean, there's been no pressure on me to go back to work.

Contrasting with this positive account of health and employment service support for his condition, was Mel's story. Mel was a single man aged 40 with a history of mental health problems. When surveyed, he described himself as long-term sick/disabled, and had not been in full-time employment for five years – signing on as unemployed for the first three. Mel had left school in 1973 and had a continuous sixteen-year record of steady employment with a major insurance company, starting as a clerk and working his way up to financial adviser. In 1989, he had moved to another insurance company and then to an estate agent, where he worked briefly as a financial planning consultant. His problems began in 1990–91 when he was off work for nearly a year following a 'nervous breakdown'. After this, he worked for a while as a self-employed financial adviser, before moving to another large firm in 1992. He was 'asked to leave' this job eight months later when he was found to be negotiating with another employer about changing jobs. This led to a two-year spell of unemployment. Mel blamed the job centre for the two further breakdowns and other mental health difficulties he experienced during this time:

I think the pressure of actually looking for work, and all the pressure I was getting from Employment Service, ultimately led to the breakdown. I found that once I did have the breakdown and the illness, things became considerably easier. I was on an easy street then, because I didn't have to account to the Employment Services.

When interviewed, Mel was receiving Income Support including disability premiums, and Disability Living Allowance. He felt there had been a 'long struggle with bureaucracy' before he had been able to secure the latter. He regarded his current income as quite comfortable compared with the 'dire circumstances' of 'surviving' on basic Income Support. Mel was under a psychiatrist when interviewed and had not seen the disability employment adviser, explaining that he was experiencing periods of hyperactivity and lethargy which made him very unreliable. He felt he needed to 'sort out his health situation' before he could recommence looking for work.

For a large number of the men in our survey, ill-health had been an important reason for quitting their last job, and continuing or new health problems were a key feature stopping some of these men from searching for another position. The detailed accounts outlined in this chapter show the complex way in which poor or deteriorating health interacts with other conditions in the labour market to produce seemingly intractable situations of labour market detachment. The relationship between health and detachment is thus far from straightforward. Undoubtedly, as White conjectured in the 1980s, some men capable of limited types of work, but with real health problems, have been 'shaken out' of employment; the new research reported in this book shows just how many of these men now figure in long-term sickness and disability statistics. This is not fraudulent claiming, as long-term sickness and disability benefits can only be claimed by those whose condition has been medically verified. White may have been correct, in 1983, to observe that such men, mainly manual workers, were appearing as long-term unemployed when once they would have been retained in some form of light work. Since that time, as the present study shows, they have come to feature prominently in the illness and disability figures, particularly in regions where significant job losses have occurred.

As indicated earlier in this chapter, ill-health and disability are both concepts responsive to subjective assessment and social determination, and are defined in ways which change over time. This research shows that the extent to which they are recognised within a population affects perceptions of both employment and unemployment. Just as the availability of suitable, and especially physically undemanding, work may disguise ill-health in a population, so its unavailability may increase the visibility of health problems, and in so doing conceal the extent of unemployment.

The new evidence from our study also suggests that many men with health difficulties are deterred from seeking work by a belief that employers recruiting staff will not select anyone with ill-health or a disability, and that, coupled with age discrimination, this becomes a serious barrier to seeking work. As we have seen, some men had given up seeking work entirely, on the grounds that no one would want to employ them because of their past or current health problems; such men are perhaps more accurately described as 'excluded from' rather than 'detached from' work. Our interviewees felt that mental health problems present particular difficulties, and seriously reduce 'employability', as employers define it. It remains to be seen whether Britain's relatively new and still evolving legislation on disability, and the introduction in 1999 of a voluntary code on age discrimination, will be adequate measures to address this problem.

It is clear that ill-health and disability are factors causing labour market detachment and preventing re-attachment in some cases. The issues outlined in this chapter draw attention to the need for continuing vigilance that working conditions are safe and healthy. At present, for too many, they are not, and individuals, their families, and the wider society, are all paying the price for unhealthy working environments. Other forms of ill-health, including mental health problems, also feature prominently, underlining the wider social importance of public health concerns and the need for more effective policies in this area. Health is not the *only* factor causing premature detachment from the labour force among men, and there is much 'hidden' unemployment lying beneath the figures, but at the outset of the new century, it is clear that the need for healthy working conditions should remain firmly on the public policy agenda.

Rob Macmillan

Introduction

For most working-age people, earnings constitute the 'norm' in terms of making ends meet. This is sometimes supplemented by other sources of income, but individuals and households largely 'get by' through earnings from work. Whole societies and economies are arguably predicated on this norm, which has had immense symbolic significance (Bauman 1998) even if it tends to downplay or overlook the role of unpaid work such as domestic labour, unpaid care and voluntary work (Levitas 1998).

For the Labour government in the UK, for example, employment has become a central plank of both economic and social policy. Commentators increasingly refer to an 'employment-centred' social policy based on the promotion of work and the work ethic (Jordan 1998, Annesley 2001: 202–18), encapsulated in the now familiar refrain regarding the focus on 'work for those who can, security for those who cannot' (DSS 1998a: iii). Not only does the focus on employment and employability have important economic consequences, it is also suggested to be the most effective 'escape route' from low incomes and social exclusion.

In attempting to make employment-centred social policy a reality, policies regarding income maintenance for those of working age have focused upon the introduction and development of a range of in-work benefits. New tax credits for working families, for child care costs, and for employment have been introduced or are in development. These in-work benefits are designed to 'incentivise' social security benefits for working-age people as a means of 'making work pay' when compared with unemployment and economic inactivity. The aim is to encourage movement from welfare into work by widening the gap between incomes available through work supported by in-work benefits, and incomes available when out of work.

This raises important questions about how those who have come out of employment, or who are otherwise not in employment, can 'get by', what sources of income are available to those without work, and what this means for living standards.

A key concern for policy-makers also arises: the link between the ability to 'get by' without work, and the incentive to participate in the labour market. The issue here is whether and to what extent 'getting by' without work affects how individuals and households consider potential job opportunities and labour market activity. It is sometimes suggested that if a reasonable 'living' can be made outside the labour market, those not working might consider that work 'isn't worth it' or might search for work less intensively and for longer than might otherwise be the case (Layard, Nickell and Jackman 1991).

This chapter begins to consider this issue by examining the financial circumstances of economically inactive and unemployed men. How do individual men 'get by' while out of work, and what impact might this have on their labour market participation?

An assessment of this evidence makes a contribution to the continuing debate regarding the nature of economic inactivity and labour market participation, which has often been conducted in somewhat abstract terms. Here a fundamental hypothesis is that an individual or household's financial situation is a key (if not *the* key) determinant of labour market activity. In this view, the more money you have out of work, from whatever source, the less likely you are to see the need to carry on working, seeking work or wanting work. This perspective makes the assumption that no rational individual would work unless there was a financial imperative or incentive to do so. If a tolerable standard of living can be had outside the world of paid work then it may be that people rationally choose to distance themselves from the labour market. This perspective provides a working hypothesis through which to explore some of the financial circumstances of the men we interviewed in this research. Not surprisingly, the analysis suggests that the hypothesis does not capture much of the reality as expressed by men in different circumstances.

The chapter focuses on the eighty-seven respondents in the in-depth interviews. The appendix provides more information about how respondents in the in-depth interviews were selected. The chapter opens with a brief overview of the financial circumstances of economically inactive men. It then considers the respondents' own assessments of 'making ends meet', and the main financial strategies employed by those out of work: 'reducing spending' and 'increasing income'. It goes on to explore the circumstances of men who were not receiving social security benefits and of the 'comfortably off', and concludes with a section on the experience of claiming social security benefits.

The financial circumstances of economically inactive men

The eighty-seven respondents in the in-depth interviews displayed a re-markable variety of financial situations and circumstances. Typically, 'getting by' without work is based around one or more of the following potential resources or 'cushions':

- social security benefits;
- private or occupational pensions;
- interest from savings or lump-sum investments, including redundancy payments;
- informal work 'on the side';
- a partner's income/earnings.

In addition, some men who come out of full-time employment have sought to pursue part-time employment.

For men in the in-depth interviews, the social security system formed the main form of financial support, although some were not receiving social security benefits at all. Of those receiving benefits, some were receiving income-related (means-tested) benefits and others contributory benefits. Other sources of income are significant also, particularly partners' earnings and pensions. Chapter 4 provides generalisable statistical data on some of the financial circumstances of the economically inactive and unemployed men.

It is worth considering the varied financial circumstances of men who describe their labour market status in different ways. Those who describe themselves as 'unemployed' tend to be recipients either of income-based JSA or of no benefits at all. This reflects the fact that JSA is paid on the basis of previous NI contributions only for six months, after which it becomes means tested against other income and savings in the household, including a partner's income. The men who described themselves as unemployed but who were not receiving any benefits reported that they relied on interest from savings and investments and some had partners in work. These tended to be older couples with no dependent children. Those men receiving income-based JSA were mainly younger single men with no other sources of income, or younger couples with dependent children.

Those describing themselves as 'long-term sick or disabled' were over-whelmingly entitled to IB. In contrast to the unemployed group, there were very few who were not receiving benefits at all. However, among the group receiving IB, a wide variety of circumstances was evident. Here the main dividing line was between those long-term sick or disabled men who received income support in addition to their IB, and those that did not.

Not surprisingly, given the rules around means-testing, the divide was based around those with additional sources of income and those without. Those men receiving Income Support as a top up tended not to have other sources of income, and their partners, where applicable, were not in employment. The latter group, receiving IB but not Income Support, tended to have other sources of income. These included partners' earnings from employment, private and occupational pensions, savings and investments, and other additional benefits for industrial injury.

Of the men who described themselves as 'early retired', most were not receiving social security benefits at all, while the remaining few were receiving IB alongside other sources of income. For those without benefits, income mainly comprised private or occupational pensions, savings and investments and partners working.

The final group included men who described themselves in 'part-time employment' (including some men not receiving any benefits); and 'carers' who were looking after families or disabled relatives (most receiving Invalid Care Allowance).

From this brief overview of the financial circumstances of the sample of non-employed men, it becomes clear that just as they cannot be said to be a coherent or homogeneous group in terms of their labour market circumstances, so they cannot also be described in this way in terms of their financial circumstances. 'Getting by' out of the labour market involves a range of different financial 'packages', with diverse and complicated combinations of benefits and other sources of income. Importantly, some of these financial circumstances cut across the categories that the respondents have chosen to describe their labour market status. For example, there are recipients of IB in a number of different categories (e.g. long-term sick/disabled, early retired, etc.), and respondents not receiving benefits also describe themselves in a number of different ways. This may have significance for some of the assessments men make of their financial situations, and on their own views of their prospects for securing work. We look at how men out of the labour market assess their overall financial circumstances in the next section.

Making ends meet

'We're not living . . . we're just about managing.' (Tony, aged 37)

Reviewing evidence produced from a large number of research projects commissioned by the Joseph Rowntree Foundation, Kempson (1996) has comprehensively described the financial experiences of many different groups of people living on low incomes. Although the examples in her review are not solely linked to labour market concerns, many of her conclusions are applicable to the circumstances we have found from our in-depth interviews conducted here. Kempson (1996: xi) concludes that 'Managing on a low income requires great skill: costing and controlling a tight budget; setting priorities; juggling bills; making difficult choices; cutting out all but the essentials and sometimes going without these necessities too.' These findings are largely echoed in the interviews with non-employed men.

We asked respondents to provide a general assessment of their financial circumstances, as well as some further detail of their income sources. A minority of the men referred to their overall financial circumstances as 'reasonable', 'comfortable' or 'well off'. Their circumstances are described more fully later in this chapter. Most men, however, assessed their situations more in terms of a struggle: as somehow 'managing' or 'coping', but not without great difficulty. This assessment cut across a wide range of financial circumstances (e.g. those on income-replacement benefits of various kinds, having lost a full-time wage; those living on an occupational pension or a part-time wage; those with savings and those without; as well as those with differing lengths of time living on a lower income). Typically respondents referred to the fact that they were just about 'getting by' or 'scraping by'. A large number of respondents made frequent references to the particular daily struggles to make ends meet, tinged with references to an array of associated sacrifices: there were, for example, difficulties with large bills, and with the costs of providing for and entertaining children. On several occasions respondents referred to the fact that there were 'no such things as holidays', and with seemingly characteristic understatement, no 'jet-setting, no cars and no luxuries'.

Respondents spoke generally of being unable to enjoy the things that others might take for granted or that they once themselves took for granted, e.g. holidays, daytrips, going out to restaurants and simply a little bit of money to spend on what you like. There was some evidence that the *change* of income through coming out of work was felt particularly acutely. Alongside respondents no longer being able to afford the things they used to, there were frequent references to the disruption of pre-established patterns of budgeting and ordinary spending money for housekeeping. Pat's view illustrates this.

Pat, aged 55

Pat is an unemployed man from Barnsley who lives with his wife (who works full time) and their 21-year-old son. Pat was self-employed but has been unemployed for a year after he ceased trading. As he receives no benefits, the family live only on his wife's earnings. The loss of his self-employed earnings has created some difficulty in managing household finances:

> I think the problem we've found is that basically my wife's wage was counted for ... Have this, have that. Holidays. So my money was the day-to-day spending ... weekly spending money. And that's gone now. So we're finding it very hard because we've still got the same commitments, and I think the last twelve months we've lived off credit cards which is fatal because it all has to be paid sometime. It seems a good idea at the time. You know 'well, we've got to have this, we've got to have that'. All of a sudden the monthly repayments on the credit cards are creeping up a little bit. So it's been a struggle.

Having to watch every penny you spend is a particular strain. One recently out of work respondent, who had been used to a reasonably good wage and a dual income, referred to the fact that he now had to 'think twice' about spending anything. For others, however, it was a situation of knowing there was no need to think twice about whether you could afford something; you knew immediately that you could not. Craig provides a vivid example of the frustration at the 'daily grind' of living on a low income.

Craig, aged 31

Craig lives alone in a housing association flat in Barnsley. He has been out of work for between four and five years after he was made redundant from a voluntary organisation which was making financial cutbacks. Since then he has injured his back and spent nine months receiving IB. More recently he has had to claim income-based JSA after a medical test found that he was no longer unfit for work. He and his doctor dispute this, but he has not appealed against the decision. His weekly income (1998–9 rates) has changed from £57.70 per week (IB) to £50.35 per week (JSA), and his rent of £55 per week is covered by Housing Benefit.

> I think the thing that gets me more than anything is spending money. Just having some money to go out and spend rather than saying this is for this; this is for this; and then you've got a fiver left at the end of your giro. You can't even get a pizza with that! Just a bit of spending money. The occasional treat. I mean there have been times when I've got my giro and spent it all. Got my food and that, no bills – if anybody says anything, well, they can come back in a fortnight. I've done that occasionally. You shouldn't do it, but it does keep you sane. Having that break from constantly paying out.

Of the specific difficulties mentioned by people, the extra costs of children were particularly demanding. Typically respondents in receipt of social security benefits refer to the fact that they can just about get by on the benefit amounts they receive, but the difficulties arise around the spiralling costs of young and growing children. There is some evidence of parents depriving themselves of basic things in order that their children did not suffer (see also Kempson 1996). References here included the high one-off costs associated with school uniforms and school trips, which prove difficult when you are pared to a minimal weekly or monthly income and there is little scope for saving. Sid's case exemplifies this.

Sid, aged 49

Sid was widowed in 1991, and he has been a single parent bringing up his son (now aged 10) and daughter (now aged 7) ever since. For most of his working life he was a miner, but increasing breathing problems meant that he was forced to retire. He is no longer considering work because of the need to care for the children and because of his deteriorating health. He receives a pit pension and Industrial Injuries Benefit in addition to IB. He lives in a council house in Chesterfield but does not receive Housing Benefit for his rent of £52 per week because his income is too high. He finds that the costs of bringing up two children are a struggle:

I can manage now, but there's no such things as holidays. You've got to watch every penny you spend. There's lots of things that I'd like but I haven't got the money. I'm not one of them who'd set it on and then worry about paying for it after. But with not being able to work and bring a good wage in . . . I can put up with it, but really it's my kids that's missing out.

Sid describes the daily difficulty of shopping with children, bearing in mind their own perspectives and the pressures from school:

I've not got to let the kids know I've been to Netto. Because they won't eat crisps from Netto, they won't drink lemonade from Netto, because they get teased at school you know. It's terrible, we've even bought lemonade and put it in Morrison's empty bottles! It's a struggle. I can just get through, but I don't like to think about the future because it's quite depressing. I mean I'd love to take them on a bloody good holiday.

Particularly evident here is a strong concern to ensure that your children are treated the same as everybody else's, and especially the need to ensure that they do not miss out on the latest things available in the shops or seen on the television. The pressure felt by parents of the need for their children to be seen to have the latest things seems particularly acute. If the kids do not have the latest brand names they are likely to feel the stigmatising effects at school, as described by Steve.

Steve, aged 43

Steve became a single parent when he took over the primary care for his 13-year-old son from his ex-wife in 1996. He was unemployed at the time, having been made redundant from his job as a welder in 1991. Now he describes himself as a full-time carer and is not looking for full-time work. He lives in a housing association house in Barnsley. Surviving on Income Support for himself and his son (£91.45 per week at 1998–9 rates) is not easy, and the costs of 'kitting out' his son with the latest things is one of the greatest difficulties:

It's terrible. It's hard because kids nowadays want brand names. You know when he's turning round and asking me for a pair of trainers, he doesn't just want an ordinary pair of trainers, he wants £50 trainers, because that's what they've all got. So it puts a lot of pressure on you. You know, sometimes it makes you mad.

Financial strategies

Faced with the situation of living without a wage, a person could in theory try to match income with existing financial commitments either by increasing the former or reducing the latter. Typically increasing income may arise through seeking alternative work (part time or full time), by a partner taking up or increasing work, by working informally 'on the side', by attempting to maximise benefits or by borrowing from friends, relatives or others.

In reviewing the evidence from the in-depth interviews, however, 'getting by' without work amounts in most cases to a concentration on the approach of reducing spending rather than increasing income. Opportunities for increasing income were felt to be limited and to a large extent difficult or out of one's control. Hence men seek instead to 'tailor' their expenditure and to 'cut their cloth'. There are few other viable possibilities. In the discussion below, 'reducing expenses' as a strategy is explored first before considering the possibilities for increasing income.

Strategies for making ends meet: reducing spending and 'cutting your cloth'

As we have seen, 'getting by' without a wage invariably means getting by on less money, and so largely going without certain things. Repeatedly, non-employed men speak, with a combination of resignation and frustration, of 'tailoring' their living expenses. For some this is characterised by a sense of realism rather than explicit criticism, indicating the fact that if you cannot afford something you simply do not have it. One man described how the money would only stretch so far, and therefore you have to reduce your expectations and not 'expect the earth'.

Jack, aged 54

Jack is a full-time carer living in Chesterfield. He gave up work as a long-distance lorry driver in 1992 to care for his wife who has multiple sclerosis. He receives Invalid Care Allowance, and this is supplemented by Income Support. His wife receives Disability Living Allowance. Jack described how the amount paid in recognition of this caring role is minimal: 'We've had to get used to living it, so it's a case of "needs must". You do what you can and what you can't, you don't. Nobody would do it for the money.'

In terms of money management several men report that they have to be very careful in order to keep 'heads above water' and the 'wolf from the door'. This is sometimes a process of intensely close budgeting, typically over a short time-frame – usually from week to week. Respondents thought that they could just about manage on the money they received, but not without difficulty and not without being resourceful. One respondent described the difficulty of managing on such a close week-to-week budget. Trying to manage on a benefit payment for two weeks often involved 'skimping away money from next week'. Another described the process of struggling to live from one Monday to the next. This would involve ensuring that all the essentials – bills and food – were accounted for, but this would leave virtually nothing left at the end of the week. A similar process is described quite vividly in the example below.

Brian, aged 54

Brian has been unemployed for between three and four years, and receives income-based JSA of £44 per week. He lives in Chesterfield in rented accommodation, and he is also entitled to full Housing Benefit to cover his rent. Brian graphically describes how he apportions his fortnightly benefit to ensure that all bills are paid:

What I do with that money, when I get it . . . it's a set routine with me. The rent is about £5 – plus my water rates, so that's about £10. I've got my gas and my light, that works out about – between them – round about £20. I'm looking at that [pointing to a big jar with coins in the corner of the room], because I economise with it all, and there's my money. Obviously I go to the cheapest places – I go to Netto – and I budget. I work out, when I've done paying my bits and bobs out, what I've got to spend. So at the end of the fortnight, I might have a few coppers spare, and they go in here [rattles the glass jar]. That's my luxury jar. I put all my coppers in there – so that when I empty that out... I mean last Christmas – it took me a year to save up – it's sad, isn't it? – I had about £40. But that took me out on Christmas Eve, you know and I had a good night with it. And I enjoyed it. But at no detriment to anything else in the house. My bills were still paid, I don't worry about the Council. I get by on it.

Close budgeting cycles mean that there is little financial room for manoeuvre, not only for emergencies and larger contingencies (e.g. replacing appliances or items of furniture, buying new shoes or uniforms for the children), but also for ordinary living expenses. Fluctuations in weekly expenditure meant that there were several references to 'robbing (or borrowing from) Peter to pay Paul', including mention of a variety of ways of borrowing to even out fluctuating costs. There were several references to the use of 'accessible', no strings/no credit checks, finance companies and use of the social fund, but not of membership of credit unions. The need to borrow in the face of a limited income implies that for some respondents the situation of 'cutting your cloth' becomes so difficult that you simply cannot cut back any further.

For a sizeable number of respondents (fifteen out of the eighty-seven interviewed in depth), being out of work was associated with varying degrees of debt. The severity of these situations varied. Some examples of house repossessions and bankruptcy were mentioned, along with smaller debts associated with rent arrears, utility bills and credit cards. For many, difficulty with debt results from the drop in income experienced when coming out of work. Manageable repayments for loans and credit cards became problematic when men lost their jobs. The commitments remained, but income had decreased.

For another group of men, however, debt seems more an inevitable consequence of living on a low income for a length of time. Typically there are no savings to draw upon; as one respondent aptly put it, 'the cupboard's bare'. Levels of social security benefits came under repeated criticism here. Invariably sources of credit for this group included the doorstep callers and leaflets advertising 'no strings' (but high-cost) financial services.

David, aged 36

David lives with his wife and their five children in a council house in Chesterfield. They receive Income Support as a supplement to his IB and Child Benefit. He described himself as a full-time carer for his wife who suffers from severe depression and anxiety. In total they receive approximately £239 per week.

> We manage on the money we have with great difficulty at times. At other times we seem OK. But it's the times when you get the telephone bill, when the kids need new clothes for school, or shoes or whatever. It can become a bit of a struggle. I mean at times we've had to use finance companies which help the burden then, but of course they're stretched out over such a long period. And it's a vicious circle because then things need replacing again before you've actually got the money to pay for it. So they'll come and say, 'Well, we'll help you', you know, which then just increases the length of time. Because the DSS give you a minimum that you're allowed, basically when you've bought your food, paid your rent . . . and your electricity, your gas what have you, there is just enough left for basics. I mean we don't go out, we don't drink, we don't smoke . . . hence the state of the house. You just can't. You just can't do it.

When available, a number of men receiving lump-sums from redundancy or retirement take the opportunity to 'clear the decks' by using some of this money to pay off outstanding debts. In some cases this can include paying off all or part of a mortgage. This was particularly evident among those men who had left the mining industry with substantial redundancy payments.

For some, cutting their cloth amounts to buying things as cheaply as possible, involving exceptionally careful shopping in low-cost supermarkets, use of second-hand shops, car boot sales and jumble sales. A couple of respondents expressed pride in the fact that they could shop for and cook decent meals out of practically nothing and at very little expense.

Strategies for making ends meet: increasing income

Living without a wage involves some opportunities for increasing income, but these are relatively few, in many cases undesirable and not always available. A number of strategies are evident. Many men continue to try to find paid work, including part-time work. In some cases partners also take an opportunity where possible to increase their work activity as a response to men coming out of work. This can include taking a part-time job, or trying to increase hours, or seeking out training opportunities. Otherwise, though, these strategies for increasing income include maximising benefit entitlements by pursuing other benefits which men may be entitled to, or through taking advice about such benefits, working 'on the side', and reliance to some degree on relatives.

Such strategies for increasing income are not always explicitly calculated. Relying on occasional or one-off contributions from parents or other relatives was described more as a crisis resolution in difficult circumstances than a reliable ongoing source of independent income. Similarly, maximising benefits entitlements appears to be an option for only a few people. This was because men were receiving their maximum entitlements already, or because of a lack of know-how concerning how to find out about these things. Although there were a couple of striking cases involving men who were very knowledgeable about benefits and who actively sought information and advice about claiming, including dogged pursuit of appeals, knowledge of social security benefits and access to information regarding entitlements is at best only partial. In many cases people described situations where they misunderstood or appeared to have been misinformed about benefit rules. Often knowledge about benefits amounts merely to a chance awareness (for example, through a conversation with a friend) of a possibility that you might not be getting the right benefits at the appropriate level for your circumstances.

Very few men refer to the level of benefit they received as being somehow 'comfortable'. Two were single men – one living with his parents, another receiving Income Support with a severe disability premium and the highest rate of Disability Living Allowance. A third man had been out of work for over ten years and described having learnt a range of 'survival techniques'. He received income-based JSA for himself, his wife and their four children and considered that the amount was more than was required. These examples were by far the exception, however. For most respondents who have to make ends meet on social security benefits, levels of benefit are at best merely adequate for adults making regular sacrifices and cutbacks, but not for everyday living, or for the extra costs of children, or for larger one-off expenses.

Of the eighty-seven men we interviewed at length, ten referred to working cash-in-hand 'on the side' at some point in the past, but only four spoke of currently working on the side. Of these one man had a regular and frequent supply of work. For the others, the work amounted only to small-scale and occasional odd jobs. The range of work done on this basis covered the building trade, either for a subcontractor on a site or as a local handyman/carpenter/painter/decorator, as a window cleaner, a gardener, in a nightclub and for security firms. Jobs came about through friends or relatives and, in some cases, by the spread of a man's name as a reliable and inexpensive worker. For those who had worked on the side but were not currently doing so, the fear of getting caught or 'shopped' by a neighbour was a recurrent reason for stopping, although other men mentioned situations where a particular need (for example to pay off a loan or large bill) came to an end. In one case the conditions in a job became unbearable so the respondent decided to quit.

Although there were no evident 'systematic' factors behind working on the side (in terms of for example age, household circumstances, current circumstances, etc.), frequent references are made by men in this situation to the need somehow to make ends meet in less than ideal circumstances. Difficulties finding work, and problems bringing in enough either to make a living generally, or to pay for specific things such as higher mortgage payments, loans or the odd night out, were cited as reasons for working on the side. There is a general recognition of the precariousness of such work – it is something done out of necessity rather than lightly.

Thus cash-in-hand work amounts to a less than desirable way of getting by and surviving on a low income. Here men refer both to the need to keep their benefits as a way of surviving on low wages, as well as the need to work 'on the side' as a way of surviving on low benefit levels. Benefits alone, or low wages on their own, are seen as insufficient for everyday expenses. Overall, therefore, working 'on the side' results from a combination of low levels of benefits received, few opportunities in the formal 'legitimate' job market and the low pay evident in those jobs which are available. These latter two factors might make for a greater incidence of working on the side in localities with slacker labour markets.

Since wages are said to be insufficient to make a decent living, especially in sectors where jobs seemed to be more readily available, such as with security firms, the only way to make those jobs worth taking would be to work unofficially and continue claiming benefit. In this sense an ordinary 'out-of-work' benefit such as JSA seems to be acting in these cases as a *de facto* 'in-work benefit' akin to Family Credit (now replaced by Working Families Tax Credit) which is designed to supplement lower wages. One man spoke of working in a warehouse a number of years ago without declaring it to the job centre in order to help pay his mortgage over a difficult period. The pay was low, but it became a viable option only if he could retain his Unemployment Benefit. There were few other opportunities around at the time. When the company suggested that he be taken on the books 'legitimately', which as a consequence meant that he would sign off, he turned the offer down because he would not have been able to afford it without the contribution from social security benefits.

The 'comfortably off' and those living without benefits

Clearly our sample of men covers a broad range of circumstances. Although the preceding sections have painted a broad-brush picture of the overall financial circumstances experienced by men, it cannot adequately capture the circumstances experienced by everybody. Being out of work is, as we have described repeatedly in this book, a differentiated experience, and no less so in financial terms. In short, some people find it easier to 'get by' than others. We already know that some men were not in receipt of social security benefits. This group described themselves in a range of different ways, including unemployed, early retired and in part-time employment. Not all described themselves as 'comfortably off'.

In fact, only a minority referred to their overall financial circumstances as 'reasonable', 'comfortable' or 'well off'. They were characteristically older men, who now saw themselves as early retired having left employment with a lump-sum and a pension (although there were some now in part-time work also having left full-time work). Their employment history typically involved lengthy spells in one occupation or with one firm, hence their being able to accrue sizeable pension contributions. Coming out of work for this group seems to have consisted of specific choices made when reasonably attractive financial packages were on offer.

This does not necessarily lead to a final abandonment of work, however, for several men take up part-time work or do odd bits of work for friends and former work associates (including, for example, training and consultancy work). Typically this was referred to as 'keeping a hand in' and 'keeping yourself occupied'. This confirms some of the observations about the link between early retirement and part-time working discussed in ch. 6. None the less, many of the more comfortable men are now no longer interested in working again, and are no longer looking for work. For many in this group the distance from the labour market amounts to a 'managed withdrawal', usually with some considerable financial planning, cushioned by relatively large occupational pension entitlements and lump-sums converted into investments. Mike describes one such situation below.

Mike, aged 54

After thirty-two years' service with the Post Office, Mike now describes himself as 'early retired'. He lives in Chesterfield with his wife who is also retired. He left his job in 1994 when the Post Office began to make early retirement packages available to men who had reached 50. He decided to take the option since he saw that the Post Office was undergoing rapid change. He felt that the package was substantial enough to support him and his wife, and now they live on the occupational pension and the interest from the invested lump-sum. He describes this here:

I have a general idea of what our expenditure is at our time of life. You've paid your mortgage off and you've no major expenses and so two-thirds of what I thought was necessary to live on I thought was being provided by my occupational pension scheme. We'd taken note of our investments and a portfolio had been drawn up. We'd taken some of the income from some of that investment initially, a small amount of it, and so we found that was sufficient. I found that the occupational pension and the interest from investments was quite adequate for what we required.

When he first left work, Mike was looking for part-time work to provide an additional income, but after a year he decided to sign off and 'properly retire'. He is no longer looking for work and does not want a full-time job.

It is important to note, however, that it is not just the prospect of a reasonable income out of work for these men which explains their apparent detachment from the labour market. First, some men refer to the fact that large financial commitments – typically associated with mortgages and children – are no longer pressing. Mike above refers to this scenario. The judgement around needing or not needing to find work appears to be based on an assessment of some of the demands of these commitments. A contrasting example from Geoff illustrates this situation.

Geoff, aged 57

For Geoff, a large mortgage formed the main reason for continuing to seek work. Despite having taken early retirement from full-time teaching in 1996, he has returned on a part-time basis to work to supplement his pension. He is clear that he needs to earn an extra £11,000 per annum in order to cover his remaining financial commitments, including the mortgage. He lives in Northampton with his wife, who works full-time, and their two teenage sons, one of whom is still at school:

I wouldn't work at all if I won the lottery. I don't work for my soul or for the enjoyment of it. I work because I need to pay my mortgage. So I would work no hours at all if I could. Zero work is my desire. I'm still stuck with a big mortgage at 57. I certainly haven't organised my life and my times and certainly my finances very well. Because everything could have been different [laughs]. I could have packed up teaching like these people do pack up jobs, and you read about them. A little while ago they were the big purchasers of our society weren't they? Fifty-something, mortgage gone, children gone, top of their salary, ready to spend . . . but that's not me.

A second factor relates to a long working career coming to an end. Among men who had worked for thirty years or more, often in the same industry or firm, a common feeling was that by taking early retirement they were simply taking a well-earned rest. The hope was that they could enjoy life in retirement while they were still in reasonable health.

Vince, aged 55

Vince has recently taken early retirement when he reached the age of 55. He started as an apprentice in an engineering firm when he was 16 and had worked there ever since until his retirement as a senior manager. He lives with his wife, who works part time, and their 16-year-old son in an owner-occupied house in Northampton. Since leaving work he has returned to the firm to undertake a short piece of consultancy work. He decided to retire early after he had a health scare when he was in his mid-40s. He wanted to stop work at an age where he could enjoy life with his family. The total household earnings are approximately £40,000, and he has invested part of his pension which was paid as a lump-sum:

Everything that went into the thinking of going at 55 was the fact that I had worked hard for 38 years and I felt that I needed a break. If nothing else, I needed a break and nine months later having experienced another three months of intense working I'm still of that sort of feeling. I'm financially reasonably well off. I don't have to look for work.

Lastly, for a few men, there is some evidence that the calculations around the possibility of making ends meet without work rely to some degree on their partners continuing to work. Without these continuing earnings, it seems, there might have to be more cloth-cutting than would otherwise be the case.

In terms of labour market attachment, it would seem that, with due regard to those circumstances indicated above, the evidence from this group of 'comfortable' respondents points to a general conclusion that they have less of a financial imperative to work or seek work. As we have seen, this is not just because they have secured a reasonable out of work income. Because they are at a stage of life where (in most cases) heavy financial commitments are drawing to a close, and because in most cases they have put in what they consider to be 'a fair whack' at work over their working life and have a secure income, they have no great need to join or remain in the queue for work. For them the queue for work becomes less important.

The experience of claiming social security benefits

If some of the 'comfortably off' have less of a financial imperative or incentive to continue working or seeking work, this is not generally the case with those on lower incomes and those receiving social security benefits. We have seen already the ways people describe how they are 'just about managing' on their incomes, and have explored some of the difficulties this presents. The general experience here is that living on a low income is not a 'comfortable' experience, but is more a matter of necessity, from which certain financial strategies have to be adopted to survive.

In addition to asking men to describe their overall financial circumstances and experiences, we asked those receiving social security benefits to assess their own experiences of claiming these benefits.

A clear divergence emerged between men on the one hand who had fewer qualms about claiming social security benefits and, on the other, those who felt that it was much more discomfiting. Overall, the latter view was more common, involving what men perceive to be a loss of status and dignity. Some strong opinions were voiced here about how the process was felt to be degrading. The perceived legitimacy or otherwise of claiming benefits was also linked to geographical considerations of the local labour market.

Claiming social security benefits is felt to be less of a problem by those who typically talk about the contributory nature of benefits. Having paid NI contributions and general taxation during a lengthy working life, many men feel that claiming benefits is simply an entitlement under an assumed contract with the state.

Gordon, aged 54

After working for nearly thirty years, including twenty-three years in the mining industry, Gordon took redundancy in 1988. He now claims IB and Disability Living Allowance and describes his circumstances as 'long-term sick/disabled'. He lives in Barnsley with his wife who works part time. Gordon was clear that his benefits were simply something for which he had paid in during his working life:

Personally myself I don't feel too bad about [claiming benefits] because I've worked all my life, and I've paid into the system. I've looked after them, and they should look after me a little bit. That's what I think. Like if I'd never worked, and been on it all time I might have felt different, but, no, I was paying £30 odd a week tax when I was working, and my stamps and that. It's like swings and roundabouts, isn't it?

As well as simply receiving at a later date an entitlement based upon what you paid earlier, some men also referred to the fact that they had worked in a physically demanding industry (for example, mining) for which there was a need for some kind of recompense. Separately, some referred to the circumstances surrounding leaving the workforce or continuing to be out of work. For example, some men mentioned that they had been forced out of work either through personal circumstances (to be a full-time carer) or redundancy (or 'robbed of a career by the government', as one ex-miner put it). In addition, their perspectives seemed to be related to their current situations. Thus claiming social security benefits was not felt to be illegitimate because there were no jobs available or because respondents were not fit to work in any case.

In these last examples, the underlying assumption is that the 'norm' of full-time employment for men retains a pervasive influence on their feelings and attitudes. The basic assumption is that a man of 'working age' should be in work, and it is only where there are no jobs available or where a man is physically incapable of work that being out of work is acceptable. However, the work ethic strongly underpins the predominant view expressed by men, in which claiming benefits is described variously as 'like charity', 'like pinching from the state', 'like being a burglar', 'embarrassing', 'upsetting', 'degrading', 'like being beholden to others' and 'like begging'. Underlying this is a preference for being in work and earning a wage. The two examples below provide an illustration of this.

Joe, aged 60

Joe has been out of work since 1988 after a road accident when he was a haulage driver. Earlier that year he had taken voluntary redundancy from the mining industry. He lives in the Barnsley area with his wife and claims IB, Disability Living Allowance and his miner's pension:

This is the bit that's upsetting, you know. You're having to claim when really I'd much prefer a job. And I'd be able to say, 'Well, I've earned my money. It's my money now. I'll do what I want with it.' Whereas when you're receiving state benefits, you're thinking 'I'm beholden to someone', because there's somebody out there working and paying taxes.

Brian, aged 54

Brian, introduced earlier in this chapter, is unemployed and receives a fortnightly payment for income-based JSA. He feels that he does not have the pride of receiving money he has personally earned:

A lot of people expect this money to come through the letter box – they just expect it to be there. I don't. I never expect it to come through, because

> I know somebody else has had to pay that money in, like I used to pay it.
> And – it's a very difficult thing for me – because it's like somebody's giving
> you something – and I've not earned that. I've not earned that money. I've
> not gone out and earned it and got a bit of pride that you get. You know, when
> you go to the bank and you get the money out, you get a bit of pride. You
> don't get that with a Giro.

Clearly work retains its associations with independence, participation and making a valued contribution to society. To live without paid work, especially where that involves the need to claim social security benefits, is thus couched with discomfort and fear that your legitimacy is under question.

Many men also feel at the mercy of prevailing public and media attitudes towards claiming benefits. Such debates are deeply stigmatising. Use of terms such as 'scrounger' and the fact that benefit fraud often seems to be the only debate of interest to the media is felt strongly by those forced to live on benefits for a variety of reasons. Barry illustrates this.

Barry, aged 36

After his wife was diagnosed with a severe mental illness, Barry had to give up work in 1994 to become a full-time carer and to look after their two teenage daughters. They live in Northampton, and because of his overall care responsibilities and the unpredictability of his wife's condition, Barry is not presently looking for work. However, he would like to return to work when he can. In the meantime though they live on Invalid Care Allowance and Child Benefit supplemented by Income Support. Barry's wife also receives Disability Living Allowance. Barry was frustrated at being made to feel illegitimate for claiming benefits and not being at work:

You can hardly miss it, can you? It is in all the papers all the time, calling us scroungers and everything. We've had every reason to claim. You read it in the papers all the while, don't you? Anybody who is on benefit is a scrounger. They don't seem to understand that some people have to be on benefit. It annoys me. All these people with work saying, 'We don't want to pay our taxes.' Fine. I wouldn't want to pay tax if I was working but I don't have that choice.

From this exploration of the attitudes and feelings of those claiming social security benefits, a number of themes can be identified. First, that feelings of discomfort and anxiety are part of the territory for those living on benefits, although for many men this is mitigated by feelings of now taking out what had previously been contributed during a longer period of work. In addition, claiming benefits is seen by men as an uncomfortable position that they are forced to endure, given that there are few possibilities for them to return to work (through lack of jobs or personal circumstances). Interestingly, it was in the stronger labour market, in Northampton, where feelings of stigma and discomfort were strongest. This is perhaps not surprising: if there are fewer people out of work because of a tight local labour market, the prevailing opinion which indicates that there are 'plenty of jobs out there' for people that want them, would be felt all the more strongly for those without work. In this view one 'legitimate' reason for being out of work is weaker, and the stigma of living on benefits might be felt more strongly.

Most men are not happy about their situation and in most cases would prefer to be working. Tim exemplifies this in stark terms.

Tim, aged 49

Tim has been out of work for about three years. Otherwise he has largely worked all his life in a variety of jobs, including running his own successful business. After being in a relatively prosperous position, his health has declined, he has had to give up work, his house has been repossessed and he now lives in private rented accommodation in Northampton. He has continuing debts in excess of £20,000. Because he has osteoarthritis he is no longer able to work, and he suffers from depression. His wife is now taking an access course in the hope of taking a social work qualification. For Tim the overall change in his circumstances has been seen as a downfall about which he is deeply distressed:

It is very hard to know that your bank statement has a £200 credit put in it from the welfare state every fortnight, but had it not been for that we'd be dead. We have nothing! We want off the system. We can't live like this. We don't like living like this. We don't like it. There's no alternative. You've got to live like this, but our attitudes are not the same. We're not happy people. We're working towards it. To get some independence.

Conclusion: income and barriers to work

In this chapter we have looked at the detailed in-depth evidence regarding the financial circumstances of non-employed men. The picture which has emerged is one of differentiation. Just as non-employed men exhibit a variety of different orientations to the labour market, their financial circumstances are no less diverse. There is no single uniform picture of what 'getting by' without work involves. This is not to say that no general statements can be made from the qualitative analysis. In summary, we have suggested that:

- Non-employed men rely on a wide range of income sources, both within and beyond the social security system. Although social security benefits of one form or another are the most widely used 'cushion', private pensions and (where possible) partners' employment patterns are also significant.
- For most men coming out of work involves a considerable impact on living standards. Making ends meet is a challenge, involving the need to increase income where possible, but more significantly to 'tailor' living expenses. The result is typically that men and their families go without things they would normally have, go without things others might take for granted, and some struggle with debt and everyday budgeting on a low(er) income.
- Some non-employed men are not entitled to social security benefits, and some men describe themselves as 'comfortably off', although these two groups are not exactly the same. For the more secure or affluent, an occupational pension and a lump-sum retirement or redundancy package received at a time when major household expenses (children, mortgages) are drawing to a close has for some lessened the attachment to the labour market. These men tend to regard themselves as early retired.
- For others, the process of claiming social security benefits is felt by most to be one of stigma, loss of self-esteem and discomfort. Many refer to the fact that they have contributed during a working life and are therefore fully entitled to claim, but otherwise men typically refer to being forced to claim (through lack of jobs, ill-health or caring responsibilities) when they would rather be working.

This last reference, to being forced to claim rather than work, brings us back to our original working hypothesis, namely that detachment from the labour market is a function of the income available while out of work. The evidence presented here suggests that the hypothesis stated in such stark terms needs to be modified or abandoned. Men do not report that they are living particularly well, and mostly do not like having to live on benefits whose legitimacy is always under question.

Clearly for some of the more affluent men there is a feeling that with no financial pressure or incentive to work, their activity or participation is likely to decline. Not having to work, alongside having worked for many years, translates into not looking for work and taking 'early retirement' instead. But this is not a general experience of non-employed men. The search for answers to why men's labour market participation has declined has to look elsewhere. Given these conclusions, it would seem that the availability of an income out of the labour market will affect some people or groups in some contingent circumstances more than others. The overall sense from the evidence of the in-depth interviews is that financial considerations do not affect respondents in any simple uniform manner.

10   Back to work?

Stephen Fothergill and Rob Macmillan

The preceding chapters mainly explored how men have become detached from employment. However, as chs. 2 and 3 explained, re-attaching the unemployed and inactive to the labour market has become a key preoccupation of governments in the UK and elsewhere. Indeed, it is often now the guiding principle in restructuring social security systems away from an essentially 'passive' model, geared to individual need, towards an 'active' model aimed ultimately at moving claimants off welfare altogether.

This chapter examines how non-employed men assess their labour market position and the possibility of returning to work. It does so primarily by drawing again on the in-depth interviews that were the basis of chs. 7, 8 and 9. The chapter concentrates on two groups of men: the long-term unemployed and the long-term sick. In the UK context these groups mainly comprise the men in receipt of JSA and IB, though the overlap between how men describe themselves and the benefits they are actually claiming is not perfect, as ch. 4 showed. These two groups make up about two-thirds of the 'detached male workforce', as we have defined it in this book, and the long-term sick are particularly numerous. As ch. 4 also showed, nearly 90 per cent of the long-term unemployed and around half the long-term sick say they would like a full-time job. Far fewer of the early retired – the other large group among the detached male workforce – express an interest in returning to work.

The chapter begins with a general discussion of the position of the jobseeker within the wider labour market. This is important because the men who are detached from employment are a highly diverse group and they face a labour market segmented by occupation, location, age and gender. The chapter then considers the perspective and experiences of the long-term unemployed and of the long-term sick, before concluding with a discussion of the implications for labour market policy.

Two perspectives on the labour market

The labour market can be viewed from two different vantage points. Many economists, in particular, tend to concentrate on the view 'from above', that is of aggregate demand for and supply of labour. An alternative perspective looks at the world 'from below', from the vantage point of the experience of ordinary people.

In aggregate 'from above' terms, getting people back to work is usually seen as being about matching supply and demand. There are jobs (demand) and there are potential people to fill them (supply). The key questions therefore concern the number of jobs and number of people, their potential mismatches and their various geographical and other characteristics. Wage levels are particularly important; in economists' theoretical models, wage adjustment is supposed to bring labour demand and supply into balance. In this framework the problem of unemployment (and wider non-employment) is about the failure of the market to clear, or in other words the persistence of obstacles that prevent the matching of those who are out of work with the opportunities that are available in the economy. The UK Treasury, for example, takes the view that with an estimated 1 million vacancies in the economy and with 1 million claimant unemployed, the problem is one of equipping the million jobseekers with the capabilities and motivation to take the million jobs (HM Treasury 2000). There is an important debate about whether this is a matter of 'skills matching' (the non-employed not having the skills required by vacancies) (Layard 1999) or of 'spatial matching' (the non-employed not being able to get to the vacancies) (Green and Owen 1998).

But considering the labour market 'from above' is not the only way of trying to understand how it operates. By moving from aggregate numbers to individual experiences a quite different perspective is added that takes account of how people respond to opportunities on a day-to-day basis. What we end up with is a more complex picture of supply and demand. In particular, the view that the problem of labour demand and supply is merely one of adjusting wage levels looks especially misleading.

In practice, each individual faces a range of opportunities that is restricted in a number of ways. There may be a million vacancies in an economy at any given time, but this is not the same as the flow of job opportunities faced by individuals, which will be much smaller, given geographical limits to their area of job search, the skills they are able to offer and the pay and conditions they feel able to accept. Furthermore, the chances of obtaining a given vacancy depend on how many other jobseekers are in a similar situation.

As ch. 5 explained, the 'queue for jobs' is unlike a conventional queue in which you take your place and wait your turn. Newly unemployed people tend to join near the front rather than the back because employers tend to look more favourably on those who have only recently come out of work. The longer individuals have been in the queue, the lower the chance that they will find employment. Movement in the queue for jobs is thus less like an orderly queue in which individuals gradually move forward, and more one where there is a lot of movement and 'churning' at the front and far less at the back. At the front, the individuals with the most 'employable' attributes tend to take the jobs that come up. Towards the back, the people with fewer employable attributes and other disadvantages face the prospect of continually losing out in the competition for jobs.

Individuals in search of work have to ask themselves a series of questions about each job opportunity they encounter. Is it in an accessible location? Is it the sort of work I can do? Have I got the right skills, qualifications and experience? Are the hours of work acceptable? Is the job compatible with my other commitments, for example at home? Is the pay acceptable? What are the long-term prospects? Most jobs fall at one or more of these hurdles. If job applications are submitted, employers ask a series of questions of their own. Is this person the best qualified for the job? Is he reliable? Is he fit and healthy enough to do the work? Would he fit in? And all too often, is he the right age? These are the realities of the fine grain at which the labour market operates on a day-to-day basis.

The point is that getting men 'back to work' is about more than just getting the macroeconomic variables right. A greater supply of jobs in the economy as a whole would certainly be immensely helpful. It would mean that non-employed men would have more jobs to choose from and employers would have less scope to be fussy about exactly who they took on. But at the fine grain of the labour market there is an altogether more complex task of matching what individuals are able to offer with the sorts of opportunities that might come up.

The degree to which re-engagement with employment depends on the overall level of demand for labour or on obstacles at the level of the individual varies from case to case, as will become apparent. However, the general rule is that the further back in the queue for jobs, the greater the stimulus to labour demand that is needed to secure re-employment, and the greater the need as well for intervention to overcome personal obstacles.

The long-term unemployed

The long-term unemployed are the men for whom in theory labour market re-attachment should be easiest to achieve. As we noted earlier, nearly

90 per cent of long-term unemployed men say they would like a full-time job and most say they are currently looking for work. Our survey findings, reported in ch. 4, also suggest that the proportion looking for work does not fall away much as the duration of unemployment grows – for example, the share looking for work when their last job ended was just over 80 per cent, compared to just over 75 per cent at the time of the survey. The chances of returning to work are also greater for unemployed men in receipt of JSA than for most other non-employed groups because JSA claimants are required to demonstrate that they are looking for work in order to retain their benefit entitlements.

Economic statistics confirm that there should be hope for this group. The number of claimant unemployed fluctuates with the trade cycle – a rather obvious point, but a trend that stands in contrast to the seemingly inexorable rise in the number of economically inactive men (see table 4.1). So if economic growth can be fast enough and sustained enough – as indeed it was in the UK between 1993 and 2001 – it should be possible to bring down claimant unemployment. Furthermore, within the stock of claimant unemployed the number of long-term claimants tends to fall along with the headline total, and the rate of long-term unemployment is generally lower in the areas where the overall rate of claimant unemployment is lowest (see Turok and Webster 1998).

We carried out our in-depth interviews during 1998 and 1999, at a time when claimant unemployment was falling and was well below its peak of the early 1990s. Even so, the shortage of suitable job opportunities was the barrier to work mentioned most frequently by long-term unemployed men. The sub-sample we interviewed was not selected to be statistically representative – rather, the aim was to cover a sufficient number of non-employed men in a range of different circumstances – so it is important to be cautious about making generalisations. However, the frequency with which a shortage of suitable jobs was mentioned is entirely consistent with another quite separate survey of men we carried out in other localities during 1999 (Breeze, Fothergill and Macmillan 2000). The sorts of problems to which men referred were not just the absolute shortage of jobs but also their unsuitability in terms of pay, short-term contracts and part-time working.

It is perhaps to be expected that unemployed men will blame a shortage of jobs for their predicament because it shifts the responsibility for their joblessness firmly on to the external labour market rather than any individual shortcomings. However, the interviews revealed no unwillingness on the part of men to acknowledge their own limitations where they thought this provided part (or indeed the whole) of the explanation for their joblessness. Men often show no hesitation in recognising shortcomings in their qualifications, skills and experience, or in acknowledging health constraints on the work they are able to do. Care and family responsibilities, lack of confidence and motivation and financial considerations (such as loss of benefits) were mentioned where they seemed appropriate. Seen in this context, many men's insistence that there are not enough suitable job opportunities needs to be given some weight. It is a simple and obvious explanation for unemployment, but that does not necessarily make it incorrect.

A key aspect of job shortages is, of course, that they vary in severity from place to place. It is no surprise, therefore, that a shortage of local job opportunities was mentioned more often in the Barnsley and Chesterfield survey areas, where non-employment rates are relatively high, than in Northampton where they are relatively low (see the appendix). The contrasting perception and experiences of two men, both of whom had been unemployed for a very long time, illustrates this point. Tony lives in Barnsley and sees no realistic way forward.

Tony, aged 37

Tony lives in a council house with his wife and their three school-age children. He receives income-based JSA plus Housing Benefit and Council Tax Benefit. He has been out of work for fourteen years, and his wife is not in paid employment either. His last job was as a butcher, but when his employer made staff cutbacks he was 'last in' and so 'first out'. He had worked there for four years. He remembers thinking that he would have a reasonable chance of getting further employment, but found that employers either wanted more qualifications than he had, or only school leavers. During the years without work Tony has had only two job interviews. 'For unskilled there's practically no work. Any jobs that there is then you've to fight for them because there's that many unemployed in the Barnsley area... There's that many unemployed it's a lucky dip really.'

He is looking for work locally and he would like to go back into full-time employment, into any kind of job provided it was a job that he could do or could be trained to do. He is particularly interested in outdoor work. He cannot drive and so this has sometimes limited his options when van driving and delivery jobs come up. He would learn to drive straight away if he had the money. Tony thinks he looks for work less intensively than when he first came out of work:

When I first became unemployed then I looked more. Possibly because there were more jobs available for what I was looking for. But as time's gone on there isn't. So I go to the Job Centre once a fortnight when I've got to sign on. I have a look on boards. I have a look in newspapers...I think as time's gone on...you get in a situation where you can get as you're not bothered...Unless there's a miracle happens then I don't think there probably will be [a realistic chance of finding work] in the near future. Hopefully yes, but being realistic no.

Gary, from Northampton, describes a contrasting situation to Tony's. He is also married with children, and his wife is not in employment, but Gary faces an apparently growing labour market and buoyant local economy.

Gary, aged 47

Gary lives in a council house with his wife and four children, two of whom have now left school and started work. He claims income-based JSA plus Housing Benefit and Council Tax Benefit. He has not worked for approximately eleven years. He has had four unsuccessful interviews in the previous two years and is waiting for the outcome of four job applications. He was looking for positions to reflect his previous experience as a service engineer and manager, but has now decided to look for less senior positions, such as in warehouse administration and stock control. His weekly income from social security benefits decreased significantly when his two eldest children left school, and the booming economic situation in the local area is changing his perspective about finding work:

It's the economic growth within the town as well that's proved to be more a carrot. I mean now I know I can go out to work and I can earn the money, whereas before it was 'how the devil will I make ends meet?' – We can't, and so that was a very big factor. It said to me: 'Stay away.' Over the last five years now the wages have gone up horrendously, because the jobs are out there, and people are screaming and every time you look round another factory has gone up. I haven't had so much scope in the past. So the changes are happening daily.

Gary admits that his financial situation has been one of the main reasons why he has been out of work, but this is now changing. Until recently the earnings that he might have been able to command were always considered to be too low for his everyday household expenses:

Lets face it: a man with a family. The paramount concern is with security. And it did affect how I looked on the world. I can honestly say that out of the eleven years that I've not been working, I didn't look for a job for nine of them. I never physically went out and applied for any jobs. Because it was purely financial. Because they were asking such ridiculous money . . . Finance has been a big, big problem . . . trying to get a job that was paying me as much as the state was almost impossible . . . A few years ago I could quite easily have gone out and got a job, but I'd have been out of pocket.

Both these men are of 'prime working age'. They are not youngsters struggling to gain a foothold in the labour market, nor men drawing towards the close of their working lives and looking forward to retirement. Both had been able to endure such extraordinary long periods of unemployment because their household circumstances – a non-employed partner, school-age children and rent to pay – meant that they were entitled to a package of means-tested benefits that was equal to, or greater than, the wages they felt able to command. For both men the shortage of jobs therefore made itself felt specifically as a shortage of sufficiently well-paid jobs. Neither could afford to take just any low-paid job. The introduction of Working Families Tax Credit, subsequent to our interviews, will have changed the precise calculation, making work more financially rewarding. Nevertheless, the basic point remains valid – there are not always enough jobs paying high enough wages to support a family.

However, Tony and Gary's perceptions diverge in looking to the future. Both would like to find a job, but in a slack labour market such as Barnsley, Tony holds out little hope. In the altogether stronger labour market of Northampton, Gary is a lot more optimistic. The point is that even for men with extended periods of unemployment and facing a major loss of benefits if they take a job, the local demand for labour remains central in influencing their chances of returning to work.

Beyond a shortage of jobs, the other barrier that is mentioned most frequently by unemployed men is age – or more specifically, the ageism practised by employers and the employment services. Two further examples illustrate these feelings, though as is so often the case, neither man sees ageism as the sole problem he faces in getting back to work. In Alan's case the problem is a combination of ageism and lack of personal transport.

Alan, aged 55

Alan has been out of work for just over a year. He was unexpectedly made redundant from his job as a warehouse manager just as he was about to move to Northampton. His wife works full time, so her earnings disqualify him from income-based JSA, though he still signs on. Alan can drive but at the moment can't afford the money to buy a car:

I am convinced that there's ageism in the marketplace. I'm 55. I'm a fit healthy 55 but I'm quite sure, you can see it advertised in the paper, they don't want people over 45 . . .

I would retrain in any areas, but unfortunately if you're over 25 the Job Centre's not particularly interested in training you in anything anyway. The big push on with the Labour government is getting all these young people into work. I think they've reorganised the Job Centre up there. There's this special big area all for getting the young people into work . . . They were closed for two or three weeks while they were remodelling and redesigning the place and the first thing I said when I went in was 'Where's the special area for people over 45?' It's basically a big push for the young people, and no push for the older folk . . .

It's a catch-22 situation . . . because unless I've got a car I can't get a job and unless I've got a job I can't get a car. I discovered the transport system is absolutely hopeless. The buses go everywhere but at very inconsiderate and inconvenient times. You can sometimes get to work in the morning but you can't get back at night. Or you can't get there in time in the morning, you can maybe come back at night easy enough, but you can't get there in time for your work . . . If I had wheels I'd probably be working now.

Brian lives in Chesterfield – not as weak a labour market as Barnsley, but certainly not in the Northampton league. He experiences the key barriers to work as being a combination of his age and the intense competition for the jobs that come up.

Brian, aged 54

Brian has been out of work since his job in a foundry came to an end. As we saw in ch. 9, he receives income-based JSA and lives in a rented house. He moved to the area in the hope of finding similar work but has not been successful, although he has been on a couple of government-sponsored environmental training schemes.

If you go to the job club or the dole and look at the list, if there's any jobs in my line of work, which is basically labouring, you know there are going to be at least three or four hundred people after that. So the gaffer's sat there. He's going to pick the cream. And then again, the ageism creeps in again. He's got a young lad there, just left school, or round about twenty, who's willing to learn. He'll have him. He doesn't want me. I will apply for the job, in the hope that he might do. He might say 'Oh, this guy's got a bit of intelligence, he's had some experience, he's punctual, he's loyal, we'll have him.' But a lot of the time, they go for a young kid in these situations . . .

I went to an employment agency in town, and this young lass, bless her, she just looked me up and down and shook her head. I didn't say anything, I just walked in and she just looked and smiled. She said, 'I'm sorry', Age. She said it. She might deny that now, but she said 'are you over 35?' . . . I'm

> 54 now, coming 55, no particular skills. I can acquit myself in the foundry, but no particular skills. They won't tell you to your face, that you are 54, they don't want to know about your experience.

Ageism in recruitment processes is sometimes hard to prove, but Alan and Brian illustrate how it is experienced by older men looking for work. Just like the 'shortage of jobs' that is quoted so often by unemployed men, the issue of 'age' is mentioned so often that it seems impossible to dismiss it as an illusion or as a convenient excuse for joblessness. Furthermore, ageism in the labour market seems so pervasive that it is hard to believe that voluntary codes of practice, such as that introduced by the UK government in 1999 (DfEE 1999), will by themselves make much difference. A cultural shift is required, and just as with racism and sexism this probably needs to be backed up by legislation and enforcement.

What the examples of Alan and Brian also illustrate is that for many unemployed men, even those on the receiving end of ageism, there is rarely just a single barrier to returning to employment. As a general rule, the further back in the queue for jobs the more numerous or acute the barriers become. Two further examples illustrate this point. Interestingly, these are men at different ends of the age range – one in his mid-20s, the other in his late 50s – but both face multiple hurdles which suggest that neither is likely to be a candidate for early re-employment.

Andy, aged 25

Andy lives with his girlfriend and their three young children on a council estate in a village a few miles from Chesterfield. He worked as a burner in a scrap yard but injured his hand and had to leave his job. It is eighteen months since the injury and he has not worked since. After claiming IB for a while, he moved on to income-based JSA when he recovered from his injury and is now looking for a job, as a labourer or in some other line of work that does not require qualifications.

I'm looking all the time. But there's nothing going. That's the problem with having no qualifications, do you know what I mean?
  [The] hardest part about it is I've got no transport. That's where I'm let down. I've got a car licence like but I just can't get a car at the minute. No transportation, except a pushbike. I've had a few jobs at town I could've had, but its just like buses they're not very clever you see, especially in the morning. I just can't get there. In the morning, without a car, it's a bit awkward . . . You can't rely on a bus. Gotta get a car. You're stuck without a car. Desperate. You could look further out for a job and could get there quicker.

Andy is keen to be back at work and takes a proactive stance in approaching employers directly, but only within a radius of three miles or so. These are the larger factories in the area that he knows he can get to. However, this has not been successful because the firms report waiting lists of people to be 'set on'. Andy faces multiple obstacles to getting back to work – his lack of formal qualifications, a shortage of suitable jobs in the Chesterfield area, and the fact that he does not have a car. Added to this, Andy's financial predicament is very similar to that of Tony and Gary, described earlier. With three small children, a non-employed partner and his housing costs largely met by Housing Benefit, he is not in a position where he can afford to accept the lowest paid jobs. In 1999, when he was interviewed, Andy said that he might be willing to accept a job at £140 a week so long as this could be topped up with in-work benefits or substantial overtime pay, but realistically he felt he needed £180 a week and he was only too aware that few labouring jobs in the vicinity paid that much.

At least Andy's age did not work against him. Davy, from Barnsley, illustrates a cocktail of problems – his age, the redundancy of his skills, his declining health and a difficult local labour market.

Davy, aged 58

Davy has not worked for over ten years and is registered unemployed. Despite declining health, he continues to claim income-based JSA rather than IB. He lives alone in a council house. He took redundancy after thirty-three years as a miner:

I was made redundant. It was classed as voluntary but it wasn't really voluntary. They shut all the pits down. And you more or less had to take it at my age. We weren't forced to take it, you could move to another pit, but after that you went to another pit. They were gradually shutting them all down.

I don't think there's a lot of work for blokes of my age. I went for an interview, but there were only young people that were interviewing me. You knew straight away you'd no chance. You can sense it. At the back of your mind, you know. There were a young feller sitting at the side of me waiting to go in, and you knew who'd get the job in that sort of industry.

At 58 I think they've had the best out of you . . . in the pits and that. Young lads can do it twice as better as me. Labouring and anything like that. I don't think I'd be able to manage labouring now.

It seems to be changing fast, you know, to what we knew. Computers and everything, you know. I should think it is easier for a young feller coming out of school in a way. To go into some sort of training, it's more or less straightforward for them isn't it? When you've been in mining all your life you've no academic qualifications or anything like that, and that's all it's been in this area: mining and industry. I know there's a few new [factories] opening

> now like, but it's different work now... computers and all like that isn't it? I feel I wouldn't have a chance. I can't see the point in retraining at 58, say into computers or things like that.

Among the claimant unemployed, Davy must be near the back of the queue for jobs. The strong up-turn in aggregate employment levels in Britain during the middle and late 1990s had still left him marooned with no obvious opportunities to return to work. For Davy, a realistic opportunity to work again would not only require a strong national economy but also the vigorous regeneration of his own local labour market – Barnsley – and a measure of retraining tailored to his own needs and aspirations.

The range of complex and intractable labour market problems faced by many long-term unemployed men means that they frequently see little prospect of a return to work. Overcoming these barriers would seem to present an immense challenge for employment policy.

The long-term sick

The long-term sick and disabled are an especially difficult group to re-attach to employment. As ch. 4 showed, a degree of health limitations on the ability to work is reported just about universally by men in this group, as might be expected. Health problems add a further obstacle to re-employment to those that men may already face because of age, poor skills or location.

Of course, some long-term sick men can never be expected to work because their health presents an absolute and insurmountable obstacle. There are others, too, whose health problems are so severe that it would require special circumstances – a supportive employer, a specially adapted workplace or flexible working arrangements, for example – to enable them to return to work. But equally, the tremendous variation in the nature and severity of the health problems of the long-term sick should not be overlooked. The All Work Test, for example, which is the gateway to IB for long-term claimants, is a crude tool which, despite its name, does not measure the inability to do all work in all circumstances. As we saw in ch. 5, only a minority of IB claimants say they cannot do any work at all. For the majority, their health limits exactly what work they can do, or how much.

Let us therefore be clear that the health problems of the long-term sick are real enough, and that for some men the health problems are sufficiently serious as to preclude employment in most or all circumstances. It would never be realistic to talk about getting all, or nearly all, the long-term sick back to work. Furthermore, even getting some of these men back to work is likely to be a difficult task given the problems they face.

The statistics on long-term sick men certainly do not suggest that labour market re-attachment is likely to be easy. As ch. 4 showed, just under half say they would like a full-time job but only 5 per cent say they are currently looking for work. The majority are clearly men who see themselves at the back of the queue for jobs. Among the long-term sick there is also a predominance of older men (nearly two-thirds are over 50) and of manual workers.

On the other hand, ch. 5 argued that there is extensive hidden unemployment among men on IB – men who could reasonably be expected to have been in work in a fully employed economy. This suggests that there ought in theory to be scope for some re-engagement with the labour market in the right circumstances. Even so, the 'hidden unemployed' are not an easily identified group that can be separated off from the rest and targeted by appropriate policies. As with the long-term unemployed, there is tremendous diversity between long-term sick individuals and often a multiplicity of obstacles to employment, related both to health and other factors.

At one end of the spectrum are those men whose health problems are so considerable that they are not only completely prevented from working but no longer wish to work either. Malcolm is an example.

Malcolm, aged 51

Malcolm used to work for the army as a land agent – a job that involved a lot of physical work. He had previously worked in other sorts of outdoor, manual jobs – farmwork, gardening and labouring. He gave up work between two and three years ago, on the advice of an army welfare officer, because of acute arthritis in his lower back. He lives in Northampton with his second wife and her two teenage sons, one of whom is now in full-time employment. His wife works part time. Malcolm receives IB plus a small pension (around £30 per week) and he and his wife own their home outright.

I was struggling to do [my job]. Some days I couldn't do it. I did work on my own quite a lot of time so I could hide the fact that I couldn't do it . . . But in the end it caught up with me . . . Basically, I couldn't do the job.

I've worked all my life, from day one. It was a shock. I mean a real shock. I didn't know what was happening to be honest.

I don't really know what I could do, because I've always done manual work whatever it be, outside, and it's all I know. And I can't do it. It's as simple as that.

There are many men in similar situations, and the comments we make about hidden unemployment should not detract from this point.

However, there is a second group of long-term sick men who say they do not want a job but for whom the reasons are less clear cut. The point here is not that the physical limitations on the work they are able to do are anything less than real, but rather that there are other factors too and their illnesses or disabilities might not in practice be an insurmountable obstacle in all circumstances.

Colin does not want a job and in any case faces a multiplicity of obstacles to working. His health is just one of them, and not self-evidently the most important. Even if he were able to work, the chances seem slim of him finding a job that is sufficiently well paid to make it worthwhile for him to move off benefits, especially as he lives in one of the country's weaker labour markets.

Colin, aged 45

Colin's caring responsibilities were mentioned in ch. 7 – he has a daughter with disabilities – but there are other factors, too, keeping him out of the labour market. He describes himself as 'long-term sick' rather than unemployed because he suffers from severe migraines and has stomach and kidney problems. He has not worked for more than ten years, apart from occasional casual work. He has difficulty reading and writing, lacks formal qualifications, and has spent time in prison. He also has five children (the oldest is 12) and his wife does not go out to work, so his IB is topped up by a range of other benefits, including Income Support, Housing Benefit and Council Tax Benefit, bringing the total to over £300 a week (in 1999). He lives in a council house in the Barnsley area.

I can't fill forms in or 'owt. Not very good at reading. That was one of the main problems getting another job . . . Way back, you didn't have to do all this filling forms in for labouring jobs, so . . . it got a bit harder for me . . . Way back, it were a bit easier weren't it? I mean, you could fall out of one job and get another job as easy as 'owt.

I have been bad, don't get me wrong. I have been bad with headaches but I've never been bad in my body . . . I've done steelworks, I've done all sorts. Hod carrying and scaffolding and concreting. I've done all sorts like that. This last couple of years I've got bad with my stomach and kidneys and things.

Once you've told them you've been in prison, they don't want to know. They want to know basically the truth. And you tell 'em. And they just don't want to know.

After you're 30 . . . that's it with work, unless you're qualified for something, which I'm not . . . I'm 45 and looking into the future a couple of years . . . I mean, there's going to be nowt is there?

For others, getting a job may not seem impossible, but in the circumstances they face – their health, existing income and the job opportunities in the local labour market – finding work is not a priority. Like Malcolm and Colin, Harry does not want a job but in his case this owes at least something to the fact that he is able to get by reasonably comfortably. Taking all things into consideration, he sees no need to try to overcome the handicap of his declining health.

Harry, aged 58

Like Colin, Harry's responsibilities as a carer were mentioned in ch. 7. Aged 50, Harry took redundancy in 1990 from his job as a bus driver in order to look after his wife, who was seriously ill. Prior to driving buses he had a long spell as a miner. Initially he claimed Invalid Care Allowance for looking after his wife, plus Income Support, but his own health deteriorated during his time as a carer – he has back and hip problems, suffers from lung disease, and has had heart troubles as well. So when his wife died in 1996 his doctor had no hesitation in placing him on IB. He also receives Disability Living Allowance, Industrial Injuries Benefit and a pit pension (about £40 per week). This means that his total weekly income is just over £200 a week. He lives alone in a council house in Chesterfield, on which he pays full rent and Council Tax.

At this moment in time I am financially alright. I'm not going back to work, I don't want to go back to work. I think I've done my share. And if there are any vacancies, let young 'uns have 'em.

I'm sure if I went out tomorrow, by the end of the week I'd have a job of some description. And then I got to thinking about it and I thought, well come on . . . at that time I was 55–56 . . . I've worked since I've been 15 year old right up to packing it in to look after my wife.

Now if I do go and take a job . . . I'm going to lose this benefit, that benefit. Financially, I've got to work out the pros and cons because I might go for a fortnight and then find out I can't do it and then I've got to start fighting all the tribunals in the country to get back to where I was before.

Men such as Malcolm, Colin and Harry are unlikely to return to employment so long as they do not want a job. A change in attitude would require a shift in either their personal circumstances or in the labour markets they face. In Malcolm's case only an improvement in his health would seem likely to make a difference. In Colin's and Harry's cases an improvement in their health would help but there would also need to be a shift in the financial attractions of going back to work rather than remaining on benefits. The wages that Colin and Harry could command would need to be a lot higher.

Another group of long-term sick men are unlikely to return to work in the near future even though they would very much like to do so. These are the men whose health problems remain a serious obstacle. In the contemporary labour market they need to find a considerate and flexible employer if their aspirations are to be met. Dean is an example of a man who wants to work but still faces considerable physical hurdles, in spite of which he was about to submit a job application at the time we interviewed him.

Dean, aged 44

Three years ago, Dean walked away from his own business as a fraud investigator. He had begun to have severe headaches, culminating in a collapse. He was diagnosed as having a tumour and underwent major surgery. He has recovered, though there is some permanent damage including extensive loss of movement in one arm and hand. He also now suffers from epilepsy and his speech is a little impaired. He is separated from his wife and lives in a council house in Northampton with his two young children. He relies on Income Support, with a premium for disability.

I would love to work...I have absolutely no outside interests other than my immediate family. And I have always been a man who has been self-driven and very goal orientated. And I've always kept on the go. I need something to do. And I would do literally anything.

Other men face physical or psychological obstacles to working that appear surmountable, both in theory and in practice. Roger is an example. He says he would like a full-time job and he has been taking positive steps to try to equip himself for getting back to work.

Roger, aged 38

Roger has been without a full-time job for between three and four years. He had to leave his last job as an NHS nurse because of anxiety and depression. He receives a pension arising from early retirement from his job, plus IB. He lives in Northampton with his wife (who works full time) and three teenage children, in a house on which they still have a substantial mortgage. Roger's tentative steps towards re-employment were mentioned in ch. 8 – he has recently been doing a part-time job placement scheme, to build his confidence, and has also returned to study for NVQs, though he remains sceptical about the value of external pressure to go back into the labour market.

> It's a very strange area, depression, anxiety. Particularly when you're anxious about work. To have that pressure put onto you that 'yes you will go back' or 'you will do this training scheme' or 'you will do this that or the other'. I don't think it will work.
>
> I thought while I'm feeling positive, get myself down to the employment agency and see what they can advise . . . I mean, I could have just carried on in the same sort of mode but it wasn't doing me any good . . . I think if I had carried on claiming Incapacity Benefit then I would have been at some time called up and put on something, but in no way did that shape any of my thinking . . . I can see some sort of future ahead although I still don't know what it's going to be.

There should be every hope that in due course a relatively young man such as Roger, living in an area where the demand for labour is strong, should be able to re-enter employment. Another one of our interviewees had actually made the move from IB into work, underlining the point that the health problems of IB claimants are not necessarily an insurmountable obstacle to all work in all circumstances.

Stan, aged 54

Stan had not had regular work for ten years when he was first surveyed in 1998, and was claiming IB. However, as we mentioned in ch. 8, when we returned a few months later to carry out an in-depth interview he had just started work in a parcel depot, as an agency employee, though he was finding the physical demands of the job to be a strain. His return to work partly reflected a change of heart by him and his wife but had also been triggered by a visit from social security officials, who had been told he was 'working on the side'. He lives in a council house in Northampton with his wife, who has health problems of her own and does not go out to work, and their three school-age children.

> I don't like drawing [benefits] anyway. I never have done. It was just economically the best way for us. Which it is with a lot of people with two or three kids that are unskilled. You just can't command the kind of wage that you need these days for two or three kids. It's impossible. I just wouldn't have been able to bring in enough for us to have any quality of life whatsoever.
>
> I don't mind [returning to work] . . . You'd be bored at home sat watching television wouldn't you? I can't stand it at all. I couldn't take any more of

> it. I always kept myself occupied because I always went out doing a bit for people. . . I can stand that kind of pain anyway [from lumbago]. It gets worse as I get older but I can stand it. There's a lot working in worse pain than me.
>   The doctors'll go mad. I went down with this [angina] about six weeks ago. I was at the doctor. 'No work. Definitely no work.' He's going to go mad when I go back!

Nevertheless, even if health-related barriers to employment do prove surmountable there remains the obstacle of a shortage of jobs in some parts of the country. This affects the prospects of the long-term sick just as much as the long-term unemployed. A man with few qualifications or skills always has difficulty finding work in a local labour market where there are lots of similar men competing for the same vacancies. A man with family responsibilities also finds that he cannot afford to take the lowest paid jobs that would leave him little if at all better off. Whereas the two previous examples – Roger and Stan – live in Northampton, Peter lives in Chesterfield, where it is harder to find suitable jobs, especially if employers get to know that you've had a history of mental health problems.

Peter, aged 36

Peter has been out of work on sickness benefits for five years. He suffers from depression and had been dismissed from his last job, in a factory, after having time off during a difficult divorce. He lives in a council house with his new partner (who is also not in employment) and their young daughter.

I go for an interview. They see me, but they don't want to know. They read that form: you're ill. It doesn't matter that you can do the job standing on your head. That doesn't apply to them. They're not interested. You've got this illness. They don't want you.
  So now I have reached the stage, I'm not looking. I refuse to look for work. . . I'm honest about it and I'm honest with the social. If they ask me 'why aren't I looking for work?' I'll turn round and say to them 'you find me work that's not security work, that's going to pay me a good wage. I'll do that.' But I'm not working for a pittance. I refuse.

It is hard to escape the conclusion, however, that for many men the move on to IB is a one-way ticket. This view is supported by aggregate statistics that show that the big increase in the number of IB claimants during the 1980s and 1990s owed less to a surge in the number of new claimants and more to the fact that the men on IB were staying there longer. In our survey, for example, 40 per cent of IB claimants had been on this benefit for at least five years. Furthermore, IB claimants are concentrated among the older age group – nearly two-thirds are over 50. In effect, for many men IB acts as a key financial bridge between the end of their working lives and the state pension age of 65.

Three final examples illustrate this point. We make no apologies for the fact that all three examples are drawn from Barnsley in South Yorkshire, and all three men are former miners. The share of men of working age who are IB claimants is much higher in parts of Northern England, Central Scotland and South Wales than in the rest of the country. Barnsley is one of these areas – in August 1999, 16 per cent of all men of working age were claiming sickness-related benefits. These were the places where traditional heavy industries, mainly employing men, were especially badly affected by job losses in the 1980s and 1990s. The coal industry typifies this collapse in employment perhaps more than most and we noted (in ch. 5) how the largest labour market adjustment in response to the loss of mining jobs has been a withdrawal of men from economic activity into recorded long-term sickness. The experiences of former miners in Barnsley may therefore shed light on the areas and the sectors where IB plays a particularly central role in supporting non-employed men.

The three examples below are all men who have never worked since leaving the coal industry, mostly a decade ago. Two of these men have never claimed unemployment benefits during their years without work and have therefore been excluded from claimant unemployment figures for the whole of this period. The third claimed unemployment benefits only briefly for a period in the mid-1990s. All three men said they would have happily carried on working in the coal industry if a job had still been there for them. However, none of these men now wants a job.

Chapter 5 argued that to be 'hidden unemployed' men do not necessarily have to be looking for work. The important point, it was argued, is whether men could reasonably be expected to have been in work in a fully employed economy. Chapter 5 also argued that there is extensive 'hidden sickness' in the labour market – men who continue in employment despite health problems, possibly because their employer is keen to retain them – and all three of the men described below held down a job in the coal industry for several years despite the limitations imposed by their health. However, the Barnsley miners' former employer has now disappeared entirely from their area, and they find themselves in a difficult labour market with few other obvious opportunities, especially given their health problems. They offer an insight into what for many may be the real experience of hidden unemployment.

Gordon, aged 54

Gordon took redundancy from the coal industry in 1988 and has never worked since. He has always had poor eyesight so he never worked underground and was employed on the surface instead, latterly as a general foreman in charge of several operations. He was offered the chance of a transfer but decided to opt for redundancy because of the travelling involved and because, apart from his poor eyesight, he also had recurring back problems. Because of his eyesight, he gained early access to his coal industry pension. On being made redundant he moved directly on to sickness benefits but did not initially give up looking for work. Gordon lives with his wife, who works part time, and two older children, who both work, and is still paying a mortgage on his home.

I think health-wise I would have stopped on if I could have done. I might have stopped on until I was 60 if I could have done.

When I finished at the pit I thought to myself I'd never work again . . . Who'd take you on when you're nearly 50? And train you up? Because they're not going to get any work out of you are they? If they set someone on at 18 they'd get some years out of him won't they? Train me up and in five years I could be on the sick.

I went for one interview and as I sat down he said 'you're really too old aren't you?' I was 47 then I think. It's all the same when you get to 45 – you're on the scrap heap.

But I'd worked all my life. I'd got this pension. I thought, I'm going to enjoy it a little bit . . . We'd like a bit more, but you've got to manage with what you've got haven't you?

Terry, aged 64

Terry worked continuously in the mining industry from leaving school until being made redundant in 1985. He has been claiming IVB and then IB, ever since. He had been able to access sickness benefits because in the 1970s he had a serious accident at the pit, after which he was moved to lighter duties above ground. He lives in a council house with his wife, who works part time, and now describes himself as 'retired' rather than 'long-term sick'. He would have liked to have stayed in the coal industry:

But they said there was no chance of being transferred. They said they'd not much chance of transferring 100 per cent fit men.

Surely there was no other employer going to bother with me. I couldn't do a physical job. I didn't bother going looking because . . . nobody else would set me on if my own employer was having doubts about keeping me on...I thought they're not going to bother with me when they've got 100 per cent fit men going and they can't get jobs in any other industry.

Bill, aged 51

Bill, whose health problems were mentioned in ch. 8, left the coal industry in 1992. He would have liked to stay on but he had taken a lot of time off (owing to neck pain and arthritis) and at a time when his employer was adopting a hard line on absentees he feared being sacked if he did not take early retirement on grounds of ill-health. He has not worked since. Initially he moved directly on to what was then IVB, but in 1994 had been 'thrown off' on to unemployment benefits. He then claimed Invalid Care Allowance instead while he looked after his mother. Although he admits that his health problems would probably not have prevented him from working when he first finished at the pit, there has been some deterioration and in 1997 he returned to IB. He also receives a pit pension of around £110 per week. A single man, Bill owns his home outright.

When I went to the appeal when I was thrown off [IVB] I was given a list of jobs that I was capable of doing with the problems I was having. Now, the only two jobs that came up they said I was capable of doing were a car park attendant and a lift attendant. Now round here, they're very rare them type of jobs, so obviously I'd no chance of getting one.

If I could have found a job which could pay me a decent wage I would probably have tried it, but there wasn't any. Especially when at the time I was on the dole, signing on, there were hundreds signing on, some I know for a fact had not had jobs in ten years.

I suppose when I first finished I thought about [working] but it went through my mind 'what can I do that doesn't involve any really heavy work?' And at the time I couldn't think of anything. But now I'm just not bothered . . . I can manage on what bit of money I've got now. At the moment I can anyway.

Conclusions

In this chapter we have looked at the real situations and stories of a small number of non-employed men. Obviously each individual has a partial view of the labour market, but overall their perspectives provide a different picture from that painted by aggregate statistics or economic theory. There are differences between places, and differences in individual biographies and work histories. These all contribute to an uneven, differentiated and complex labour market.

Individuals sometimes face a range of complex interweaving barriers to returning to work. The examples quoted illustrate barriers relating to age, health, skills, access to transport, wages and a lack of job opportunities. In response, some men are close to pursuing only a minimal strategy of job search in order to meet benefit requirements, and others have given up entirely.

The current focus of UK employment policy is directed towards getting people to broaden their horizons in looking for work, and increasing the intensity and effectiveness of their job search activity. The aim is to encourage jobseekers to adapt to the changing demand for labour. This strategy also involves upgrading and adapting their skills. So far, compulsion has been applied only to those officially classified as unemployed and receiving JSA. For those classified in other ways, for example recipients of IB, the approach has been one of encouragement rather than compulsion; the aim has been to encourage IB claimants to think of the work they can do rather than the work they cannot. The various forms of encouragement and compulsion involve looking further afield for work (thus implying being prepared to move or to travel) and giving consideration to retraining and to options that might hitherto have been considered unthinkable, such as lower wages or less secure employment.

Becoming more active in looking for work and applying for jobs does increase the chances of some individuals returning to employment. However, there are dangers in assuming that this individual experience can simply be aggregated to suggest that more people more actively searching for work will increase overall employment levels. Aggregate employment is dependent on a far greater number of variables, so unless overall employment levels rise the intensified emphasis on supply-side measures may affect only the distribution of jobs, i.e. exactly who gets employed. It may change individual positions in the queue, and give those towards the back more of a chance, but it may not itself change the overall length of the queue. This is not to say that strategies focused on individual motivation and requirements are irrelevant. Clearly, given the highly differentiated experience of non-employed men illustrated in this chapter, and the complex range of barriers they face, support needs to be tailored to fit the complex circumstances of each individual.

The clear conclusion from our interviews is that obstacles to getting men back to work are a mix of both labour demand and labour supply. Many men recognise that they face personal barriers to re-employment, but in at least as many cases they also recognise that there are insufficient jobs locally that they are likely to be able to secure, or afford to take.

Part III

The policy implications

11 New roles, New Deal

*Pete Alcock, Christina Beatty, Stephen Fothergill,
Rob Macmillan and Sue Yeandle*

The main findings

Our research has been restricted to just the UK so there must be caution about the extent to which the findings can be generalised to other Western economies. However, the observations that can be made about men's labour force participation in the UK are striking. At least six key points emerge.

First, the extent of labour market detachment among men is now very considerable indeed. It is well known that more young people are staying on in education and thereby delaying their entry to full-time employment. What our findings show is the dramatic rise in labour market detachment among the over 25s – a group largely clear of full-time education – and in particular among the over 50s. Unlike the gradual increase in the number of young people staying on in education, which goes back many decades, rising detachment among these men is a comparatively recent phenomenon and unlike extended stays in education it was never a sought after outcome of public policy. This rising detachment among older men has also happened during a period when the labour market was mostly plagued by a shortage of job opportunities.

Claimant unemployment comprises only a modest proportion of the total number of non-employed men of working age. The others – by far the majority – are traditionally described as 'economically inactive'. Early in the new century, when claimant unemployment in the UK has fallen to a twenty-five-year low, the number of economically inactive men of working age outnumbers the number of claimant unemployed men by nearly three to one. 'Economic inactivity' in all its various forms – long-term sickness, early retirement and so on – has thus become a major feature of the male labour market.

The second key point to emerge from our research is that this extensive labour market detachment among men cannot be equated with voluntary withdrawal from employment. Above all, it should not be equated with voluntary early retirement. That a substantial number of men do retire early – i.e. before the state pension age of 65 – is not in dispute. But among men in their 50s and even men in their early 60s, early retirees make up only a minority of those outside full-time employment. Among the under 50s early retirement barely figures at all.

The majority of the 25–64-year-old men who are detached from employment find themselves in this position because of unemployment, ill-health or pressing domestic responsibilities. None of these reasons can really be described as 'voluntary'. Even 'early retirement' is not always what it first seems, as our survey and interview evidence both illustrate. Sometimes the men who describe themselves as retired actually left their last job because of redundancy. Some of the early retired also looked for further employment when their last job ended, and only after their subsequent failure to find work did they become reconciled to retirement. The dividing line between unemployment and early retirement is indistinct at best.

The third key point is that many of the men who have become detached from employment still want to work. This does not just apply to the claimant unemployed, who by virtue of the rules governing their benefits have to stay in touch with the labour market. As we saw in ch. 5, around half of all IB claimants say that they would like a full-time job. Among the detached male workforce there is therefore an immense reserve of labour which could in theory be re-engaged with the mainstream economy.

Another way of interpreting this widespread desire to work is that there is extensive hidden unemployment. IB appears to be at the heart of this, partly because of the sheer number of men who now claim this benefit, partly because of their skewed distribution across local labour markets, and partly because of what the claimants say about themselves. Chapter 5 argued that the real issue is just how many of the 1.4 million men of working age in receipt of this benefit might be considered to be hidden unemployed. Estimates were presented which put the figure at approaching three-quarters of a million. The precise number is perhaps irrelevant, and in any case is open to methodological dispute. The importance is the broad order of magnitude, which seems to be substantial. Yet as the same chapter was at pains to stress, this is an unusual form of hidden unemployment. The claims for IB are not fraudulent. Nor are the physical limitations from which these men suffer anything less than real. There is plenty of interview evidence to endorse this view in ch. 8. These men are hidden unemployed in that in a fully employed economy they could reasonably be expected to have been in work.

There is an indistinct dividing line between unemployment and sickness, just as there is between unemployment and early retirement. Many of the IB claimants who say they want work do so in full knowledge of the limitations on just exactly what they are able to do. However, excepting those with the severest problems, ill-health or disability has never been an absolute bar to employment. As ch. 5 explained, in the UK nearly 3 million people with long-term limiting illnesses do hold down jobs, and further back in time the much smaller numbers on sickness-related benefits suggest that far more men with health problems did hold onto a place in the labour market. What has happened is that as the jobs which they once held have disappeared, their health problems have become visible in the sickness-related benefit statistics. Their joblessness, however, has remained hidden from the official unemployment figures.

Because of the apparent scale of hidden unemployment our research points to a quite different view of the UK economy from that which most politicians and commentators put forward at the start of the new century. Their view is typically that the mass unemployment that haunted the 1980s and 1990s has been banished, and that a shortage of workers rather than a shortage of jobs is increasingly the UK's problem. We do not dispute that unemployment, however it is measured, has fallen from its peak levels. But our findings suggest that a substantial proportion of the old unemployment problem has simply become hidden from view as the benefits system and the Employment Services have diverted large numbers of jobless men from unemployment-related benefits to sickness-related benefits, and thereby out of the official unemployment figures. Labour ministers are right in arguing that too many people have been 'parked' on IB, but they have failed to acknowledge the true distress in the labour market which is thereby being disguised.

The fourth key point to emerge from our research is the importance of place. Economists in particular can often be blind to the differences between localities. They tend to deal in crude national aggregates, as if all cities and regions behave in the same way. So while they have sometimes noted the extent of economic inactivity among men they have rarely considered the local geography or its implications. Yet what is transparent from our research is that the extent of labour market detachment among men varies enormously from place to place. Where detachment is widespread, the share of 25–64 year olds without jobs can be three or four times higher than elsewhere – from more than 30 per cent of men in some places to less than 10 per cent in others.

The geography of this labour market detachment follows familiar patterns. Broadly, in the areas where claimant unemployment has traditionally been highest, the extent of economic inactivity is also highest. In particular, the share of men claiming sickness-related benefits peaks in these same places. Whether a man remains in employment, especially beyond 50, thus depends not just on his abilities and aspirations but also on exactly where he happens to live. In the industrial parts of North East England, in South Yorkshire, Merseyside, the Welsh valleys and Clydeside, labour market detachment among men is exceptionally widespread. That these same areas were particularly badly affected by industrial job losses during the 1980s and 1990s adds fuel to the argument that the high level of economic inactivity in these places is in part a form of hidden unemployment.

The fifth point is about the redefinition of men's working lives. Whereas at one time most men expected to have to work (or at the very least look for work) from leaving school until the age of 65, the growth in labour market detachment is creating a new pattern. Finishing work early, before 65, is becoming the norm. Sometimes this is done with the support of a pension, other times not. At the same time men's life expectancy is increasing, albeit slowly, so that the relatively new prospect of an extended period beyond employment is opening up. So, too, is the prospect of taking on new roles, such as sharing in the care of grandchildren. There are elements here that surely represent progress.

However, our evidence suggests that it would be wrong to jump to the conclusion that this redefinition of men's working lives is always welcome. We have noted that labour market detachment is something that is forced on many men, even in their 50s and early 60s. It can also be associated with lower incomes and dependence on welfare benefits. There is only mixed evidence that men are happy with this new redefined structure of their working lives. Many would still prefer to be in work. There is also widespread resentment at having been discarded by employers and at perceived age discrimination. The middle-class early retirees who take up part-time work stand out as perhaps the main exception for whom the early departure from full-time employment is working well. Supported by pensions from their previous jobs, many of these men seem to have arrived at a compromise that neither dents their living standards nor sits uncomfortably alongside their aspirations. They are, however, a relatively small minority among the detached male workforce – certainly less than 10 per cent.

Quite where this redefinition of men's working lives leaves those older men who remain in employment is an interesting question. Already at one end of the age range among employees, these older workers are becoming a still smaller proportion of the active workforce. Positions of power and influence, from Cabinet ministers to company executives, are increasingly being filled by people in their 40s rather than men – and it was once nearly all men – in their 50s and 60s. Exactly what role this leaves for the active older worker is unclear. Rather than their accumulated skills and experience being valued, there is at least a danger that their increasingly small presence in the workplace makes them seem old fashioned, out of touch and left over from an earlier era of technology and organisation.

The sixth key point to emerge from the research concerns the interaction of the benefits system and men's labour market position. We have already commented on how the operation of the benefits system appears to have masked the true scale of unemployment. Much wider issues are raised by these links. However, the labour market changes reported in this book have interacted with the increasingly complex relations between means-tested and contributory benefits to move the benefits system from the relatively passive role of support for unemployment classically envisaged by Beveridge, towards a more active role in which regulations governing entitlement may be steering some claimants towards particular labour market outcomes.

This is clearest at the interface between sickness and unemployment. Many long-term unemployed men are financially better off on non-means-tested IB than on means-tested JSA. This creates financial incentives for men with health problems, especially for those who have been on IB for some while and receive benefit at the highest rate. Furthermore, once on IB men are not required to look for work and to do so could in fact prejudice their benefit entitlement by demonstrating an ability to work. So once on IB, very few jobless men do actually look for work and few seek a move on to JSA. Their position firmly outside the labour market is thus consolidated. We see here the unintended outcome of the interaction of benefit rules and a difficult labour market.

As our findings show, men's labour market detachment is actually more likely to be supported by the state, through the benefits system, than by private means such as pensions. Even for some men in receipt of a pension, the benefits system provides an important top up. Some might argue that in the absence of welfare benefits many of these non-employed men would have had no choice but to keep on looking for work, so in effect it is the state that has acted as midwife to widespread labour market detachment. But this is a simplistic view, not least because in an economy operating below full employment, dropping out of the labour market is often the alternative to conventional unemployment that would in any case have been supported by the state. The real debate is about the rules by which the benefits system operates and, in turn, how these affect labour market behaviour. The important message from our research is perhaps that labour market detachment among men is not only costly in terms of the potential output forgone but also that it is a substantial financial claim on the Exchequer.

Welfare to Work?

In Britain the term 'welfare to work' has become closely associated or even synonymous with the reforms implemented by the Labour government from 1997 onwards. In fact, as chs. 2 and 3 showed, the roots of welfare to work go back much further and this approach is not uniquely British. The United States, in particular, has long practised elements of welfare to work. But in Britain Labour's Welfare to Work programme does represent a step-change in the emphasis on getting people back to work, not only to reduce the benefits bill but also to promote social cohesion through participation in employment.

As ch. 3 explained, at the heart of Labour's welfare to work programme lies New Deal – a series of initiatives targeted at specific groups of claimants all of whom are currently detached from employment. By far the biggest initiative, in terms of resources, is targeted at the unemployed under 25s. This involves an initial stage consisting of guidance and advice, followed by four options – a subsidised job with an employer, work on an environmental task force (usually for benefit plus a small sum), work with a voluntary organisation (again usually for 'benefit plus') or full-time education or training. Famously, there is no 'fifth option' – in other words, under-25 New Deal participants are not allowed to remain on benefits.

The research reported in this book has focused on the over 25s. For this group of men three New Deal schemes are most relevant. The first is for those who are long-term unemployed JSA claimants. The second is for the over 50s who are long-term benefit claimants, in this case of a wide range of benefits including not just JSA but also sickness-related benefits. The third is for people with a disability. Like the New Deal for the under 25s, these three schemes involve a mixture of advice, financial support for employers and access to training. For the over 50s and the disabled, participation is voluntary.

The New Deal has resulted in some important steps forward. In particular, the personal advisers allocated to each participant represent a significant advance in tailoring services to the needs of the individual. New Deal itself is also just part of a much wider package aimed at promoting labour market attachment. As ch. 3 explained, this includes Working Families Tax Credit, Minimum Income Guarantees and the national minimum wage, all intended to 'make work pay'. There is also a greater emphasis on educational standards and attainment, intended to raise the employability of new entrants to the labour market. Whether New Deal is rooted in an accurate understanding of the causes of joblessness is, however, much more debatable, and on this front Labour's new programme has prompted a distinctly more sceptical response (see, for example, Turok and Webster 1998, Peck and Theodore 2000).

The problem is that New Deal (and the wider Welfare to Work programme) is a wholly supply-side initiative. Its underlying assumption is that the cause of unemployment is that the unemployed are either insufficiently employable or that their wage expectations are unrealistically high in relation to their low productivity. The solution to unemployment, in this view, is therefore to increase the employability of the workforce through education and training and to ensure that the tax and benefits system creates the incentive to work. These views are most clearly articulated in the Treasury document *The Goal of Full Employment: Employment Opportunity for all throughout Britain* (HM Treasury 2000) and in the employment Green Paper *Towards Full Employment in a Modern Society* (DfEE 2001b). In essence, the supply-side approach to unemployment embodied in New Deal assumes that a better supply of more employable labour will ultimately generate its own demand.

One of the favourite arguments in support of New Deal is that the jobless become increasingly unemployable the longer they are out of work. This view is particularly closely associated with Richard Layard, a key government adviser often seen as the intellectual architect of New Deal (see Layard, Nickell and Jackman 1991 and Layard 1997, 1998). The idea is that the skills of the unemployed wither and their work ethic wanes as the duration for which they are without work grows. In effect they become decoupled from the rest of the workforce. Employers cease being interested in them and accordingly this group no longer exerts any downward pressure on wage inflation in the labour market. If these long-term unemployed could be reskilled and reconnected to the labour force, the argument goes, they would put downward pressure on wage inflation and allow the economy to operate at a higher level of employment. Interest rates could be cut with less fear of inflationary consequences.

A more direct route through which increased employability could lead to higher employment is by easing skill shortages. It is undoubtedly true that from time to time some firms do encounter recruitment difficulties, and that the staff they sometimes take on are less than fully productive because of shortfalls in training or skills. A better-qualified and well-motivated pool of available labour should allow some of these firms to expand. National output and employment would be higher.

But set against these mechanisms for job creation, the supply-side approach embodied in New Deal does nothing directly to promote additional demand for labour. So although in the years immediately following its introduction employment in the UK rose and recorded unemployment fell, it cannot be assumed that the Welfare to Work programme was an important cause. Indeed, it can be argued that the apparent success of New Deal in moving under 25s into jobs and off the unemployment register mainly occurred because of buoyant macroeconomic circumstances. This was certainly the conclusion of one evaluation (Riley and Young 2000).

In weaker macroeconomic circumstances, or in locations where there is little obvious shortage of labour, the potential consequences of a purely supply-side approach to tackling unemployment are altogether less desirable. The effect of encouraging greater labour market participation, especially among the less skilled, is likely to be an increase in the competition for the relatively few available jobs. This in turn may depress wages – already low for low skill jobs – and make it easier for employers to use short-term contracts and 'hire and fire' practices, to the detriment of the job security and conditions of those already in work.

Our research offers four important comments on the validity of Welfare to Work initiatives like New Deal. The first is that the balance of funding between the existing New Deal schemes is altogether wrong. When they were initially constituted in 1997, using the proceeds of a windfall tax on privatised utilities, £200 million was earmarked for people on IB, £200 million for lone parents, £350 million for long-term unemployed adults, and no less than £3,150 million for unemployed under 25s. This balance did not shift significantly during Labour's first term in office. The massive weighting towards the young unemployed reflected the perceived importance of giving this group a fair start in the labour market, not least to help stem the growth in crime by young people. Getting youth unemployment down was one of Labour's five key pledges that helped the party win the 1997 general election.

This allocation of funding was clearly uninformed (or at best uninfluenced) by data on the number of benefit claimants. Back in 1997, 16–24 year olds who had been unemployed for six months or more (the initial target New Deal group) were a relatively small group. As youth unemployment fell they became an even smaller group. In early 2001 a total of only 260,000 16–24 year olds were unemployed and claiming benefit, and only 40,000 of these for six months or more. By contrast, our research highlights vast numbers of older men who are out of work and claiming benefits – 1.4 million IB claimants alone, hardly any of whom are under 25. Even the balance between the measures aimed at IB claimants and those aimed at the older long-term unemployed seems wrong. Among the over 25s, long-term unemployed JSA claimants are far outnumbered by those on IB.

Of course, there is no reason why each category of New Deal client should be targeted by the same per capita funding. It is perhaps right that a young person struggling to secure a first foothold in the labour market should be given priority over a 55 year old with at most only a few years before retirement. But it is important to remember that even among groups such as IB claimants a large proportion still express a desire to work. Furthermore, because of their health problems, they are likely to require more intensive practical support from the employment services, and greater flexibility from employers, in order to allow them to participate once again in paid employment. They may also require substantial retraining if the jobs which they used to do have disappeared or if their physical limitations prevent them from returning to their old occupation. Fortunately, the balance of spending on different New Deal client groups is something that could be adjusted fairly easily. All it requires is the political will.

The second comment on Welfare to Work arising from our research is an endorsement of the view that a large proportion of those who are out of work and on benefit have become so detached from employment that they no longer exert any downward pressure on wage inflation. This is especially true of the very large number of men who are IB claimants. We have suggested that many of them should be regarded as hidden unemployed in that they could reasonably have been expected to be in work in a fully employed economy. But this does not mean that they presently look for work. In fact, looking for work is something done by only a small minority of these men.

There is a huge reserve army of men on sickness-related benefits that could in theory provide a major source of labour for a growing economy. As we noted, many people with long-term illnesses do continue to hold down jobs, and in the past the much smaller number of sickness-related claimants indicates that far more people with health problems did in fact work. It should not be assumed, therefore, that because men or women are claiming IB they are incapable of all work in all circumstances. Indeed, most of the men we surveyed said this was not the case. One of the problems in the UK benefits system is that the 'All Work Test', which determines access to IB beyond the first six months, makes a crude distinction between those who 'can work' and those who 'cannot work at all'. The effect is that it marginalises many IB claimants far more than is necessary. So at the times and in the places that their contribution to the labour force would be valuable, the benefits system contrives to rule it out.

'Personal capability assessments', introduced in 2001, aim to restore some balance in this respect. The 'All Work Test' remains the gateway to IB itself, but IB claimants now have to attend an interview with an adviser which explores what work they are actually able to do and what specialist training or support they may need. At last, therefore, IB claimants are no longer written off so comprehensively, but whether personal capability assessments really do begin to alter claimants' perceptions of the opportunities available to them, and whether the back-up training resources are ever provided, still remains to be seen. The assessments may yet prove to be just another bureaucratic procedure to be gone through.

The third comment on Welfare to Work arising from our research is the importance of tailoring policies to the needs of the individual. In so far as this is the intended role of the 'personal adviser' within New Deal our findings again provide a cautious endorsement of Labour's approach. What is evident, particularly from in-depth interviews, is that the circumstances confronting individuals and the obstacles to their re-employment are often complex. Surprisingly few men are simply 'unemployed' in the sense that they just cannot find work. Certainly, a shortage of jobs is an on-going problem, especially in some areas. But often the difficulties men face in securing appropriate employment are compounded by degrees of ill-health, by the interaction of their benefit entitlement and the wages they can command, and by domestic responsibilities, as well as by the shortcomings in training and skills which New Deal is so keen to target. Higher levels of employment overall would mean that there would be a greater choice of opportunities and a greater likelihood that the jobless could find something suitable for them. Nevertheless the difficult task of matching job opportunities to the individual would still remain.

Our findings also demonstrate the blurred distinction between categories of jobless men. The dividing line between sickness and unemployment is a case in point, and so is the distinction between unemployment and early retirement. This emphasises the need for policies that avoid the rigid categorisation of people. New Deal seems to be badly designed, with its continuing emphasis on discreet and non-overlapping groups of claimants, each with its own set of rules for support.

The fourth and final comment on Welfare to Work concerns the geography of joblessness. Here our observations are altogether less favourable. It is clear that supply-side initiatives like New Deal work best in local labour markets where there are plenty of jobs. In these strong labour markets the task is to ensure that the jobless are able to fill the vacancies that are available. In these areas it is also much more likely that residual unemployment reflects a skills mismatch rather than a fundamental imbalance between labour demand and supply. Yet our research shows not only that non-employment among men extends far beyond just claimant unemployment but also that jobless men, especially those hidden from the official unemployment figures, are disproportionately concentrated in the weakest labour markets. We documented the distribution of non-employed men across the country as a whole in ch. 4, and the geographical concentration of the men on sickness-related benefits (including the 'hidden unemployed') in ch. 5.

What this means is that Labour's New Deal makes sense in parts of South East England but as a solution to the unemployment problems of much of the rest of the country, especially Northern industrial Britain, it looks fundamentally ill conceived. The scale of joblessness among men in parts of Northern Britain is far greater than is likely to be removed by labour-supply measures alone. In these areas, the main solution would undoubtedly be a greater supply of jobs.

The Labour government's enthusiastic embrace of New Deal is rooted in a very London-centred view of the country, shared by top politicians, senior civil servants and the national media. In London at the turn of the century the day-to-day experience of the economy is that it is strong with plenty of available jobs. Any continuing joblessness therefore seems explicable in terms of lack of skills or other personal obstacles to employment. This view is compounded by flawed unemployment data that suggests that most of the country is not lagging too far behind the capital. The reality is that these perceptions fall well short of an accurate view of Britain as a whole, where the truth is that for men in particular the destructive recessions of the 1980s and 1990s have left lasting damage. In Northern industrial areas the remaining jobs for manual workers often number just a fraction of what there used to be, and new job creation has not occurred on a sufficient scale to plug the gap left by the old industries. As a result, exceptionally large numbers of men in the worst affected areas still find themselves marginalised from the labour market.

Compared to the priority attached to New Deal, policies aimed at raising labour demand in lagging areas are a distinctly poor relation. The Conservative governments of the 1980s and early 1990s wound down what had previously been a quite vigorous set of regional policies, based at the core on strong financial incentives to firms to locate in areas of high unemployment. Labour has so far fought shy of reviving the regional policies of old, which, although expensive, did have a track record of successfully diverting large numbers of jobs to where they were needed (see Moore, Rhodes and Tyler 1986 in particular). Labour continues to make regional selective assistance – financial aid to firms – available on a discretionary basis in the assisted areas, which cover 28 per cent of the UK population, but its spending on this form of regional support remains well below the ceilings permitted by EU rules. Labour also places faith in the new Regional Development Agencies in England, but only a small part of their budgets is new money and the rest merely a diversion of existing regeneration spending from central government departments.

The full employment that New Deal aspires to deliver can in reality now be achieved only if it is linked to strong regional policies designed to remove imbalances in labour demand. The at-or-near full employment attained in the early 2000s in parts of the South of England limits the opportunity for further macroeconomic expansionary policies. The scope for lower interest rates, in particular, is limited by fears of fuelling inflation in an overheated South. Further job creation in the UK therefore needs to ensure that new employment is located in the areas where there continues to be a large labour surplus. It is not clear, however, that this has yet become the conventional wisdom among ministers.

From hidden to recorded unemployment?

Although one of the central propositions of this new research – that sickness-related benefits hide unemployment – is controversial, it has actually been accepted within government. The spiralling number of IVB claimants was a key reason for the changeover to IB in 1995, with its more rigorous medical tests to determine eligibility. At the same time, IB became taxable for new claimants and certain additional allowances for dependants were dropped. The effect of these reforms is already evident. After 1995, the relentless increase in the number of men of working age claiming sickness-related benefits finally levelled off.

A further round of reform was initiated in 1998. This time ministers made the link with unemployment explicit:

Incapacity Benefit has strayed from its real role of helping people who have lost their income when they were forced to stop work by illness or disability. It is increasingly being claimed by people who have been unemployed – sometimes for years. (DSS 1998c)

This new round of reform involved four measures. A 'single gateway' to access the benefits system, including IB, now provides advice on employment opportunities and training as well. The 'All Work Test' for IB claimants has been supplemented by personal capability assessments focusing on what the individual can actually do, enabling targeted advice to be provided on employment and training. Tougher rules deny access to IB by individuals without recent employment-based NI contributions. And means-testing has been introduced for IB claimants with substantial private pensions. In 2001 ministers announced a further change – most IB claimants would in future have their entitlement re-assessed every three years, instead of haphazardly or not at all, as had been the case. However, in what can be regarded as a wise political step, all these new rules apply only to new claimants. Existing claimants are unaffected.

The focus on new claimants means that the full impact of the reforms will take some years to be felt. Taken together with the 1995 reforms, however, the net effect is to make access to IB more difficult, to reduce the financial incentive to claim this particular benefit, and to increase the pressure to stay in touch with the labour market. In future, there is therefore a distinct possibility that as a result of these reforms less unemployment will be hidden from view by this part of the benefits system.

Means-testing in response to private pensions reduces the incentive to claim IB. Our survey evidence, in ch. 5, showed that just over a third of male IB claimants have pension income. Official figures indicate that in the late 1990s the average pension income for IB claimants was £85 per week (DSS 1998b). Since some of this pension income is still discounted and the rest remains means tested at a higher rate for JSA claimants, the main effect of the new reforms is likely to be a reduction in IB payments rather than a shift to JSA. However, the effect of the claw-back is to eliminate IB entirely for those with larger pensions.

Our survey findings showed that 20–25 per cent of men claiming IB moved directly from unemployment – some 300,000–350,000 men. Because of the new rules on NI contributions fewer men will now be entitled to IB, regardless of their capacity or incapacity for work. The government estimates that in the long run the effect of this will be to reduce the number of people on IB by 170,000 (DSS 1998b). In so far as they remain unemployed, they may qualify for JSA. The combination of the single gateway, the new personal capability assessments and the three-yearly reassessments, is also likely in theory to reduce the number of IB claimants who are considered in some way to be fit for work.

In addition there may be perverse effects. Because long-term unemployment now disqualifies an individual from IB there is an added incentive for some individuals to move quickly on to IB rather than linger on JSA. Because more claimants will be thrust on to means-tested JSA there will be less reason for their partners to remain in work, since their earnings would reduce benefit entitlement. More households could therefore become entirely workless.

However, the eventual impact of the reforms could be substantial. Given that we have estimated that there are approaching three-quarters of a million hidden unemployed men on IB, it would not be unreasonable to suppose that over ten to fifteen years the number of men claiming this benefit might be reduced by up to half a million. This assumes that the reforms are effective in reducing the flow on to IB and that many of the existing claimants clustered in their 50s and early 60s gradually reach retirement age. A similar proportional reduction among women would reduce the number of claimants by up to a further quarter of a million. While this may be good news from the point of view of public finances, such a big reduction is not costless.

First, there is a risk of impoverishment. New IB claimants with larger private pensions do face a reduction in benefits. Those claimants who find themselves on means-tested JSA will also generally receive less than if they had been on IB. Second, if there is no corresponding increase in job creation (and there is certainly no reason why this should be automatic), the effect of the reforms will be to increase claimant unemployment. Some of this additional unemployment will be among the jobless who are denied access to IB. Some of the increase will occur as men and women with disabilities are steered away from benefits and into vacancies that would otherwise have been filled by other jobseekers.

Perversely, at one level an increase in claimant unemployment as a result of these reforms would be welcome because it would bring recorded unemployment in Britain closer into line with the reality of joblessness. Via the requirement of JSA to look for work, the number of ILO unemployed should also rise, again bringing it closer in line with reality. A shift from IB to JSA is implicit in the reforms, but it is not obvious that the government is braced for the scale of the impact. If just two-thirds of the possible reduction in the number of IB claimants mentioned above were to feed through to additional JSA claims, the increase in claimant unemployment would be around 500,000.

The reforms to social security rules are also likely to lead to widening regional disparities in recorded unemployment. We have noted how hidden unemployment among IB claimants appears to be widespread in localities where the labour market is weak and where claimant unemployment is already highest. Following the reforms the existing IB claimants in these places are allowed to retain their present status, but the generation following them is much less likely to have the IB option available to them. If they cannot find work, more of them will be compelled to remain on JSA. The effect will be to concentrate the increase in recorded unemployment in places such as the Welsh valleys, North East England, Clydeside and parts of Yorkshire and the North West. In these places a 50 per cent reduction in the number of IB claimants, of which two-thirds fed through to an increase in the number of JSA claimants, would add no less than 6–10 percentage points to claimant unemployment.

Two misconceptions characterise virtually all debate about the UK labour market at the start of the twenty-first century. The first is that unemployment is fading as an economic problem. On official figures, at the start of the century the UK has lower unemployment than at any time since the 1970s and lower unemployment than most of its European neighbours, or so the argument goes. The second misconception is that within the UK regional disparities have narrowed. On official figures again, unemployment in many traditionally lagging regions is now no higher than in parts of London.

What the evidence presented in this book shows is that these perceptions are flawed. Nearly all commentators have ignored the interaction between the benefits system and the labour market and its impact on the way that joblessness is recorded. Our evidence shows that in Britain one of the main effects has been to disguise unemployment among men, especially in the areas where the demand for labour is weakest. Older, male manual workers – the group worst hit by redundancies in traditional industries – have been the most likely to fall out of the ranks of the conventional unemployed into other forms of joblessness.

In the UK, the government is already trying to move benefit claimants of working age back into employment. But it is not obvious that the government is aware of the scale of the change it is trying to set in motion or the extent to which it is likely to reveal the true level of distress in many of Britain's weakest local labour markets. It is also not obvious that the government has yet given much thought to how enormous numbers of older, often poorly qualified men with varying degrees of ill-health, can in future be given a meaningful role in the labour market.

A new approach to policy

The research reported in this book has led us to express concerns about the practicability and desirability of some core features of current UK government policy on the promotion of employment and on the measures adopted to ensure a movement from 'Welfare to Work'. Our conclusions go beyond just a critique of the details of current policy. They suggest the need for more general changes in the approach that underlies the development and delivery of government support.

For a start, it is clear that the challenge facing employment policymakers is not just claimant unemployment but the more general and diverse problem of labour market detachment among working-age men. As we have shown, detachment can take a number of forms and the experience of detachment differs a great deal between individuals. In general, however, a consequence of detachment is that some men find themselves towards the back end of our metaphorical queue for jobs – and what is more, find themselves stuck there. The challenge for policymakers is to ensure that the men who want to work are supported to move forward in the queue.

It is also clear, especially from the in-depth interviews which explored the experiences of individual men, that policies which seek to address labour market detachment need to start from the circumstances, experiences and needs of detached workers, rather than from the ideals, objectives or hopes of policy-makers. Unfortunately the policy legacy in employment and social security is one of top-down planning and, more significantly, of top-down thinking. Benefit entitlements and benefit rules, as we saw in ch. 3, have been adjusted in the light of assumptions about labour market needs and the incentives and supports needed by unemployed workers. More recently, employment support and training packages have been designed and implemented for specific groups. These include the New Deal programmes that we discussed above. They offer much to some individuals seeking employment, but the regimes of support they provide are driven by categories of benefit claimants (young unemployed, lone parents, the disabled) determined and defined by programme designers. Such categories need to be questioned and opened up, or perhaps even avoided altogether.

There is no doubt that the personal adviser system adopted within the UK's Welfare to Work and New Deal services is a step in the right direction, as research on the operation of the New Deal confirms (Millar 2000). However, this system still operates within the constraints of tightly defined groups, who are offered particular policy packages on the basis of how they are labelled rather than on an assessment of what as individuals they might actually need.

The explicit objective of current UK employment policy is to encourage as many people of working age as possible to be active participants in the labour market – holding jobs, running businesses or making a living through self-employment. If this is ever to be achieved, our research suggests that policy needs to be based on a regime which starts with individuals and the particular hurdles, barriers and pitfalls that stand in the way of their move (back) to employment or self-employment. This means treating all men (and women) as individuals, through a regime of personal interview and advice – and building on the adviser model could be an important move forward here. It also means tailoring responses to individual circumstances through a regime of personal packages of assistance and support for those who need help. Further, it means recognising that employment, especially full-time employment, may not be appropriate for everyone – for instance some of those with health problems, with caring responsibilities or with legitimate retirement aspirations. In a nutshell, employment policy should be person centred.

What is also clear from our research, however, is that policies must be more than person centred; they must also be context sensitive. This means responding to the local and regional variations in labour market opportunities that are so pivotal in understanding the scale of labour market detachment. The balance of resources deployed in different parts of the country needs to reflect the particular local incidence of obstacles to labour market participation – which means an emphasis on economic development and job creation in the areas where labour demand is weak, and on training and retraining where skill shortages are the main obstacle. The balance between these different approaches also needs to shift through time as economic circumstances change. In particular, in periods of recession and higher joblessness the rationale for focusing on supply-side measures like training grows weaker and the case for promoting the demand for labour grows stronger.

Finally, as we saw in ch. 2, men's labour market detachment is not just a UK phenomenon. In particular the problems experienced by workers in the UK can be found in most other EU countries. Across the EU (and beyond) employment policy is taking up the challenge which this detachment poses through the development of strategies to re-engage workers and promote labour market participation. The UK can learn much from policies developed elsewhere, and international experience reinforces some of the messages emerging from our research – in particular the message that modern nations need to shift their concern away from narrow definitions of unemployment to a broader view of labour market detachment. What all this points to is the need to reverse some of the trends in late twentieth-century employment practice:

- The trend towards early involuntary withdrawal from the labour market needs to be turned back, and ageist discrimination against older workers needs to be openly combated.
- The focus on youth in the provision of employment support, to the detriment of people of prime and older working age, is neither sensible nor defensible and should be replaced with flexible measures for all, according to aptitudes, aspirations and needs.
- The assumption that men can meet family responsibilities only through breadwinning should be finally abandoned, and recognition given to men whose family roles include care for children or dealing with illness or disability within the family.
- Men whose own ill-health or injury involves an inability to continue in their occupation should no longer be classified exclusively as either 'incapacitated' or 'unemployed'; rather the benefits system and the support provided by the employment services should reflect not just the work they are unable to do but also the potential contribution that in the right circumstances they are still able to make.

- The solution to the extensive labour market detachment arising from illness and disability lies principally with supporting moves back into employment, including through economic regeneration in the worst affected areas, not with cuts in disability benefits.

These proposals pose a challenge to much of the current thinking and practices of politicians and policy-makers. Coupled with a new approach based on person-centred and context-sensitive employment support, however, they could offer hope to many of those male workers who at the start of the twenty-first century find themselves detached from a labour market in which once they might have expected to thrive.

Appendix: research methodology

The survey covered men aged 25–64 who were economically inactive or at the time of the survey had been unemployed for most or all of the preceding six months. It also covered part-time workers on the basis that this type of work is non-traditional for men. Taken as a whole, this is the group which we refer to as the 'detached male workforce'.

The survey was carried out in seven localities:

- Barnsley, in the heart of the former Yorkshire coalfield, an area badly affected by industrial job losses in the 1980s and 1990s. This metropolitan borough has a population of 230,000, comprising Barnsley town and surrounding mining villages;
- Chesterfeild, in Derbyshire, which shares some of the industrial job losses found in Barnsley but has a more diverse and resilient economic base. Chesterfield borough has a population of 100,000, mostly in the town itself;
- Northampton, a county town in the Midlands just seventy miles from London, which enjoyed expansion as a result of New Town status and which has a relatively buoyant local economy. Northampton has a population of 190,000;
- West Cumbria, as an example of a rural area with a declining industrial base;
- North Yorkshire, as an example of an upland rural area (the survey area was within the North Yorks Moors);
- North Norfolk, as an example of a rural economy with an important seaside/tourist component;
- South Shropshire, as an example of a lowland rural area.

The locations of the survey areas are shown in fig. A.1.

Figure A.2 shows how each of the survey areas ranks in terms of the composite indicator of male labour market detachment presented in figs. 4.3 and 4.4 earlier. This diagram arranges all districts across Britain from the highest to the lowest in terms of labour market detachment (on

Figure A.1   Location of survey areas

the vertical axis) and shows the cumulative male population in the 25–64-year-old group (on the horizontal axis). The positions of the seven survey areas in the ranking are marked. Barnsley was chosen as being representative of the top 10 per cent of districts (in population terms) where labour market detachment among men is particularly high. Chesterfield was chosen as representative of the next 40 per cent, and Northampton of the bottom 50 per cent. The four rural areas were chosen to provide a good mix of the different types of rural area found across England, including in terms of labour market conditions.

Collectively, the seven areas cover a range of circumstances spread across five UK regions. The significant omission is an area within one of Britain's conurbations – the original three towns were intended to be representative of the middle of the country's urban hierarchy. Vitally, however, the survey areas do extend from one where labour market detachment is very high (Barnsley) through to one where it is relatively low (Northampton).

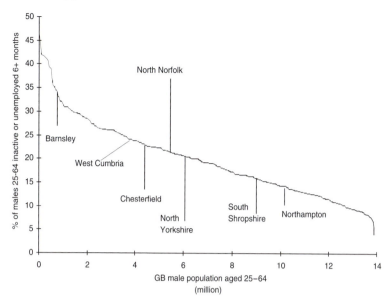

Figure A.2   Male labour market detachment in survey areas, 1996–7
Source: Census of Population, DfEE, DSS.

All the interviews were carried out between the autumn of 1997 and summer of 1998. Within each locality the interviews took place in a representative sample of wards or Enumeration Districts (ED).

In each of the three towns a representative sample of EDs was chosen. This was accomplished by creating the same composite indicator of male labour market detachment for all EDs within the district. The EDs were then ranked by this indicator. An initial number of EDs was selected to cover enough households to achieve the target number of interviews in each area. Subsequent representative booster samples were selected as necessary until approximately 400 completed interviews were achieved in each area. An address list was compiled for every household contained within each ED to be surveyed. A letter was sent to each address to explain the purpose of the survey and say that an interviewer would call. Every household within each ED was visited by a professional interviewer. Where initially no contact was made with a member of a household a second visit was made on a different date and time. In a small number of EDs where the contact rate was less than 75 per cent after two visits a third visit was made to bring the contact rate up to at least this level.

The approach taken in the four rural areas differed slightly. The rural sample used a representative sample of wards rather than EDs, and some outlying addresses were excluded. A target of approximately 125 interviews was set in each of the rural areas.

When contact was made with a member of the household a short screening questionnaire was carried out to identify household members in scope, i.e. men aged 25–64 who were economically inactive, in part-time employment, or unemployed for most of or all of the past six months. If a man in the household was in scope then the main questionnaire was completed with him if he was present at that time. If a man was in scope but not actually present at the time when the interviewer called an appointment was made and the interviewer returned to complete the questionnaire with him at a later date. The interviews were therefore carried out with the men themselves (not partners or other household members). The interviews followed a tightly structured format and usually lasted fifteen to thirty minutes.

In all areas the questionnaire sought detailed information for each respondent including:

- present position (sick, retired, unemployed, etc.);
- marital status;
- social class/occupation;
- qualifications;
- housing status;
- duration of non-employment;
- work history;
- reasons for job loss;
- previous experience of non-employment;
- job aspirations and job search;
- obstacles to re-employment;
- self-assessed health;
- financial circumstances (pensions, redundancy, etc.);
- benefit status;
- household composition;
- economic status of other members of the household.

Only 3 per cent of households refused outright to participate in the survey. The refusal was sometimes with the screening questionnaire, sometimes in moving forward to the full questionnaire. In addition there may have been some instances when the interviewer was deliberately and misleadingly told that there was no one in scope in the household. However, in all areas relatively few households – typically below 10 per cent – contain men within scope of the survey. Most households instead contain men in work or over the retirement age or only women. Interviews were therefore carried out at only a small minority of the addresses visited. In total more than 45,000 addresses were initially targeted.

The 1,703 completed survey interviews were distributed as follows: Barnsley 394, Chesterfield 407, Northampton 393, West Cumbria 122, North Yorkshire 125, North Norfolk 119, South Shropshire 143.

THE IN-DEPTH INTERVIEWS

In-depth interviews were carried out with a sub-sample of survey respondents. These men were selected from respondents in Barnsley, Chesterfield and Northampton. The interviews took place in the second half of 1998 and the first part of 1999.

At the time of the survey, all respondents were asked if they were willing to be contacted at a later date by a member of the research team. Of the 1,194 respondents in Barnsley, Chesterfield and Northampton, 714 provided contact details and were willing to participate further in the research. Of these, 625 were actually considered for interview and 148 were contacted to see if they were still willing to take part in the next stage of the research. In total, eighty-seven survey respondents were revisited and interviewed in depth. The interviews were evenly spread across the three areas with thirty completed in both Barnsley and Chesterfield and twenty-seven completed in Northampton.

Selection was made on the basis of key characteristics to enable the qualitative interviews to cover the full age range, to include men in all different economic inactivity statuses as well as unemployment, and to include men in different family situations. The database containing the main survey results was interrogated in order to select a sample of men with various characteristics who had also provided contact details. The intention was not to be statistically representative. Rather, the aim was to ensure that a sufficient number of men in each broad category was included.

The interviews were carried out by Alison Herrington, Rob Macmillan and Sue Yeandle from the core research team. Most interviews lasted between one and one and a half hours, and all were conducted using a common aide memoire to ensure that key topics were explored in all cases, and addressing the following points:

• survey details were checked for accuracy and updated as appropriate;
• how interviewee came to be in current situation;
• job search activities and limitations of job search;
• reasons why any job offers were turned down;
• details of any retraining undertaken or offered;
• getting by – income sources, attitudes to benefit, changes over time;
• barriers to getting work – local labour market situation, family situation, health, motivation, financial circumstances (including desired wage levels);
• attitudes to any possible return to employment, and associated activities;
• current activities, including voluntary work, domestic work and 'jobs on the side';

- attitudes to government policy – Welfare to Work/New Deal; reform of disability benefits.

The interviewers took great care to allow the men to present their situation in the way they felt was most important, and some interviews thus departed from the topics in the aide memoire. All interviews took place in the home of the interviewee by prior arrangement. Interviews were tape recorded (with the consent of participants) and fully written up, with transcription of key passages (including substantial verbatim quotation) and detailed notes. In addition to these notes (typically fifteen to twenty pages in length) a one-page summary of work history, health and benefit details was produced for each case, together with a short 'pen portrait' of the circumstance described by each man.

An indexing scheme was devised early in the in-depth interview phase, working on full transcripts of the initial interviews. The scheme contained nineteen major categories, each with between one and ten sub-categories, and the full notes for each of the eighty-seven cases were indexed. A method of computer-aided retrieval of this indexed material was also devised. This approach ensured that all cases relating to any topic or theme could be accessed.

Material used in this book from the in-depth interviews has been anonymised. For each interviewee a pseudonym has been created. These pseudonyms are consistent throughout the chapters, so that, for example, discussion of 'Colin' in ch. 7 relates to the same person as references to 'Colin' in ch. 10. Any very specific details of each interviewee's circumstances have been changed in order to safeguard anonymity, but this does not substantively change the points being made.

References

Ainley, P., 1988, *From School to YTS: Education and Training in England and Wales 1944–1987*, Milton Keynes: Open University Press.

Alcock, P., 1996, 'The advantages and disadvantages of the contribution base in targeting benefits: a social analysis of the insurance scheme in the United Kingdom', *International Social Security Review*, 49.1: 31–51.

1997, *Understanding Poverty*, 2nd edn, Basingstoke: Macmillan.

1999a, 'Employment and social exclusion: the policy context and the policy response in the UK', in Lind and Møller.

1999b, 'Poverty and social security', in R. M. Page, and R. Silburn (eds.), *British Social Welfare in the Twentieth Century*, Basingstoke: Macmillan.

Alcock, P., and Pearson, S., 1999, 'Raising the poverty plateau: the impact of means-tested rebates from local authority charges in low income households', *Journal of Social Policy*, 28.3: 497–516.

Allatt, P., and Yeandle, S., 1992, *Youth Unemployment and the Family: Voices of Disordered Times*, London: Routledge.

Amerini, G., 2000, 'Social protection in Europe', *Statistics in Focus: Population and Social Conditions*, Theme 3–15/2000, Luxembourg: Eurostat.

Annesley, C., 2001, 'New Labour and welfare', in S. Ludlam and M. J. Smith (eds.), *New Labour in Government*, Basingstoke: Macmillan.

Armstrong, D., 1999, 'Hidden male unemployment in Northern Ireland', *Regional Studies*, 33.6: 499–512.

Ashdown, C., 2000, 'The position of older workers in the labour market', *Labour Market Trends*, 108.9: 397–400.

Baldwin, S., and Falkingham, J. (eds.), 1994, *Social Security and Social Change: New Challenges to the Beveridge Model*, Hemel Hempstead: Harvester Wheatsheaf.

Barker, G., and Hancock, R., 2000, 'The income dimension', in D. Hirsch (ed.), *Life after 50: Issues for Policy and Research*, York: Joseph Rowntree Foundation.

Bauman, Z., 1998, *Work, Consumerism and the New Poor*, Buckingham: Open University Press.

BBC Television, 1998, *Panorama* 'On the Sick', broadcast 9 February 1998.

Beatson, M., 1995, 'Progress towards a flexible labour market', *Labour Market Trends*, 103.2: 55–66.

Beatty, C., and Fothergill, S., 1996, 'Labour market adjustment in areas of chronic industrial decline: the case of the UK coalfields', *Regional Studies*, 34.7: 627–40.

1997, *Unemployment and the Labour Market in Rural Development Areas*, Rural Research Series no. 30, London: Rural Development Commission.

1999a, *The Detached Male Workforce*, CRESR, Sheffield: Sheffield Hallam University.

1999b, *Labour Market Detachment in Rural England*, Rural Research Series no. 40, London: Rural Development Commission.

1999c, *Incapacity Benefit and Unemployment*, CRESR, Sheffield: Sheffield Hallam University.

Beatty, C., Fothergill, S., Gore, T., and Herrington, A., 1997, *The Real Level of Unemployment*, CRESR, Sheffield: Sheffield Hallam University.

Beatty, C., Fothergill, S., and Macmillan, R., 2000, 'A theory of employment, unemployment and sickness', *Regional Studies*, 34.7: 617–30.

Beck, U., 1992, *Risk Society: Towards a New Modernity*, London: Sage.

Becker, U., 2000, 'Welfare state development and employment in the Netherlands in comparative perspective', *Journal of European Social Policy*, 10.3: 219–39.

Bell, D., 1976, *The Coming of Post-Industrial Society*, New York: Basic Books.

Bellaby, P., and Bellaby, F., 1999, 'Unemployment and ill health: local labour markets and ill health in Britain 1984–1991', *Work, Employment and Society*, 13.3: 416–82.

Benefit Fraud Inspectorate, 1999, *Securing the System: Annual Report of the Benefit Fraud Inspectorate*, London: Department of Social Security.

Berthoud, R., 1998, *Disability Benefits: a Review of the Issues and Options for Reform*, York: Joseph Rowntree Foundation.

2000, 'Introduction: the dynamics of social change', in Berthoud and Gershuny.

Berthoud, R., and Gershuny, J. (eds.), 2000, *Seven Years in the Lives of British Families: Evidence from the British Household Panel Survey*, Bristol: The Policy Press.

Beveridge, W., 1942, *Report on Social Insurance and Allied Services*, Cmd 6404, London: HMSO.

1944, *Full Employment in a Free Society*, London: George Allen and Unwin.

Blondal, S., and Pearson, M., 1995, 'Unemployment and other non-employment benefits', *Oxford Review of Economic Policy*, 11: 136–69.

Blundell, R., and Reed, H., 2000, 'The employment effects of the Working Families Tax Credit', *Benefits*, 29: 21–2.

Braverman, H., 1974, *Labor and Monopoly Capital: the Degradation of Work in the Twentieth Century*, New York: Monthly Review Press.

Breeze, J., Fothergill, S., and Macmillan, R., 2000, *Matching New Deal to Rural Needs*, London: Countryside Agency.

Burghes, L., and Lister, R. (eds.), 1981, *Unemployment: Who Pays the Price?* Poverty Pamphlet 53, London: Child Poverty Action Group.

Campbell, N., 1999, *The Decline of Employment among Older People in Britain*, CASE Paper 19, London: London School of Economics.

Cohen, G. (ed.), 1987, *Social Change and the Life Course*, London: Tavistock.

Commission of the European Communities, 2000, *Social Policy Agenda*, Communication from the Commission, Luxembourg: Office for Official Publications of the European Communities.

2001, 'Council Decision of 19 January 2001 on Guidelines for Member States' employment policies for the year 2001', *Official Journal of the European Communities* (2001/63/EC).

Connell, R. W., 1995, *Masculinities*, Cambridge: Polity Press.

Cousins, C., 1999, *Society, Work and Welfare in Europe*, Basingstoke: Macmillan.

Cousins, C., Jenkins, J., and Laux, R., 1998, 'Disability data from the Labour Force Survey: comparing 1997–8 with the past', *Labour Market Trends*, 106.6: 321–36.

Crompton, R. (ed.), 1999, *Restructuring Gender Relations and Employment: the Decline of the Male Breadwinner*, Oxford: Oxford University Press.

Dawes, L., 1993, *Long-Term Unemployment and Labour Market Flexibility*, Centre for Labour Market Studies, Leicester: University of Leicester.

Deacon, A., 1976, *In Search of the Scrounger: the Administration of Unemployment Insurance in Britain 1920–31*, London: Bell and Sons.

2000, 'Learning from the US? The influence of American ideas upon "new Labour" thinking on welfare reform', *Policy and Politics*, 28.1: 5–18.

Deacon, A., and Bradshaw, J., 1983, *Reserved for the Poor: the Means-test in British Social Policy*, Oxford: Basil Blackwell.

Denman, J., and McDonald, P., 1996, 'Unemployment statistics from 1881 to the present day', *Labour Market Trends*, 104.1: 5–18.

Department for Education and Employment, 1999, *Age Diversity in Employment: a Code of Practice*, Nottingham: DfEE Publications.

2001a, *UK Employment Action Plan*, London: The Stationery Office.

2001b, *Towards Full Employment in a Modern Society*, London: Department for Education and Employment.

Department of Social Security, 1998a, *New Ambitions for our Country: a New Contract for Welfare*, Cm 3805, London: The Stationery Office.

1998b, *A New Contract for Welfare: Support for Disabled People*, Cm 4103, London: Department of Social Security.

1998c, press release.

1999, *A New Contract for Welfare: Safeguarding Social Security*, Cm 4276, London: Department of Social Security.

2000a, *The Changing Welfare State: Pensioner Incomes*, DSS Paper No. 2, London: The Stationery Office.

2000b, *The Government's Expenditure Plans, Departmental Report*, table 10, London: The Stationery Office.

2000c, *Income-related Benefits: Estimates of Take-up in 1998/99*, London: The Stationery Office.

2000d, *IB204: A Guide for Registered Medical Practitioners*, appendix 2 'The Personal Capability Assessment', DSS website: http://www.dss.gov.uk/publications/dss/2000/medical/app2_001.

Department of Social Security and Department for Education and Employment, 1998, *A New Contract for Welfare: the Gateway to Work*, Cm 4102, London: The Stationery Office.

Department of Trade and Industry, 1998, *Fairness at Work: a White Paper*, Cm 3969, London: The Stationery Office.

2000, *Work and Parents: Competitiveness and Choice – a Green Paper*, Cm 5005, London: The Stationery Office.

Dex, S. (ed.), 1999, *Families and Work: Trends, Pressures and Policies*, London: FPSC.

Ditch, J. (ed.), 1999, *Introduction to Social Security: Policies, Benefits and Poverty*, London: Routledge.

Donnison, D., 1997, *Politics for a Just Society*, London: Macmillan.

Dorsett, R., Finlayson, L., Ford, R., Marsh, A., White, M., and Zarb, G., 1998, *Leaving Incapacity Benefit*, DSS Research Report no. 86, London: Department of Social Security.

Drake, R., 2000, 'Disabled people, New Labour, benefits and work', *Critical Social Policy*, 20.4: 421–39.

Düll, N., and Vogler-Ludwig, K., 1998, 'Germany', *Employment Observatory Trends*, no. 30: 20–6.

Edgeley, J., and Sweeney, K., 1998, 'Characteristics of JSA claimants who have joined the claimant count from Incapacity Benefit', *Labour Market Trends*, 106.2: 79–83.

Esam, P., and Berthoud, R., 1991, *Independent Benefits for Men and Women*, London: Policy Studies Institute.

Esping-Andersen, G., 1990, *The Three Worlds of Welfare Capitalism*, Cambridge: Polity Press.

    1993, 'Post-industrial classes: an analytical framework', in G. Esping-Andersen. (ed.), *Changing Classes: Stratification and Mobility in Post-industrial Societies*, London: Sage.

European Labour Force Survey 1999, 'Table 65: Inactive population aged 15 years or more, by willingness to work and by reasons for not seeking employment', Luxembourg: Eurostat.

Evans, M., 2001, *Welfare to Work and the Organisation of Opportunity: Lessons from Abroad*, CASE Report 15, Centre for Analysis of Social Exclusion, London: London School of Economics.

Fenwick, D., and Denman, J., 1995, 'The monthly claimant unemployment count: change and consistency', *Labour Market Trends*, 103.11: 397–400.

Ferrie, J. E., Marmot, M. G., Griffiths, J., and Ziglio, E., 1999, *Labour Market Changes and Job Insecurity: a Challenge for Social Welfare and Health Promotion*, WHO Regional Publications, European Series no. 81, Copenhagen: World Health Organisation Regional Office for Europe.

Field, F., 1995, *Making Welfare Work: Reconstructing Welfare for the Millennium*, London: Institute of Community Studies.

Fieldhouse, E., and Hollywood, E., 1999, 'Life after mining: hidden unemployment and changing patterns of economic activity amongst miners in England and Wales, 1981–91', *Work, Employment and Society*, 13: 483–502.

Fina-Sanglas, L., 2000, 'Europe's population and labour market beyond 2000: main issues and policy implications', in A. Punch and D. L. Pearce (eds.), *Europe's Population and Labour Market Beyond 2000*, vol. I, Population Studies no. 33, Strasbourg: Council of Europe.

Finland, 2001, *National Action Plan for Employment*, http://europa.eu.int/comm/employment_social/news/2001/may/naps2001_en.html.

Finlayson, L., Ford, R., March, A., Smith, A., and White, M., 2000, *The First Effects of the Earnings Top-up*, DSS Research Report no. 112, London: Department of Social Security.

Finn, D., 1998, *Working Nation: Welfare Reform and the Australian Job Compact for the Long Term Unemployed*, London: Unemployment Unit.

France, 2001, *National Action Plan for Employment*, http://europa.eu.int/comm/employment_social/news/2001/may/naps2001_en.html.

Franco, A., 2000, 'Labour Force Survey: principal results 1999', *Statistics in Focus: Population and Social Conditions*, Theme 3 – 5/2000, Luxembourg: Eurostat.

Fraser, D., 1973, *The Evolution of the British Welfare State: a History of Social Policy since the Industrial Revolution*, London: Macmillan.

Gallie, D., and Vogler, C., 1994, 'Unemployment and attitudes to work', in Gallie, Marsh and Vogler.

Gallie, D., Marsh, C., and Vogler, C. (eds.), 1994, *Social Change and the Experience of Unemployment*, Oxford: Oxford University Press.

Germany, 2001, *National Action Plan for Employment*, http://europa.eu.int/comm/employment_social/news/2001/may/naps2001_en.html.

Gershuny, J., 1978, *After Industrial Society: the Emerging Self-service Economy*, London: Macmillan Press.

Gershuny, J., and Marsh, C., 1994, 'Unemployment in work histories', in Gallie, Marsh and Vogler.

Giddens, A., 1994, *Beyond Left and Right: the Future of Radical Politics*, Cambridge: Polity.

1998, *The Third Way: the Renewal of Social Democracy*, Cambridge: Polity.

Gilbert, B., 1966, *The Evolution of National Insurance in Great Britain*, London: Michael Joseph.

Gineste, S., and Ait Kaci, A., 1998, 'France', *Employment Observatory Trends*, no. 30: 39–49.

Goodin, R. E., 2000, 'Crumbling pillars: social security futures', *Political Quarterly*, 71.2: 144–50.

2001, 'Work and welfare: towards a post-productivist welfare regime', *British Journal of Political Science*, 31.1: 13–39.

Goodin, R. E., Headey, R., and Dirven, H. J. (eds.), 1999, *The Real Worlds of Welfare Capitalism*, Cambridge: Cambridge University Press.

Green, A., 1999, 'Insights into unemployment and non-employment in Europe using alternative measures', *Regional Studies*, 33.5: 453–64.

Green, A. E., 1997, 'Exclusion, unemployment and non-employment', *Regional Studies*, 31.5: 505–20.

Green, A. E., and Owen, D., 1998, *Where are the Jobless?: Changing Unemployment and Non-employment in Cities and Regions*, Bristol: Policy Press.

Gregg, P., and Wadsworth, J., 1996, 'More work in fewer households?', in J. Hills (ed.), *New Inequalities*, Cambridge: Cambridge University Press.

1998, *Unemployment and Non-employment: Unpacking Economic Inactivity*, Economic Report vol. 12, no. 6, London: Employment Policy Institute.

Handler, J., and Hazenfeld, Y., 1997, *We, The Poor People: Work, Poverty and Welfare*, Newhaven and London: Yale University Press.

Harris, C. C., 1991, 'Recession, redundancy and age', in P. Brown and R. Scase (eds.), *Poor Work: Disadvantage and the Division of Labour*, Milton Keynes: Open University Press.

Haskey, J., 1984, 'Social class and socio-economic differentials in divorce in England and Wales', *Population Studies*, 38.

Health and Safety Executive, 2000, *Health and Safety Statistics 1999/2000*, London: National Statistics.

Hennock, E. P., 1987, *British Social Reform and German Precedents*, Oxford: Clarendon Press.

Hepple, B. A., and Fredman, S., 1986, *Labour Law and Industrial Relations in Great Britain*, London: Kluwer Law and Taxation Publishers.

Hill, M., 1990, *Social Security Policy in Britain*, Aldershot: Edward Elgar.

1999, 'Insecurity and social security', in J. Vail, J. Wheelock, and M. Hill (eds.), *Insecure Times: Living with Insecurity in Contemporary Society*, London: Routledge.

Hills, J., Ditch, J., and Glennerster, H. (eds.), 1994, *Beveridge and Social Security: an International Perspective*, Oxford: Clarendon Press.

HM Treasury, 2000, *The Goal of Full Employment: Employment Opportunity for all throughout Britain*, London: HM Treasury.

Jenkins, C., and Sherman, B., 1979, *The Collapse of Work*, London: Eyre Methuen.

Jessop, B., 1994, 'The transition to post-Fordism and the Schumpeterian welfare state', in R. Burrows and B. Loader (eds.), *Towards a Post-Fordist Welfare State*, London: Routledge.

2001, *The Future of the Welfare State*, Cambridge: Polity Press.

Jordan, B., 1998, *The New Politics of Welfare: Social Justice in a Global Context*, London: Sage.

Jozefowicz, A., and Pearce, D. L., 2000, 'Europe's population and labour market beyond 2000: an assessment of trends and projections', in A. Punch and D. L. Pearce (eds.), *Europe's Population and Labour Market Beyond 2000*, vol. I, Population Studies no. 33, Strasbourg: Council of Europe Publishing.

Kempson, E., 1996, *Life on a Low Income*, York: Joseph Rowntree Foundation/York Publishing Services.

Kvist, J., 2001, 'Nordic activation in the 1990s', *Benefits*, 31: 5–10.

Kyi, G., and Charlier, H., 2001, 'Employment rates in Europe – 2000', *Statistics in Focus: Population and Social Conditions*, Theme 3 – 8/2001, Luxembourg: Eurostat.

Lampard, R., 1994, 'An examination of the relationship between marital dissolution and unemployment', in Gallie, Marsh and Vogler.

Land, H., 1980, 'The family wage', *Feminist Review*, No. 6.

Layard, R., 1997, 'Preventing long-term unemployment', in J. Philpott (ed.), *Working for Full Employment*, London: Routledge.

1998, 'Getting people back to work', *CentrePiece*, autumn: 24–7.

1999, *Tackling Unemployment*, Basingstoke: Macmillan.

Layard, R., Nickell, S., and Jackman, R., 1991, *Unemployment: Macroeconomic Performance and the Labour Market*, Oxford: Oxford University Press.

Levitas, R., 1998, *The Inclusive Society? Social Exclusion and New Labour*, Basingstoke: Macmillan.

Lilja, R., 1999, 'Finland', *Employment Observatory Trends*, no. 33.

Lind, J., and Møller, I. (eds.), 1999, *Inclusion and Exclusion: Unemployment and Non-Standard Employment in Europe*, Aldershot: Ashgate.

Lødermel, I., and Trickey, H. (eds.), 2001, *'An Offer You Can't Refuse': Workfare in International Perspective*, Bristol: The Policy Press.

Lonsdale, S., Lessof, C., and Ferris, G., 1993, *Invalidity Benefit: a Survey of Recipients*, Department of Social Security Research Report no. 19, London: HMSO.

MacKay, R., 1999, 'Work and nonwork: a more difficult labour market', *Environment and Planning A*, 31: 1919–34.

Marlier, E., 1999, 'Dynamic measures of economic activity and unemployment: 2. Status in terms of the amount of time spent', *Statistics in Focus: Population and Social Conditions*, Theme 3 – 18/1999, Luxembourg: Eurostat.

Marshall, T. H., 1975, *Social Policy*, 4th edn, London: Hutchinson.

Martin, R., and Wallace, J., 1984, *Working Women in Recession: Employment, Redundancy and Unemployment*, Oxford: Oxford University Press.

McCormick, J., 2000, *On the Sick: Incapacity and Inclusion*, Edinburgh: Scottish Council Foundation.

McKay, S., and Rowlingson, K., 1999, *Social Security in Britain*, Basingstoke: Macmillan.

Merritt, G., 1982, *World out of Work*, London: Collins.

Millar, J., 1999, 'Obligations and autonomy in social welfare', in R. Crompton (ed.), *Restructuring Gender Relations and Employment: the Decline of the Male Breadwinner*, Oxford: Oxford University Press.

2000, *Keeping Track of Welfare Reform: the New Deal Programmes*, York: Joseph Rowntree Foundation.

Moore, B. C., Rhodes, J., and Tyler, P., 1986, *The Effects of Government Regional Economic Policy*, Department of Trade and Industry, London: HMSO.

Morris, L., 1990, *The Workings of the Household*, Cambridge: Polity Press.

1995, *Social Divisions: Economic Decline and Social Structural Change*, London: UCL Press.

Moss Kanter, R., 1990, *When Giants Learn to Dance: Mastering the Challenges of Strategy, Management and Careers in the 1990s*, London: Unwin Hyman.

Netherlands, 2001, *National Action Plan for Employment*, http://europa.eu.int/comm/employment_social/news/2001/may/naps2001_en.html.

de Neubourg, C., 1997, 'Social security and the unemployment–poverty trade-off', in W. Beck, L. van der Maesen and A. Walker (eds.), *The Social Quality of Europe*, Bristol: The Policy Press.

Novak, T., 1988, *Poverty and the State*, Milton Keynes: Open University Press.

Observer, 2001, *The Sickest Town in Britain*, 22 July, London: Guardian Newspapers.

Office for National Statistics, 1997, *Labour Force Survey Historical Supplement*, London: The Stationery Office.

1999, *Social Trends 29*, London: The Stationery Office.

2000, *Labour Market Trends*, 108.7: 311.

Oppenheim, C., 1999, 'Welfare reform and the labour market – a "third way"?', *Benefits*, 25: 1–6.

Peck, J., and Theodore, N., 2000, 'Beyond "employability"', *Cambridge Journal of Economics*, 24: 729–49.

Performance and Innovation Unit, 2000, *Winning the Generation Game*, London: The Stationery Office.

Peters, M., 1998, 'Netherlands', *Employment Observatory Trends*, no. 30: 63–9.

Piore, M. J., and Sabel, C. F., 1984, *The Second Industrial Divide: Possibilities for Prosperity*, New York: Basic Books.

Raynor, E., Shah, S., White, R., Dawes, L. and Tinsley, K., 2000, *Evaluating Jobseeker's Allowance*, DSS Research Report no. 116, London: Department of Social Security.

Riley, R., and Young, G., 2000, *The New Deal for Young People: Implications for Employment and the Public Finances*, Employment Service Research and Development Report ESR62, Sheffield: Employment Service.

Ritchie, J., and Snape, D., 1993, *Invalidity Benefit: a Preliminary Qualitative Study of the Factors Affecting its Growth*, London: Social and Community Planning Research.

Ritchie, J., Ward, K., and Duldig, W., 1993, *GPs and Invalidity Benefit*, DSS Research Report no. 18, London: HMSO.

Roche, M., and Van Berkel, R. (eds.), 1997, *European Citizenship and Social Exclusion*, Aldershot: Avebury.

Rowlingson, K., and Berthoud, R., 1996, *Disability, Benefits and Employment*, DSS Research Report no. 54, London: Department of Social Security.

Royal Statistical Society, 1995, *Report of the Working Party on the Measurement of Unemployment in the UK*, London: Royal Statistical Society.

Santamäki-Vuori, T., 1998, 'Finland', *Employment Observatory Trends*, no. 30: 80–5.

Schwartz, J. E., 1998, *Illusions of Poverty: the American Dream in Question*, New York and London: W. W. Norton.

Seabrook, J., 1978, *What Went Wrong? Working People and the Ideals of the Labour Movement*, London: Victor Gollancz.

1982, *Unemployment*, London: Quartet Books.

Showler, B., and Sinfield, A. (eds.), 1981, *The Workless State: Studies in Unemployment*, Oxford: Martin Robertson.

Sinfield, A., 1981, *What Unemployment Means*, Oxford: Martin Robertson.

Sly, F., Thair, T., and Risdon, A., 1999, 'Disability and the labour market: results from the winter 1998/9 LFS', *Labour Market Trends*, 107.9: 455–66.

Smith, A., Youngs, R., Ashworth, K., McKay, S., and Walker, R., 2000, *Understanding the Impact of Jobseeker's Allowance*, DSS Research Report no. 111, London: Department of Social Security.

Smith, N., 1972, *A Brief Guide to Social Legislation*, London: Methuen.

Spain, 2001, *National Action Plan for Employment*, http://europa.eu.int/comm/employment_social/news/2001/may/naps2001_en.html.

Taylor, M., 2000, 'Work, non-work, jobs and job mobility', in Berthoud and Gershuny.

Thane, P., 1996, *The Foundations of the Welfare State*, 4th edn, Harlow: Longman.

Toharia, L., 1998, 'Spain', *Employment Observatory Trends*, no. 30: 34–9.

Trickey, H., Kellard, K., Walker, R., Ashworth, K., and Smith, A., 1998, *Unemployment and Jobseeking: Two Years On*, DSS Research Report no. 87, London: Department of Social Security.

Trickey, H., 2001, 'Comparing workfare programmes – features and implications', in Lødermel and Trickey.

Turok, I., and Webster, D., 1998, 'The New Deal: jeopardised by the geography of unemployment?', *Local Economy*, 13: 309–28.

Turok, I., and Edge, N., 1999, *The Jobs Gap in Britain's Cities: Employment Loss and Labour Market Consequences*, Bristol: The Policy Press.

Waldfogel, J., 1997, 'Ending welfare as we know it: the personal responsibility and work Opportunity Act of 1996', *Benefits*, 20: 11–16.

Walker, A., 1981, 'The level and distribution of unemployment', in Burghes and Lister.

Walker, R., 1999, '"Welfare to Work" versus poverty and family change: policy lessons from the USA', *Work Employment and Society*, 13.3: 539–53.

Walker, R., and Howard, M., 2000, *The Making of a Welfare Class? Benefits Receipt in Britain*, Bristol: The Policy Press.

Webb, S., 1994, 'Social insurance and poverty alleviation: an empirical analysis', in S. Baldwin and J. Falkingham (eds.), *Social Security and Social Change: New Challenges to the Beveridge Model*, Hemel Hempstead: Harvester Wheatsheaf.

Webster, D., 2001, 'Inequalities in the labour market', paper presented to the British Association Festival of Science, Glasgow, 4 September 2001.

Weir, D., 1973, *Men and Work in Modern Britain*, Suffolk: Fontana/Collins.

White, M., 1983, *Long Term Unemployment and Labour Markets*, Report no. 622, London: Policy Studies Institute.

White, M., and Lakey, J., 1992, *The Restart Effect: Evaluation of a Labour Market Programme for Unemployed People*, London, Policy Studies Institute.

Yeandle, S., 1991, 'Couples in the labour market: an analysis of work histories in South Wales', in W. R. Heinz (ed.), *The Life Course and Social Change: Comparative Perspectives*, Weinheim, Germany: Deutscher Studien Verlag.

1993, 'Intersections of biography and history in couples' working lives', in C. Born and H. Krüger (eds.), *Erwerbsverlaüfe von Ehepartnern und die Moderniesierung weiblicher Lebensverlaüfe*, Weinheim, Germany: Deutscher Studien Verlag.

1999, 'Gender contracts, welfare systems and non-Standard working: diversity and change in Denmark, France, Germany, Italy and the UK', in A. Felstead and N. Jewson (eds.), *Global Trends in Flexible Labour*, London: Macmillan.

Index